EFFECTIVE RESPONSE TO
SCHOOL VIOLENCE

EFFECTIVE RESPONSE TO SCHOOL VIOLENCE

A Guide for Educators and Law Enforcement Personnel

By

TONY L. JONES

Charles C Thomas
PUBLISHER • LTD.
SPRINGFIELD • ILLINOIS • U.S.A.

Published and Distributed Throughout the World by

CHARLES C THOMAS • PUBLISHER, LTD.
2600 South First Street
Springfield, Illinois 62704

© 2001 by CHARLES C THOMAS • PUBLISHER, LTD.

ISBN 0-398-07188-8 (hard)
ISBN 0-398-07189-6 (paper)

Library of Congress Catalog Card Number: 2001023085

Printed in the United States of America
MM-R-3

Library of Congress Cataloging-in-Publication Data

Jones, Tony L.
    Effective response to school violence : a guide for educators and law enforcement
personnel / by Tony L. Jones.
        p. cm.
    Includes bibliographical references and index.
    ISBN 0-398-07188-8 (hard) -- ISBN 0-398-07189-6 (pbk.)
    1. School violence--Prevention--United States. 2. School crisis management--United
States. 3. Schools--United States--Security measures. I. Title.

LB3013.3 .J69 2001
371.7'82'09733--dc21   2001023085

This book is dedicated to the people who have experienced school violence. These people have experienced the incalculable costs of death, emotional distress, physical injury, facility destruction, disruption of classes, negative public perception, civil/criminal lawsuits and the resulting embarrassment these acts generate. These people need to know that they are not alone; nearly everyone in a community, if not the nation, is touched in some way.

Their sacrifice has not been in vain. Entire communities now have a better awareness and understanding of school violence. The benefits from this act are both long-term and short-term. Over the long term, community awareness and involvement will help reduce school violence. In the short-term, it is vital that people realize that school violence can occur in their community.

Finally, society has come to understand that school safety is everyone's job. Teachers, administrators, parents, community members, and students all have a stake in proactive measures focused on identifying troubled students, intervening when required, quickly and efficiently responding to school violence in progress and addressing the tragic aftermath that will follow.

INTRODUCTION

G ranted, most schools are safe. Fewer than one percent of all violent deaths of children occur on school grounds; however, no school is immune from school violence. As a result of the recent armed assaults targeting learning institutions, many school administrators and government entities are searching for proactive solutions. Indeed, educational entities can no longer afford the false assumption that "nothing has ever happened here and nothing ever will." This false assumption ignores the changing contemporary circumstances of politics, demographics, sociological views, target criticality, and vulnerability. Indeed, violence can happen at any time, anywhere, and include anyone's son or daughter.

Furthermore, school violence incidents often generate fear and concern among victims, survivors, and the broader public, and have the potential to escalate into copy-cat actions. Recent school shootings have changed the face of school security forever and serve as harbingers of a new era in school violence. It is an era when violence is both random and carefully executed, ambitious and without conscious, horrifically deadly and yet perpetrated by the child next door. Twelve shootings in U.S. schools brings this point home. They include the following:

1. February 19, 1997–Bethel, Arkansas–A 16-year-old student fatally shoots a fellow student and the principal, and wounds two other students.

2. October 1, 1997–Pearl, Mississippi–A 17-year-old boy kills his mother and shoots nine students, two fatally.

3. December 1, 1997–West Paducah, Kentucky–Three students are killed and five others wounded by a 14-year-old student.

4. March 24, 1998–Jonesboro, Arkansas–Four girls and one teacher are shot to death and ten people wounded when two boys, 11 and 13, open fire from the woods after setting off a false fire alarm at a middle school.

5. April 24, 1998–Edinboro, Pennsylvania–A science teacher is shot to death, another teacher and two pupils are wounded in front of students at an eighth-grade graduation dance. A 14-year-old student awaits trial.

6. May 19, 1998–Fayetteville, Tennessee–An 18-year-old honor student opens fire in a high school parking lot, killing a classmate who was dating his ex-girlfriend.

7. May 21, 1998–Springfield, Oregon–A 15-year-old boy opens fire

killing two students and injuring more than 20. His parents are found slain in their home.

8. April 16, 1999–Notus, Idaho–A high school sophomore fires two shotgun blasts in a school hallway. No injuries.

9. April 20, 1999–Littleton, Colorado–Two young men, ages 17 and 18, dressed in black trench coats, open fire, killing 12 students and one teacher.

10. May 20, 1999–Conyers, Georgia–A 15-year-old boy armed with two guns, opens fire on students–wounding six. The suspect surrendered to the assistant principal.

11. November 19, 1999–Deming, New Mexico–A young boy, dressed in camouflage clothing, shoots and critically wounds a 13-year-old female classmate in the lobby of a middle school. The victim dies two days later. The boy also pointed the gun at the principal and assistant principle before surrendering.

12. December 7, 1999–Fort Gibson, Oklahoma–A 13-year-old boy, armed with a handgun shoots four students as they attempted to enter a middle school before classes started. The boy fired 14 rounds before dropping the handgun.

NOTE: Please keep in mind, the above described incidents are actual shootings, they do not include the numerous threats and other types of violent confrontations that are made throughout the country every day. In fact, the author was going to record and include all incidences of school violence, but they have become so numerous that gathering information would be a huge tasking which would have no foreseeable end point.

There are few accurate up-to-date statistics tracking how many firearms or other weapons have been found in schools or discovered before entry into schools. Further, there are many studies in the statistical pool. Some studies reveal discrepancies, however, most studies reveal a great deal of concurrence. One example, an Executive Summary titled *Indicators of School Crime and Safety 1998*, prepared by the U.S. Department of Education and the U.S. Department of Justice, has shed some light on many statistics concerning school violence.

For example, in 1996, students ages 12 through 18 were victims of about 225,000 incidents of nonfatal serious violent crime at school and about 671,000 incidents away from school. In 1996, 5 percent of all 12th graders reported that they had been injured with a weapon such as a knife, gun, or club during the previous 12 months while they were at school, and another 12 percent reported that they had been injured on purpose without a weapon while at school. Additionally, in 1996-97, 10 percent of all public schools reported at least one serious violent crime to the police or a law enforcement representative. Furthermore, school principals also reported a number of serious violent crimes including murder, rape or other type of sexual battery, suicide, physical attack or fight with a weapon, or robbery. Finally, 76 students were murdered or committed suicide at school during the combined 1992-93 and 1993-94 school years (the latest period for which this type of data is available).

Some additional data compiled by the U.S. Department of Education in 1996 concerning violence and security in public schools includes: 10 percent of all public schools experienced one or more serious violent crimes (i.e., murder, rape, suicide, physical attack or fight with a weapon) that were reported to police or other law enforcement officials; 45 percent of elementary schools, 74 percent of middle schools and 77 percent of high schools reported one or more violent incidents, and 78 percent of schools reported having some type of formal violence-prevention or violence-reduction program.

The U.S. Department of Education also broke these statistics out into categories; they include elementary schools, middle schools, and high schools. Elementary schools reported the following criminal incidents to the police: 1 percent reported rape/sexual battery; 1 percent reported robbery; 2 percent reported physical attack or fight with a weapon; 31 percent reported vandalism; 19 percent reported theft or larceny; and 12 percent reported physical attack or fight without a weapon. Middle school statistics include: 5 percent reported rape/sexual battery; 5 percent reported robbery; 12 percent reported physical attack or fight with a weapon; 47 percent reported vandalism; 44 percent reported theft or larceny; and 51 percent reported physical attack or fight without a weapon. High school statistics include: 8 percent reported rape/sexual battery; 8 percent reported robbery; 13 percent reported physical attack or fight with a weapon; 52 percent reported vandalism; 55 percent reported theft or larceny; and 55 percent reported physical attack or fight without a weapon.'

Additionally, in 1997, the Department of Education polled 1,234 regular public, elementary, middle, and secondary schools systems located throughout the United States and found that 18 percent of students polled reported carrying a weapon such as a knife, gun, or club at any time in the past 30 days. About 9 percent of the students polled reported that they had carried a weapon on school property in the past 30 days. Further, males were about three times more likely than females to carry a weapon on school property. Furthermore, students in lower grades were more likely to have carried a weapon anywhere in the previous 30 days than students in higher grades. Finally, some agencies estimate that over three million crimes occurred in schools during this time frame. One can see this figure is far beyond the reported and recorded figures.

Finally, *USA Weekend's* 13th Annual Teen Survey conducted in the Fall of 1999 questioned a total of 129,593 students in grades 6-12 and found that six in ten students believed that it was possible that a violent event on the scale of Columbine could occur at their school. Further, one in five students stated they had felt afraid at school since the Coulmbine High School killings, with younger students and girls being the most fearful. One in four said they had been intentionally hit at school with nearly four in ten boys stating they had been struck. Seven in ten stated they would feel happier if schools were safer and more than half said they would learn more. Three in four reported that a glance, a slight, or bumping into people caused most conflicts at school. Nearly three in ten had been physically threatened. Eight in ten reported seeing a school fight and one in ten said students carry weapons at school. Nearly four in five had been robbed of something worth more than ten dollars at school and two in three students said there were cliques that were picked on. When asked for solutions, one in five students said that metal detectors would make schools safer, four in ten wanted bad kids sent away, and one in five wanted conflict resolution training.

The above statistics clarify why violence is a major concern to parents, students, teachers, and the administration of any school. These statistics are even more disconcerting when one considers the fact that many criminal acts are not reported due to the fact that some school administrators do not want the public to think they run a "bad school" or have "bad children." For example, the author has been advised of more than one incident involving the discovery of firearms in school buildings which were not reported. Furthermore, school personnel may be reluctant to take actions against miscreants in their care because they believe that their is no such thing as a bad child or that it is their mission to straighten the student out. School staff may also fear a lawsuit if they take disciplinary action. Finally, teachers and staff may be fearful for their own and their families' safety from student retaliation.

As a result of these statistics, there are a great number of proactive measures being developed and implemented to make the introduction of weapons into a school building as difficult as possible. Many of the valuable proactive measures include training teachers to identify troubled youths; counseling programs; students signing contracts to stop violence; students wearing ribbons to pledge support in stopping violence; installation of closed circuit television surveillance systems (CCTV), alarm systems, metal detectors and explosive device screeners; and the hiring of a police presence. Crisis response planning is integral to enhancing any school security effort. The best planning effort starts with prevention and awareness.

The above preventative measures are adopted to create a safe school environment. However, school administrators cannot count on these measures to completely prevent school violence unless security measures approach the level of a correctional system. Consider the fact that firearms even find their way into correctional facilities. Further, school violence occurs in a unique context in every school and every situation making the adoption of any one proactive program impossible. Moreover, school communities can do everything recommended and still experience violence. "There is no single answer, no simple solution, and no guarantees."

To reiterate, many proactive measures are sound; however, many school systems can do more to enhance school security. Any safety/security program is incomplete if an effective crisis response plan is not developed to deal with violence prevention program failure. Proactive measure failure has been demonstrated by the recent school shooting in Georgia. To refresh the reader's memory, the school in Georgia had installed a new CCTV system and had hired a police presence. Neither of these concepts prevented the student (perpetrator) from entering the school with a firearm or stopped this individual from initiating his shooting spree.

Indeed, many proactive solutions can be effective; however, one of the most important proactive solutions concerns the development of a crisis response procedure. This plan is designed to provide school communities with reliable and practical information about what can be done to assist first responders in handling a school violence crisis. Focal points of concern include intervening during a crisis and responding in the aftermath of tragedy. A crisis response plan offers the most efficient path to effective rapid response operations assisting special response police forces, fire department personnel, medical aid personnel and ancillary support personnel saving the lives of hostages, students, teachers, support personnel, visitors, ancillary responders, police officers, and perpetrators. Additionally, these plans should reduce collateral damage typically generated by high threat operations. Further, response plans should also generate a detailed analysis valuable for formulating effective contingency plans. Finally, response programs will prove exceptionally valuable the more crisis situations change and the more chaotic the situation becomes.

One of the most common mistakes personnel make when developing crisis response programs is attempting to make a plan without sufficient information. Make no mistake, existing or projected natural emergency plans are not designed to accomplish this essential mission. Many school administrators believe existing or "tweaked" natural emergency plans are adequate response measures when firearms denial programs fail. Nothing could be further from the truth. The main point of the crisis response plan revolves around the principle of "Saving lives when all other proactive means have failed." Crisis response plans should focus on the elements of rapid containment, area control, and the resecuring of the effected area. Remember, time equates to lives—the longer the perpetrators remain active, the higher the likelihood that additional people will be killed.

What parents want, and what the country demands is a solid plan to enhance school security. Crisis response plans must be site specific and designed to streamline the planning efforts of all emergency responders, heightening personnel survivability and mission success by reducing time-on-target mechanics prior to mission initiation. Indeed, time equals lives–the longer it takes law enforcement officials/emergency responders to act, the higher the likelihood will be that additional people will be killed. The incalculable costs of death, facility destruction, disruption of classes, negative public perception, civil/criminal lawsuits, and the resulting embarrassment of these acts easily exceed the time and cost of any crisis response plan development.

Indeed, school violence incidents have a unique impact on society which may be compounded in many ways. There may be additional fear generated for victims because they were chosen as a target for a specific purpose. Because the basis for attack is often due to their identity, victims may experience a deep personal crisis. Thus, victims may reject the aspect of themselves that was the target for their attack. Assumptions about life may be shattered forever. Terror may be exacerbated because society may be slow to respond in effective ways heightening feelings of vulnerability to repeat attack. Grief may be more intense because victims may lose their sense of community or feel betrayed by educational systems. School violence often appears to be senseless and random making explanations and forgiveness difficult. Students may become afraid to associate with other members of a group that has been targeted. The detrimental impact of school violence incidents necessitates the development of aggressive proactive measures.

In conclusion, for some schools violence may be a minor issue; for others it may be a daily presence. Though the most extreme forms of violence are rare, the threat of all kinds of violence can keep students away from school, prevent them from going to after-school events, and leave them in fear every day. Thus, educational entities can no longer afford the false assumption that "nothing has ever happened here and nothing ever will." Indeed, it has come to the point where schools have to change their attitude about school violence. Many schools think they have a handle on this problem when they don't. Most of the systems that have been put into place are inadequate at best. School administrators cannot simply rely on any existing or projected security/safety systems to completely prevent the introduction of a weapon into the school environment, nor can they expect to thwart all of the efforts of a violent student.

Crisis response plans designed to dovetail into external agency mission concepts are a mandatory life saving concept. Crisis response plans represent a vital part of the school safety trilogy (identification, intervention, and response). Indeed, the development of a crisis response program will demonstrate to community organizations and individual citizens that school personnel and law enforcement entities are aware of security concerns and are proactively involved in addressing these issues. Further, students, educators, parents, law enforcement entities, and community members often feel secure as a result of a well-conceived plan. Finally, hopefully the information covered in this book will play a role in furthering efforts to protect America's children.

CONTENTS

LIST OF FIGURES

LIST OF RESPONSE PLAN EXERCISES

EFFECTIVE RESPONSE TO SCHOOL VIOLENCE

Chapter 1

IDENTIFYING THE OFFENDER

Many citizens tend to believe that school violence is a spontaneous act; however, this is not the case. Students build up to their violent acts and behaviors; they display signs and show a preponderance toward this behavior. Indeed, violent youngsters continue to plague America. The Southern Poverty Law Center, in their publication, "The Intelligence Report," found that the arrests of juveniles for violent crimes skyrocketed 79 percent between 1987 and 1994 (a period in which the population of juveniles in the United States rose only 7 percent. To this day, arrest rates are still well above the levels of the 1980s. Crimes committed by those under 18 years old also are more violent in the 1990s than they were earlier, with young people accounting for larger percentages of all murders, rapes, robberies and aggravated assaults than in the 1980s.

Agents in the Secret Service's National Threat Assessment Center have been researching 40 incidences of school violence and released a report to schools in the fall of 2000 on how to detect potentially violent students. Agents have found that predicators are vague by the nature of individual differences. Furthermore, agents have discovered attacks are often preceded by violent comments and are usually planned rather than spontaneous.

It is more important than ever for teachers, educational professionals, and other school officials to be trained to recognize students at risk of perpetuating violent behavior and initiate intervention programs when applicable. The goal is to identify the troubled student and then intervene by using proper support systems. Indeed, an act of violence can be prevented, but it rarely, if ever, can be predicted. Thus, it is vital for school systems to also prepare crisis action plans in the event a troubled student is not identified or intervention efforts fail.

Early Warning Signs

These enumerated early warning signs are presented with the following qualifications: they are not all inclusive, equally significant, or presented in order of seriousness. The following are some warning signs (researched by the Behavioral Science Unit of the FBI, the Department of Education, and the Department of Justice) a student may display or be subjected to which may precede a potentially lethal act:

1. A history of violence.
2. A close family member has committed a violent act.
3. A history of alcohol or drug abuse.
4. A precipitating event such as a failed romance or the perception of a failed romance.
5. Availability of a weapon or the means to commit violence.
6. Recent attempts to commit suicide or

violence.

7. A lack of coping skills or strategies to handle personal life crisis.
8. A lack of inhibition to display anger or the absence of a positive way of releasing anger.
9. No apparent support system.
10. Indications of low self-esteem.
11. Previous acts of cruelty to animals.
12. Fire setting.
13. Bed-wetting beyond a normal age.
14. Being abusive to adults.
15. A fascination with firearms.
16. Lack of discipline.
17. Possessing a narcissistic view or favorable views about self.
18. Feeling rejected, persecuted, or picked on.
19. Perception of being different from others and the dislike of those who are different.
20. Appears to be a loner.
21. Appears to be an average student.
22. Appears sloppy or unkept in dress.
23. May be influenced or used by manipulative students.
24. May have a history of mental health treatment.
25. May have a propensity to dislike popular students or students who bully others.
26. May have expressed interest in previous incidents of killings.
27. May have felt powerless and always perceives self as being the victim.
28. May have openly expressed a desire to kill others.
29. Expression of violence in writings and drawings.
30. Shows a lack of interest in school.
31. Displays an absence of age-appropriate anger control skills.
32. Demonstrates a persistent disregard for or refusal to follow rules.
33. Talks constantly about weapons or violence and/or is obsessed with things like violent games and TV shows.
34. Displays signs of depression or mood swings.
35. Talks about bringing weapons to school.
36. Has a history of bullying. Some studies show that one in four children who bully will have a criminal record before the age of thirty. Bullies often have a small group of children (a pseudo gang) who follow them around. They are a type of violent leader, are outgoing, manipulative, and instigate fights.
37. Displays misplaced or unwarranted jealousy.
38. Is involved or interested in gangs.
39. May be socially inept and tend to be out of the norm or out of the mainstream of the school population.

Early Warning Sign Misinterpretation

Remember, early warning signs may or may not indicate a serious problem. These signs do not necessarily mean that a child is prone to violence toward self or others. Rather, early warning signs provide an impetus to check out concerns and address the child's needs. Early warning signs allow school communities to act responsibly by getting help for the child before problems escalate. However, it is important to avoid inappropriately labeling, stigmatizing, or profiling an individual student because he or she appears to fit a specific profile or set of early warning indicators. **Note**: Suspect profiling is being challenged in the legal systems as this book is being written. Results and civil penalties are pending.

A good rule of thumb to follow is to assume that warning signs, especially when present in a cumulative fashion, indicate a need for further analysis in order to determine an appropriate intervention response. Indeed, the more signs that are identified, the greater the chance that the child needs help. When a number of these signs are observed, the educational professional should start background checks and notify the appropriate support personnel.

Unfortunately, there is a real danger that early warning signs may be misinterpreted. Indeed, overreaction and the jumping to conclusions will likely prove counter-productive. Thus, educators should apply the following principles to avoid the misinterpretation of warning signs: do no harm; understand violence and aggression within a context; avoid stereotypes; view warning signs within a developmental context; and finally, understand that children typically exhibit multiple warning signs. It must be reiterated that while an act of violence may be prevented, it rarely can be predicted. Indeed, predicting violent behavior is very difficult due to all of the human variables involved.

In conclusion, it is inappropriate and potentially harmful to use early warning signs as a checklist against which to match individual children. Early warning signs should be used as an aid in identifying and referring children who may need help to support systems. Thus, school communities must ensure that staff members and students relegate early warning signs to identification and referral purposes. Finally, only trained professionals should make diagnosis in consultation with the child's parents or guardian.

Imminent Warning Signs

Unlike early warning signs, imminent warning signs indicate that a student is very close to behaving in a way that is potentially dangerous to self and/or others. Typically, the student's aggressive behavior will be viewed as "out of control." In orthodox psychiatric terms, anger and resulting aggressive behavior originate within a small child when basic needs or drives are not met. The anger each person feels in the present is said to be founded in past angers and disappointments originating within their families and individual life experiences. Aggression explodes when anger grows great and individuals do not possess strong enough internal defenses (anger management skills) to control it.

Indeed, some students may believe that aggression and violent behavior are their only choice. Chances are this student learned this lesson at home. Parents may teach their children to be violent by example and by exhortation. Violence is taught and reinforced when parents are violent with each other and with their children. Some parents may openly and deliberately teach their children to resolve disputes with other children through the use of brute force. For example: these parents routinely threaten to punish their children for not fighting; advise their children on how to fight; label not fighting as babyish and/or unmasculine; and these parents may allow fights to continue long after other parents would have intervened. The result of this parental indoctrination to aggression and violent behavior may result in the creation of children who do not know how to cope with angry feelings in ways that are not violent. Indeed, these students may harbor no faith that aggression and violence can be prevented. Finally, children may be quick to choose violent aggression, if in the past, they themselves have been the subject of someone else's rage.

Further, males are typically more violent than females and many chemical substances, for example, alcohol, PCP, methaphetamines, and cocaine, etc., have been associated with aggression. There are a number of studies and theories associated with the use of these chemicals and aggression. These theories show a strong association between the above-listed chemical substances and subsequent displays of aggression and violent acts.

Perhaps the age group most prone to committing violent acts is the 12-20-year-old individual. From a developmental standpoint, a certain attraction to violence is seen by many mental health experts as a normal trait. For example, the insecurity the 12-20 year old feels feeds their needs to take risks, heightens their energy level, generates a sense of invincibility, and may propel them toward behavior many adults might label as foolhardy. However, students displaying imminent warning signs often represent a more serious condition. For example, these students may experience non-specific feelings of anger which are easy to ignite. Indeed, any small provocation may cause an eruption of aggressive feelings, causing the individual to strike out at the nearest target.

The above age group represents a period of life requiring a great deal of adjustment. Almost nothing stays constant, a world once viewed as simple has suddenly grown into a complex environment. Some of these changes include body growth, sexual interest, emotions, ideas, gender identification, relationships, etc. As a result of these changes, students often see themselves as persons separated from their parents and siblings, search for independent identities, learn to think for themselves, and make decisions for themselves. For many teenagers and their parents, the adolescent years are filled with intense emotional struggle.

The kindness most adults show small children is often withdrawn from teenage boys whose challenging attitude toward authority and growing physical prowess may be seen as threatening by men and frightening to women. Fathers, teachers, principles, police officers, and other authority figures may feel compelled to show young males who is boss or desire to "teach them a lesson." Experimenting and risk-taking are a normal part of adolescence as the student adopts new styles, new personalities, new opinions, new friendships, and new romances.

Adolescents may display an inflated self-confidence, tend to overestimate their own talents, and underestimate the risks that await them. Adolescents may feel a need to prove themselves by fighting to protect a mother's honor, a girlfriend's fidelity, or to build a reputation. The problem is magnified when weapons are used in lieu of fighting. Of course, not all young men are equal in jeopardy, some are more at risk than others. For example, what father figures teach adolescent's can be negative; for example, drinking, drugs, illegal activity, fighting, and domestic violence. Thus, many mental health experts believe that aggressive, anti-social adolescents are not born, they are slowly made over many years.

Imminent warning signs usually are presented as a sequence of overt, serious, hostile behaviors or threats directed at peers, school staff, or other individuals. Imminent warning signs may include the following:

1. Serious physical fighting with peers or family members. If fighting continues from the early years into the elementary school years, there is a likelihood of continued violence. Most fighters are said to be identifiable by the age of eight or nine. Fights in school are often categorized as fights over territory, game rules, toys, playground equipment, and for retaliation.
2. Severe destruction of property.
3. Severe rage for seemingly minor reasons.
4. Detailed threats of lethal violence.

5. Possession and/or use of firearms ·and other weapons.
6. Other self-injurious behaviors or threats of suicide.

Imminent warning signs require an immediate intervention response which typically requires mental health assistance. Many mental health providers believe that the right therapeutic intervention can teach individuals new ways of behaving and relating to others. Indeed, many of these behaviorally-oriented therapies are supported by research data which depict precisely to what extent a specific course of therapy alters attitudes and behaviors. Thus, intervention along these lines may prove to be very effective.

Teaching Students to Kill

The United States is said to have more violent crime than any other industrialized nation; likewise, the popular culture is more violent than that of most other countries. The question remains: does the popular culture inspire many children to commit violent acts? Consider the following: movies; broadcast talk; television drama; children's TV; toys; video games; sports; music for adolescents; electronic links; violently descriptive print and broadcast news concepts, and pictures. Brutality, aggression and violence are often portrayed as ordinary and amusing to the point that the population takes them for granted.

Tragically, emotion, a critical humanizing element associated with violence, is often watered down or completely neutralized. Further, violence is often made to look like a glamorous, sexy, successful, entertaining method of resolving disputes. Is it any wonder many students cannot understand that death is permanent, unalterable, final, and tragic? One can easily understand how students experiencing repeated exposure to

real-life or fictional violence can become desensitized to the wrongness of what they are experiencing or seeing and subsequently view violence as normal and/or acceptable. It is often difficult for a young mind to discern between the real and the unreal, the temporary and the permanent. The question arises: do some children act out their violent fantasies not fully comprehending the reality of the situation and accompanying tragic results?

Furthermore, there is the copy-cat aspect—one act encourages another. Researchers have established the view that copy-cat events are not an anomaly; rather, they are rare but predictable occurrences. Human beings are recognized as being a suggestible species, learning how to behave from each other. When humans see another person act, the act may become a model for others to emulate. Most researchers agree that publicity alone will not "cause" a person to engage in violent activity; however, constant exposure to information concerning violence may plant and legitimate the idea that the killing of one or more persons is an acceptable way to avenge oneself as a result of real or perceived events.

In conclusion, some children are more vulnerable to choosing violence than others. A number of mental health experts believe that aggression is a learned behavior and that our society is teaching children to kill. Children mimic what they see and react to things they are exposed to. If the child has no positive role model, he or she will more than likely develop his or her own. In many cases, this role model will be one associated with violent rap videos and/or movies. Oftentimes these role models are rebelling against authority, whether it is law enforcement, the government, or society itself. These role models often show that might is right or proport the survival of the fittest. Indeed, these role models often use violence to settle all problems. Perhaps this is why violence can appear at all levels of society and social and economic levels. Indeed, violence impacts all of us and crosses all racial and ethnic backgrounds. Further, experts believe that if aggression is a learned behavior, it can be unlearned (controlled or managed) through a number of intervention methods.

Intervention

Creating safe schools is the responsibility of the entire community in which a school or school system is located, but responsibility for maintaining these systems on a day-to-day basis lies primarily with school administrators and to a lesser extent with the local law enforcement agency. Indeed, imminent warning signs often require immediate intervention by school authorities and possibly by law enforcement officials; for example: a child has presented a detailed plan (time, place, and method) to harm or kill others, particularly if the child has a history of aggression or has attempted to carry out threats in the past. Another example would be a child who is carrying a weapon, particularly a firearm, and has threatened to use it. Of course, parents should be informed of the concerns immediately.

School communities have the right to seek assistance from appropriate agencies such as child and family services and community mental health agencies. However, all intervention actions must reflect school board policies, school policies and procedures, and comply with all federal, state and local laws. Of course, teachers and administrators will need to be supported by qualified mental health consultants who can address behavioral issues. Recognizing the warning signs and responding with comprehensive intervention systems enable concerned persons with the opportunity to

help children.

Intervention typically has three levels: primary, secondary, and tertiary. Primary steps include actions designed to prevent a crisis from happening, for example, violence prevention, suicide prevention, anger management, and diversity acceptance. Secondary steps are taken to minimize effects in the immediate aftermath of a crisis, and tertiary steps involve actions taken to provide long-term services to those most affected by a crisis.

In order to make schools safer, everyone can and must pitch in–teachers, parents, students, policy makers, law enforcement officers, local business entrepreneurs, faith leaders, civic leaders, youth workers, the juvenile justice system, and other concerned community residents.

The Responsibilities of Parents

Parents are also responsible for helping to create safe schools. However, some parents place the school in a position of raising their children. This should not be the case, schools are designed to educate children, not raise them or serve as a surrogate parent. It is meaningless to blame educators, police response methods, movies and/or video games, and students for school violence, if parents are not willing to accept responsibility for their children. School violence is a multifaceted problem and parents cannot relinquish their responsibility in helping to create safe schools.

Indeed, parents can and should support identification and intervention methods by performing a number of actions. Some of these actions require individual effort while others require a concerted effort. Furthermore, some actions address immediate issues and others address the problems that cause violence. The following information is intended to serve as ideas only and should not be considered as the only actions available. Parents should consider the following actions:

1. Discuss the school's discipline policy with their children and show support for these rules. This action will help the child understand the importance and reason for rules, regulations, and policies.

2. Involve children in setting rules for appropriate behavior in the home. If children are allowed to misbehave at home they are likely to do so at school. Parents should set clear limits on appropriate and inappropriate behaviors to include the delineation of resulting punishments and rewards. Disciplining and rewarding should be performed within a framework focusing on consistency and ultimately target self-discipline.

3. Talk to the child about the violence he or she may see on television, in video games, and possibly in the neighborhood. Discuss what violence is and is not. Answer all questions thoughtfully and thoroughly. Finally, explain the fact that violent behavior is not acceptable and won't be tolerated.

4. Teach the child how to examine and solve problems, then praise the child when he or she follows through. Children who know how to approach a problem and resolve it effectively are less likely to become angry, frustrated, or violent. Children should be taught how to deal with angry feelings in ways that are not violent, for example: counting to ten, walking away from an argument, using words instead of punches, and making a joke to defuse the tension.

5. Help children find ways to show anger that do not involve verbally or physically hurting others. When parents get angry, they should use the opportunity to model appropriate responses for their children and then talk about the situation.

6. Help children understand the value of accepting individual differences. Name-calling and teasing should be prohibited.

7. Note any disturbing behaviors in a child's behavior, for example, frequent angry outbursts, excessive fighting and bullying of other children, cruelty to animals, fire setting, frequent behavior problems at school and on the playground, lack of friends, and alcohol or drug use. Any of these behaviors may represent signs of serious problems. If identified, parents should get professional help for the child. Parents should talk with a trusted professional located in the child's school or in the community system in order to address these behaviors.

8. Lines of communication must remain open between parent and child, even when the going gets tough. An open line of communication should provide for two-way conversation forgoing judgments or pronouncements. Lines of communication should remain open an a daily basis and not solely in reaction to crisis events. Children should also be encouraged to tell parents where they will be and whom they will be with. Above all, parents need to become familiar with their child's friends. Finally, parents should strive to make the child's home an inviting and pleasant place for their child and friends to visit and use as a play area.

9. Parents should listen to children if they express concerns about friends who may be exhibiting troubling behaviors. This information should be shared with a trusted professional, such as a school psychologist, principal, school resource

officer, or teacher.

10. Parents should be involved in the child's school life by supporting and reviewing homework, talking with teachers, and attending school functions such as parents conferences, class programs, open houses, and PTA meetings. Also, parents may volunteer to perform the duties of a greeter at the entrance to school buildings and/or volunteer to work as teachers, aids in classrooms or the school library.

11. Parents should work with the child's school administration in order to make the institution more responsive to all students and families. Parents should share ideas with school personnel concerning how the school can encourage family involvement, welcome all families, and get families involved in meaningful ways in their children's education.

12. Parents should encourage schools to offer before and after-school programs complete with adult supervision. At the very least, parents should become involved in the development of standards for school-related events and out-of-school activities.

13. Parents should volunteer to work with school-based groups concerned with violence prevention. If none exist, parents should offer to form one.

14. Parents should find out if there is a community-based violence prevention group and offer to participate in the group's activities.

15. Parents should interact with the parents of their child's friends and discuss how a team can be formed to ensure the children's safety.

16. Parents should find out if their employer offers provisions for parents to participate in school activities.

17. Parents must recognize that keeping firearms in the home may put adults at legal risk as well as expose the entire family to physical risk. In many states, parents can be held liable for their children's actions, including the inappropriate use of firearms. Parents who choose to keep firearms in the home must ensure that firearms are securely locked up, store and lock ammunition in a separate location, and train their children to never touch a firearm without the parents' expressed permission and supervision.

18. Parents must realize that they are responsible for controlling their children. It has been said that there is one thing all juvenile delinquents have in common and that is the fact that there is an absence of enough parental influence to have prevented delinquency.

19. Parents should go to the school and ask every obvious question they can think of concerning school security and safety matters. School officials should have a ready answer to every one of the questions asked; if not, the mere asking of a question may compel school officials to consider the issue. The answers will reflect upon whether parents feel confident in a school's ability to provide a safe and healthy learning atmosphere for their child. School officials should not be thought of as superiors but the parents' partners or designates at the school.

The Responsibilities of Teachers and School Officials

Teachers and school officials are responsible for the safety of their students and themselves. These individuals can perform individual actions or participate in concerted efforts. These actions include the following:

1. Report to the appropriate authority as

quickly as possible any threats, signs of or discussion of weapons, signs of gang activity, or any other conditions that might invite or encourage violence.

2. Set norms in the classroom such as refusing to permit any type of violence. Parameters for acceptable behavior should be established to include fair and consistent response to transgressions.

3. Regularly invite parents to talk about their children, including any concerns they may have. Reach out to the parents or guardians and assume responsibility to learn what each student experiences when the school day ends.

4. Learn how to recognize the warning signs that a child might commit a violent act and know how to use school resources to get the troubled child appropriate help. Develop and maintain a network with health care, mental health, counseling, and social work resources in the community.

5. Encourage and sponsor student-led anti violence activities and programs such as peer education, teen courts, mediation, mentoring, and training.

6. Offer to serve on a team or committee to develop and implement a safe school plan, including how teachers should respond in emergencies. Have a plan to follow in the event a dangerous situation is encountered while in control of a group of students. Be familiar with the school's crisis response plan. If the school does not have a crisis response plan, recommend that one be written.

7. Firmly, fairly, and consistently enforce school policies that seek to reduce the risk of violence. Take responsibility for areas outside as well as inside the classroom.

8. Insist that students not resort to name-calling or teasing. Do not condone bullying. Encourage students to demon-

strate the respect they expect. Involve students in developing standards of acceptable behavior and reward good behavior.

9. Teachers should learn and teach conflict resolution, stress relief, and anger management skills. These skills should be applied in everyday life. Discuss these skills in the context of subjects taught. Be a role model for positive behavior. Refrain from acting in ways which are being discouraged and give students a living example of what good behavior is.

10. Incorporate discussions on violence and its prevention into the subject matter taught.

11. Encourage students to report crimes or activities that make them suspicious.

12. Establish "zero tolerance" policies concerning weapons and violence and spell out penalties in advance. Educate students and parents on this policy and include a way for students to report crime-related information that does not expose them to retaliation.

13. Establish a faculty-student-staff committee to develop a safe school plan and invite law enforcement officers to be part of the team.

14. Work with juvenile justice authorities and law enforcement officials on how violence, threats, potentially violent situations, and other crimes will be handled. Meet regularly to review problems and concerns. Develop a memorandum of understanding with law enforcement officials focusing on access to the school building, reporting of crimes, arrests, and other key issues.

15. Develop ways to make it easier for parents to be involved in the lives of their children. Provide lists of volunteer opportunities, ask parents to organize phone trees, and hold events on

weekends as well as weeknights.

16. Work with community groups and law enforcement officials to create safe routes of travel to and from school. Help with efforts to identify and eliminate neighborhood trouble spots.

17. Demonstrate sincerity when voicing concerns for safe schools and the students.

Note: The author has been advised that some teachers, while on school property, are carrying concealed weapons either on their person or in their vehicles. This is a violation of federal law. Not only is this act unlawful, but it sets a poor example for students. How can a teacher tell children not to carry weapons at school when the teachers are carrying weapons? Furthermore, the author has been advised of one incident where a teacher actually took his students to a privately owned vehicle parked on school property during school hours and proceeded to show the students the weapon, at which time the teacher had an accidental discharge, shooting the vehicle. Thus, this demonstrates another problem, inadequate firearms training. Are teachers adequately trained to effectively use firearms and are they knowledgeable about accompanying deadly force issues? School administrators cannot condone teachers who are carrying concealed weapons. Teachers must leave weapons and use-of-force issues to the professionals.

The Responsibilities of Students

Students should also accept some of the responsibility for their own safety. For example, students should talk to teachers, parents, and counselors to find out how they can get involved and do their part to make their school safe. Indeed, there are a number of actions students can take in order to create safe schools, some of these action include the following:

1. Students should listen to friends who are willing to share troubling feelings or thoughts. These friends should be encouraged to seek help from a trusted adult such as a school psychologist, counselor, social worker, religious leader, school resource officer or similar professional. If troubled friends are unwilling to seek help, students may consider seeking help for them. At the very least, students should voice their concerns to their own parents. Finally, students may volunteer to become a peer counselor, working with classmates who need support and help with problems.

2. Students should create, join, or support student organizations that combat violence. For example, a school crime watch program may be developed to include a student patrol in hallways, parking lots, and other areas where students congregate. These students may serve as a good source for other students to report concerns to school officials in an anonymous manner.

3. Students should work with local businesses and community groups to organize youth-oriented activities that help young people think of ways to prevent school and community violence. Ideas should be shared concerning how community groups and businesses can support these efforts.

4. Students may organize an assembly and invite the school psychologist, social worker, counselor, school resource officer, and parents in addition to student panelists in order to share ideas concerning ways to deal with violence, intimidation, and bullying.

5. Students should be involved in planning, implementing, and evaluating their school's violence prevention and response plan. Student activities and

clubs may be asked to adopt an anti-violence theme. Students may start a "peace pledge" campaign, in which students promise to settle disagreements without violence, to reject weapons, and to work toward a safe campus for all students.

6. Students should participate in violence prevention programs and employ their new skills in other settings such as the home, neighborhood, and community.

7. Students should work with their teachers and school administrators to create a safe process for reporting threats, intimidation, weapon possession, drug selling, gang activity, graffiti, and vandalism.

8. Students should ask permission to invite law enforcement officers to their school to conduct a safety audit and share safety tips. Students should interact and share ideas with the officer.

9. Students should help develop and participate in activities that promote the understanding of differences and respect the rights of all students.

10. Students should become familiar with the school's code of conduct and model responsible behavior. Students should also avoid being part of a crowd when a fight breaks out. Further, students should refrain from bullying, teasing, and/or intimidating peers.

11. Students should feel free to seek help from parents or a trusted adult such as a school psychologist, social worker, counselor, teacher, etc. if feelings of anger, fear, anxiety, or depression are experienced.

12. Students must refuse to bring a weapon to school, refuse to carry a weapon for another student, and refuse to keep silent about those students who carry weapons.

13. Students should report any crime immediately to school officials or law enforcement officials. Students should also report suspicious or worrisome behavior or talk by fellow students.

14. Students should learn how to manage their own anger effectively by finding ways to settle arguments by talking it out, working it out, or walking away. Students should also help others settle disputes peaceably. Students may start or join peer mediation programs designed to teach students ways to settle arguments without the use of violence.

15. Older students should mentor younger students to help them adjust to school. New students should also be welcomed and assisted in feeling at home. Younger and new students should be introduced to other students, and incumbent students should also strive to meet at least one student with whom they are unfamiliar each week.

16. Students should avoid joining violent gangs. Gangs may be attractive because they satisfy a whole range of adolescent needs. The most significant of these needs is peer approval and acceptance. However, violent gangs (anti-social groups) are not normal. When young people feel their lives are knit into the fabric of society at large, they do not form or join violent gangs, although they do form (pro-social groups) such as social clubs, fraternities, sororities, and other age-mate groups. Pro-social groups are valuable for satisfying an adolescents needs to belong to a group separate from s family. These groups are effective for providing young people with goals and objectives, a world view, a place where they are valued, and some purpose to life.

The Responsibilities of Law Enforcement Agencies

Law enforcement (LE) agencies may be represented on campus by random police patrols, security officers, or a full-time police officer acting as a school resource officer (SRO). A full-time law enforcement presence (SRO) is by far the most effective choice. For example, SRO's may be used to evaluate internal and external security systems, compile current and potential threat data, and establish a crime scene etiquette program for the school community. However, the SRO must be chosen carefully. This person should be qualified as a police officer and have expertise in the security field. Further, this person must have an interest in and like to interact with young people. Additionally, it takes a dedicated professional to perform what may be termed as routine security functions.

Of course, the real world reveals the fact that many communities cannot afford a full-time SRO. There are approximately 40,000 rural communities in the Untied States and in those 40,000 rural communities, many police departments aren't fully funded. Logistically, these departments cannot tie up an officer in the school all day when that officer needs to be out patrolling the community. However, regardless of logistical concerns, law enforcement representatives should at a minimum, perform the following actions.

1. Get to know students in non-confrontational settings. Law enforcement (LE) officials should be thought of as mentors, peace keepers, and problem solvers, not just an enforcers.
2. Develop a formal memorandum of understanding (MOU) with school officials concerning handling complaints, criminal events, and other calls for LE services.
3. Volunteer to serve on the school's school violence crisis response planning team.
4. Offer to train teachers, staff, and students in personal safety and security efforts.
5. Help students learn about the costs of violence to their community (financial, social, and physical). Link students with others in the community who are affected by violence to help them understand its lasting impacts.
6. Provide accurate information concerning the state's juvenile and criminal justice systems and what happens to youths who are arrested as a result of being involved in violent acts. Also explain the kinds of help that are available to students who are in distress or who are victims of crime.
7. Work to include school administrators, staff, and students in existing violence prevention programs and/or actions.
8. Work with school attendance officers to identify truants and return them to school or to an alternate facility.
9. Develop links with parents through parent-teacher associations and other groups. Educate parents on violence prevention strategies and help them understand the importance of their support.
10. Work with community groups to put positive after-school activities in place throughout the community and for all ages.
11. Start safe corridor programs and block parent programs to make the trip to and from school less worrisome for students. Help with efforts to identify and eliminate neighborhood trouble spots, using community policing and problem-solving principles.

The Responsibilities of the Community

1. Citizens can adopt a school and help students, faculty, and staff to promote a sense of community in the school and with the larger community through involvement in a wide range of programs and activities.
2. Community members should help to strengthen links between school services and the network of community services that can help students and families facing problems.
3. Citizens should join with school and law enforcement officials in the development of safe corridor programs and block parent programs to make the trip to and from school less worrisome for students. Citizens should also help with efforts to identify and eliminate neighborhood trouble spots.
4. Community members should help students with such opportunities as job skill development, entrepreneurship opportunities, and internships.
5. Community members should work with students in skills training, youth group leadership, mentoring, coaching, and other one-on-one and small group activities. Citizens should provide or establish facilities in support of these activities.
6. Employers should provide employees with training on conflict resolution, stress relief, and anger management skills. All violent behavior taking place on a business premises should be immediately addressed and rejected. By applying these skills in everyday life a climate of anti-violence may be built at home, school, and in the community.
7. Citizens should speak up in support of funding and effective implementation of programs and other resources that help

schools develop an effective set of violence prevention strategies.
8. Public health personnel, trauma specialists, defense and prosecuting attorneys, and judges may have important messages to share with students concerning the costs and effects of violence in the community.
9. Employers may help parents meet with teachers by providing flexible hours or time off. Employers may encourage employees to become involved in sponsoring or coaching students in school or after-school activities. Much of the crime and violence on school property occurs after school hours.
10. The community can develop anti-violence competitions where students win prizes. This competition may become a celebrity celebration and take the form of speeches, paintings, drawings, acting, and so forth.
11. Finally, citizens should report crimes or suspicious activities to law enforcement personnel immediately.

The Responsibilities of the Juvenile Justice System

Concern with juvenile delinquency is not new. Indeed, when troubled by the delinquency in their midst, members of every society have sought to account for that phenomenon. Thus, juvenile courts are found in every state and the District of Columbia. This system is designed to protect children from traditional punishments associated with criminal law, involves modified court procedures, and uses enlightened detention and probation practices. The American juvenile justice system utilizes two major principles in handling children: parens patriae and individualized justice. The first principle, parens patriae, focuses on the concept that states act as a wise parent in decisions regarding the child and redirection is sought in lieu of punishment. The second principle, individualized justice, is grounded in actions and methods of treatment tailored to fit the needs of each child coming before the court.

The U.S. Children's Bureau has outlined the following juvenile court standards:

1. Courts have broad jurisdiction in cases of youth under eighteen years of age who require court action or protection because of their acts or circumstances.
2. Judges are chosen because of their special qualifications for juvenile court work: legal training, understanding of social problems, and knowledge of child development.
3. Court hearings should be private, rather than public.
4. The court's procedure should be as informal as possible and should still conform to the rules of evidence.
5. Detention should be in separate detention facilities specifically designed for youth and should be used only if the following conditions exist:
   a. The minor is in need of proper and effective parental care or control and has no parent, guardian, or responsible relative; or has no parent, guardian, or responsible relative willing to exercise, or capable of exercising, such care or control; or has no parent, guardian, or responsible relative actually exercising such care or control.
   b. The minor is destitute, is not provided with the necessities of life, or is not provided with a home or suitable abode.
   c. The minor is provided with a home which is unfit by reason of neglect, cruelty, or depravity of either of his parents, or his guardian, or other persons in whose custody or care he

is relegated.
   d. Continued detention of the minor is a matter of immediate and urgent necessity for the protection of the minor or the person or property of another.
   e. The minor is likely to flee the jurisdiction of the court.
   f. The minor has violated an order of the juvenile court.
   g. The minor is physically dangerous to the public because of a mental or physical deficiency, disorder, or abnormality.
6. The juvenile court should have a qualified probation staff, with limited case loads.
7. Resources should be available for individualized and specialized treatment: for example, psychological, psychiatric, and medical facilities.
8. There should be an adequate record-keeping system which provides for both social and legal records that are safeguarded from indiscriminate public inspection.
9. Youths brought before the juvenile court for criminal acts should not be defined as criminals but rather as delinquents. The term juvenile delinquents serves as a blanket term describing a large variety of youths in trouble or on the verge of trouble. The delinquent may be anything from a normal mischievous youngster to a youth who gets into trouble by accident. Or he may be a vicious, assaultive person who is proud of his anti-social behavior. Perhaps the most effective approach to clarifying the distinction between adult crime and juvenile delinquency concerns a philosophical distinction between responsibility and accountability. In order to be brief, adults are criminally responsible for their crime where

delinquents are accountable for their acts. Furthermore, parents of these children are viewed as responsible while the child is viewed as accountable.

Finally, even though the juvenile court system has come under heavy criticism in the past several years, few people will argue the fact that society must have some agency concerned with the criminal law violations and the aberrant behavior of children. The goal of the juvenile court system is to provide requisite care for troubled children which will lead them to a healthy and productive adulthood.

In conclusion, school officials and other people who like their thinking supplied to them in convenient packages are prone to wholly oversimplifying the complex problem with which they must deal. As can be seen, school violence is a multifaceted problem requiring multifaceted solutions. Indeed, in order to make schools safer, everyone can and must pitch in–teachers, parents, students, policy makers, law enforcement officers, local business entrepreneurs, faith leaders, civic leaders, youth workers, the juvenile justice system, and other concerned community residents. Each person can and must do something to help solve the problem of school violence.

Chapter 2

STUDENTS PLANNING AN ATTACK

Types of Offenders

There are generally three types of students who plan violent attacks; they are known as reactive offenders, mission offenders, and thrill-seeking offenders. Reactive offenders have a perceived sense of entitlement regarding their rights, privileges, and way of life that does not extend to the victim. This offender may react due to a perceived threat which seemingly threatens the student's way of life, personal relationships, or privilege. Reactive offenders typically focus on protecting and defending against any perceived threat constituted by the presence of "outsiders." This offender may resort to using fear and intimidation to send a message that will repel the "outsiders." Victims of this offender often fall into the category of an individual or group who are perceived by the offender as constituting a threat. Acts of violence may occur in the offender's own neighborhood, place of recreation, or school. If the threat is perceived to subside, the reactive behavior may also subside. Reactive offenders generally feel little if any guilt because this person perceives that violent behavior is a justifiable response to personal feelings of violation.

Mission offenders are often psychotic, suffer from mental illness that may cause hallucinations, have an impaired ability to reason, and often withdraw from other people. The mission offender's motivation revolves around believing he or she has been instructed by a higher order (God, the Fuhrer, the Imperial Wizard, etc.) to rid the world of an evil. He or she may also believe that he or she must get even for any misfortunes he or she may have suffered. This offender may also perceive a conspiracy of some kind being perpetuated by the person or groups targeted for violence. This offender may also feel a sense of urgency about his or her violent mission believing he or she must act before it is too late. Victims often fall into the category of an individual or group who are perceived as responsible for the offender's frustrations. All members of a despised group may be targeted for elimination. Acts of violence are likely to occur wherever the targeted group is likely to be found. Their mission often ends in the offender's suicide.

Thrill-seeking offenders are often trying to fit into a group. Their motivation revolves around gaining a psychological or social thrill, to be accepted by peers or to gain bragging rights. Victims may constitute any person or vulnerable group, especially if they are perceived as inferior by the offender. Acts of violence are likely to occur wherever the targeted group is likely to be found. Since attacks are random, it is often difficult to identify the offender. Attacks often involve desecration and vandalism, although they can involve more violent actions. Hatred of the victim is relatively superficial; offenders may be deterred from repeating actions if there is a strong societal response condemning the behavior.

Any of these offenders may become what law enforcement professionals call "Active Shooters." These active shooters often intend to kill as many people as possible and may have no plan or intentions of escape. The active shooter may intend to do as much damage as possible and then commit suicide by his or her own hand. Additionally, the active shooter may confront the police and force action or attempt to escape the crime scene. Finally, active shooters can be expected to be heavily armed with more than one weapon and carry a large amount of ammunition.

Students Planning an Attack

There may be some readers who believe students commit acts of violence with little thought or preparation. However, this does not appear to be the case with many of the more violent incidents recently witnessed. A good example of students planning an attack is illustrated in the incident of four teenage boys plotting to conduct a Columbine-style shooting rampage at South High School in Cleveland, Ohio. The plot was discovered when a student tipped off school officials that the teens planned to open fire on October 29, 1999, the day of the school's home-coming dance and football game. The police found two maps depicting predetermined shooting positions for each shooter and a list of possible students to recruit for the planned massacre. The students were subsequently arrested and pleaded guilty to conspiracy to commit aggravated murder and/or inducing panic. Prosecutors stated that while the threat was real, the students were still in the planning process when they were arrested. Prosecutors further stated that

the students planned to open fire first in the school's office and gym. Then, the students planned to attack the school's two cafeterias and wait in the courtyard for police to arrive. Finally, prosecutors stated that the teens planned to commit suicide like the perpetrators did during the massacre at Columbine High School.

As demonstrated above, once a student or students have targeted a school for attack, an extensive planning phase may be set into motion. Granted, sophistication of an attack and the planning phase for the attack will vary in detail. However, the mechanics of an attack will likely focus on the following areas to some degree: target selection, tactics, operation style, and the completion of a plan of attack.

Target Selection

Once motivated, the student will select a target school after answering the following questions. Is the target school critical, accessible, easily restored, vulnerable, and what effect will the attack and subsequent death and destruction have on the local and national population?

A target school is deemed critical when destruction or damage will have a significant impact upon unique specialized functions. Some examples include the following: importance the local community places on the school as a meeting place; the importance of athletic functions; identifying the school as a cherished institution of learning; and recognizing the school as a healthy extension of family life. Of course, the criticality of a target school may change with political, economic, and sociologic fluctuations.

A target school is accessible when the perpetrator can easily infiltrate the target site. Students will often gather detailed intelligence concerning the school's location, physical structure, and efficiency of security measures. A target school is easily restored if restoration efforts are considered efficient and quick or if students can be easily transferred to other facilities. This is important as the offenders may consider the effort not be worth the risk. However, if restoration will be expensive, difficult, time consuming, or impractical, the target school may become a favored target for attack.

School site vulnerability focuses on whether the school is open to attack by the means and capabilities available to the offenders. Offender means include explosives or bombs, both conventional and unconventional; arson; assassination; raid type attacks; hostage taking; sabotage; insider assistance; and mob/gang actions, etc. Offender capabilities include available manpower, logistics, support networks, money, training, and the availability of weapons and explosives. A focal point of

offender capability lies in the fact that school attacks always enable streamlined assets when compared to defending assets (it may only require one or two students to successfully attack an educational facility protected by numerous security systems and personnel). Offenders will often compare their means and capabilities to the target school's location, type, security systems, security forces, and available assistance.

Finally, the offender will often consider how the public will react to the attack? Will there be economic, political, psychological, and sociological impact? Can a nation-wide educational system be affected by these attacks or at the very least, will only a certain area be affected? For example, many local economies cannot afford heightened security measures or the building of new schools. Will parents fear the prospect of sending their children to school, allow their children to use school transit, allow their children to

Figure 1. Drawings of a facility, used when planning an attack.

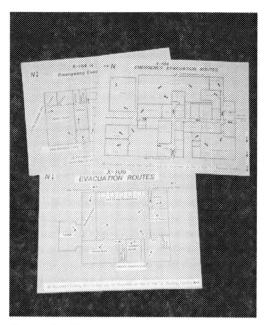

Figure 2. Evacuation routes taken from a facility—used for planning an attack.

attend school gatherings, or even allow their children to leave their homes? Will education professionals such as school administrators and teachers be afraid of going to school? Will the government and educational system become repressive in order to protect children, and will parents/children accept or even demand this type of reaction? Can sociological unrest be developed or exploited?

Naturally, each question does not require an affirmative answer for the student to choose a certain target school; however, as favorable factors accumulate, chances are a target school will be chosen for attack. Particularly desirable targets are high-profile in nature, for example, large school facilities, schools located in or around large cities, and schools representing popular landmark events for the community.

Perpetrator Tactics

In order to understand the effectiveness of student attacks, their tactics must be examined. A student may specialize using only one tactic or utilize several techniques which range from simple acts of sabotage to utilizing weapons and explosives. The tactics chosen usually corresponds to the student's abilities, philosophies, expertise, funds, or by what tactic is most effective at the time. Their purpose is to:

1. Destroy or damage educational institutions.
2. Gain control of an educational institution.
3. Eliminate students and school officials.
4. Harass educational institutions and systems.
5. Harass the community.
6. Harass educationally tied organizations.
7. Harass government organizations–this includes police organizations.
8. Attract media attention.
9. Terrorize a society.

Perpetrator tactics may include the use of subversion, sabotage (passive and/or active), threats or hoaxes, bombs, arson, assassination, media manipulation, armed raids, and hostage taking.

Subversion

Subversion is often the students' main goal and is best described as "actions designed to undermine the economic, psychological, or political strength of an educational entity." Sabotage (a very effective form of subversion) permits the selective destruction of facilities using a minimum of manpower and resources. Often sabotage is utilized by subversive students or organizations to gain recognition, momentum, support, and to recruit members.

Sabotage

There are two types of sabotage, known as passive and active. Passive sabotage uses subtle, non-violent techniques which may be difficult to recognize as a subversive activity. Passive sabotage includes mass absenteeism, boycotts of classes or educational institutions, demonstrations, protests, or organized substandard student performance. Active sabotage may be high profile and easier to recognize as an offender activity. Active sabotage includes mechanical, incendiary, explosive, and administrative methods. Mechanical sabotage is the deliberate damaging or destruction of school equipment by deliberate abuse, neglect, or the introduction of harmful additives into the critical parts of expensive or crucial equipment. Incendiary sabotage is the damage or destruction of school facilities by fire. Explosive sabotage is the damage or destruction of school facilities by explosives. Administrative sabotage is the deliberate garbling of instructions or guidance, misdirection, destruction or loss of documents, computer hacking, and the blocking or interference with communications.

Threats or Hoaxes

Threats or hoaxes are intended to force a targeted school to respond without actually carrying out a physical act. Threats or hoaxes disrupt educational productivity, normal day-to-day activity, and create fear and/or panic. This tactic can cost an educational system vast amounts of money, damage educational productivity, disrupt operating efficiency, and tie up valuable school and emergency response assets. Threats and hoaxes cost the offender

nothing. However, if an offender uses this tactic too often, the need to actually carry out violent activity may be committed in order for future threats or hoaxes to be taken seriously.

The dilemma encountered by a targeted school experiencing numerous threats or hoaxes is this: can a student threat ever be categorized as just another threat or hoax? (Remember the gamble is life–the pay off may be death.) How much is human life worth? Ultimately, the effectiveness of threats or hoaxes hinges on the value of life! **Note:** The hoax technique may also be a basic technique used by a student to "test" the effectiveness of response plans and personnel. This act may be a primary technique used by a student to assist in his or her intelligence gathering efforts when considering potential or real targets. A hoax is often not just a hoax but a serious analysis of potential targets and should never be regarded as simply "just some kooky student intent on annoying us."

Bombs or Explosives

Bombs/explosives are a favored tactic due to their propensity to maximize casualties, death, destruction, and sensationalism. An added attractiveness is the minimal use of assets and manpower. Bombs may be easily constructed on a low budget and technological base or be extremely sophisticated. A total explosive package may be commercially obtained, stolen, or constructed by improvisation. Bombs include conventional/unconventional types such as vehicle bombs; suicide bombs; letter bombs; and military weapons, i.e., rockets, mines, mortars, hand grenades, and booby traps. Increased technological sophistication and the availability of information may be seen in the use of complex timing devices and fuses.

Arson

Arson is mainly used by students to destroy school facilities through the use of flame-producing devices, but casualties or deaths are often viewed as bonuses. Arson is usually carried out by incendiary devices which are designed to ignite after the student has left the scene. Fire enhancing devices may also be left at the scene; for example, school fire extinguishers may be filled with flammable liquid in the hope they will be sprayed on the fire. Of course, unsophisticated devices may be used as well.

Assassination

A student may also employ a tactic known as assassination to kill school administrators, teachers, and other support personnel. Assassination targets are selected based upon retaliation, symbolism, and for the publicity the act will generate.

Media Manipulation

The media provides students with immediate publicity and dramatization of their cause. The media may represent an extremely powerful and effective tool used by students to enhance or perpetuate additional violent actions. Fear and intimidation may be spread nationwide and even worldwide through media coverage of a violent student act. Media vehicles include exclusive interviews, video tape, audio tape, telephone tape, and a convenient eye witness.

Figure 3. Explosive device enhanced with an accelerant.

Armed Raids

Armed raids are usually military style surprise attacks which target educational installations. The tactics involve violent combat-type actions, rapid disengagement, and swift, deceptive withdrawal or suicide. Raids are often designed to demonstrate strength, destroy and/or damage facilities, kill and/or injure personnel, and to create fear or terror.

Hostage Taking

A final perpetrator tactic, hostage taking, is a high profile activity designed to capture headlines. Hostage taking may be implemented as a retaliatory activity or to advance ideology. Students may kill their hostages and even desire to be killed themselves in order to enhance their organization or message. Negotiations may be futile.

Operation Style

Once a school has been selected for attack and a tactic has been chosen, operation style is considered. The styles to choose from are known as overt or covert. Overt operations are conducted with no attempt made to conceal either the operation or identity of the students involved. Overt operations are chosen, in order to obtain maximum publicity. Covert operations are designed, planned, and executed in order to conceal the identity of the students involved. The operation receives the publicity instead of the perpetrator.

The Mechanics of Planning and Developing a Violent Attack

The actual planning sequence will usually involve the most complete/accurate information that time allows. Timetables are usually controlled by the student. The student will often consider the schools location. The location is important for many reasons; for example, urban/suburban areas may generate more incidental or collateral damage, death and/or casualties than a rural target. A rural target may be much easier to infiltrate and exfiltrate than an urban/suburban target due to terrain features and sparse population.

Second, students may gather maps, photographs, schedules, brochures, sketches, and blueprints of the targeted school. Maps may include commercial maps, topographical maps, and school-generated maps. Photographs may include air-to-ground shots, ground level stills, or camera-recorded media cut from school-disseminated brochures, newspaper articles, magazine articles, etc. . . . Schedules include advertised tours, meetings, special activities and programs, VIP visits, and daily operating schedules. Brochures disseminated for advertisement or information purposes may be gathered and sketches may be drawn depicting line-of-site areas. Blueprints of buildings and facilities may be obtained from government entities, i.e., federal, state, county and local sources.

Third, facility power/fuel type may be of interest due to flammable, explosive, and contamination properties. Fourth, the number of students and support personnel employees on-site during regular shifts and off-shifts and work hours/days may be documented. If mass casualties are desired, the student(s) may attack during peak operational hours, or if infiltration is a priority, off hours may be chosen in order to lessen the chance of discovery.

Fifth, school transportation capabilities may be targeted for initial neutralization along with facilities. Finally, security personnel may be evaluated specifically focusing on the type, i.e., unarmed, armed, trained, or untrained. Security force strength and work schedules may also be projected. Normal duties/locations and emergency response duties/locations may be plotted. Information concerning physical screening systems, alarm systems, communication systems, and emergency access/response procedures may also be gathered.

Once all of the planning elements are gathered and completed, an appropriate attacking force may be assembled. This force may range from one student to a number of students possessing conventional/unconventional weapons and explosives. Mission scope delineates the attacking strength. Time is required for students to become motivated, answer critical questions, choose tactics, seek proper training, decide upon operating style, complete planning, and gather equipment and attacking forces. During this timespan, school facilities may operate in a lackadaisical manner believing "nothing has ever happened here and nothing ever will." This mind-set must be avoided at all cost or defending against a determined well-planned student attack will surely end in disaster.

Thwarting the Attack

To best thwart students planning a violent attack, it is imperative that school systems and law enforcement officials develop a partnership. Launching and strengthening police/school partnerships which also include civic leaders, parents, and students can positively support school violence prevention actions, spur interest in additional preventative measures, and reduce crime, victimization, and fear. The best reason for working together is the sharing of responsibility for the safety of the school and the community it serves. Schools and communities must interact because one cannot be safe unless the other is safe.

Further, school officials can find out what help law enforcement can offer and law enforcement officers can better understand school processes and problems. Emergency procedures can also be agreed upon in advance. Finally, the partnership will often generate mutual goals, bolster more power to persuade others to change and/or to get involved, and provide greater information sources for solutions.

The key partners in this endeavor are the senior school officials and senior law enforcement officials. The match should be one-to-one; the focus should be on the school and the surrounding neighborhood; and the partners should have decision-making authority even though it is realized that most policies cannot be enacted unilaterally. Senior officials should work together to establish agreements and understandings about policies and procedures; develop both preventative and problem-solving strategies; keep each other informed of activities and issues that touch on security and safety; encourage close communications between supervising agencies; and periodically review progress.

Finally, to begin the partnership, officials should set up a short initial appointment to talk about school safety and security issues; review actions that require policy changes; discuss issues or problems with respect to the school facility; identify additional community partners; review elements of collaboration among the cooperating agencies; draw up a memorandum of understanding (MOU) covering identified key issues; agree on a regular communication schedule and what data will be shared; and get the partnership moving by initiating some early action steps.

Early action steps may be divided into three areas: policies and procedures, training and public education and supporting programs. Of course, not all of these ideas will represent a viable option for all schools. Policies and procedures may include steps to take upon discovery of a weapon; the establishment of zero-tolerance programs focusing on weapons, alcohol, illegal drugs and violence; steps to enforce local laws as well as school policies; ways to share information concerning at-risk students; identifying what data needs to be gathered and shared; and establishing effective communications systems.

Additional policy and procedures may include setting forth both positive expectations and clear rules for students, including the notification of students and parents concerning their existence; penalties must be clear and faithfully employed; development of student contracts for specific improvements; requiring the storage of outer garments during school hours; developing and enforcing dress codes; conducting random searches and the use of see-through bookbags and lockers; banning gangs and gang-like behavior; establishing a policy of positive identification; developing resource lists compiling referral services; developing closed campuses during lunch periods; identifying the school perimeter; banning beepers and cellular phones on school property;and finally, removing graffiti as soon as it appears.

Training and education may include training school staff and law enforcement officers to work together when handling school emergencies or a crisis; training school officials and staff how to effectively take reports from students; training teachers how to break up fights with minimal risks; training staff members in anger management skills and how to pass these skills on to students; periodically refreshing students on school rules; learning to identify the signs of a troubled youth; effective sharing of progress reports; developing home firearm safety programs, and identifying personnel for students to approach if they are angry, depressed, or otherwise need help and/or guidance.

Programs may include involving students in anti-violence programs (mediation, mentoring, peer assistance, school crime watch, and graffiti removal); developing anonymous reporting systems; developing red flag systems to ensure reports of students who exhibit warning signs of violence get immediate attention; developing a comprehensive truancy prevention efforts; and conducting periodic security/safety audits. More programs include identifying resources that can help troubled youths; creating a safe homes campaign in conjunction with parents; providing adequate security at all school events taking place after school; establishing emergency intervention teams; and building and sustaining an educational environment that is conclusive.

Some final programs may include providing access to support groups for children who are already facing stress; ensuring that security and safety factors are fully considered in siting, designing, and building additional or new facilities; developing joint-use programming in order for community agencies to develop and conduct after school activities; mapping incidents to examine whether a policy needs to be changed; and finally, establishing a student assistance program that helps young people get help with such problems as substance abuse, violence or anger management, and bullying.

Chapter 3

INTEGRATED SECURITY SYSTEMS FOR EDUCATIONAL FACILITIES

Introduction to Integrated Security systems

Given the recent violence in schools, it is easy to understand the drastic steps being adopted in order to ensure personal and facility security. But what is the ultimate cost to school systems' budgets and students' personal freedom? Does the cost outweigh the benefits? The implementation of drastic security policies and throwing money in the direction of the latest high-tech hardware will certainly give the public the perception of new-found security, but how much of it will actually provide the best safety at the lowest cost? With limited budgets and tremendous pressure to "do something now," school administrators are facing a crisis never before seen in our schools. Administrators must ultimately ask themselves the question: "What can we afford to protect and how can the task be achieved?" This chapter targets these questions and concerns and endeavors to provide the answers.

Any suggestion that an administrator is not doing everything possible in the area of students' safety is certainly a political if not moral time bomb. Thus, the goal is to focus on core security issues and the best, most cost-effective ways to reduce risk. While the installation of the latest high-tech hardware may give everyone a quick fix feeling that "somebody is finally doing something," there is a definite need to go beyond politics, policies, and hardware. To better deal with recent school-related crimes, many schools are turning to tighter security controls and adopting more effective security programs and methods. Indeed, schools around the world are testing different security systems ranging from stand-alone methods to integrated systems.

The author has decided to place an emphasis on integrated security systems due to the fact that schools share many characteristics with other types of occupancies which focus on security concerns. Indeed, as the reader looks at semantics, he or she is sure to see a correlation between schools and other types of entities. School districts should consider following the footsteps of corporations that have already learned and embraced the concept of security system integration as a cost-controlling feature as well as a way of ensuring that the staff and students are receiving the highest level of security that technology can offer.

To begin the discussion on integrated security systems, the author has decided to cover some statistics gathered in 1999 by *Access Control & Security Systems Integration* magazine. These statistics will be broken down into the following categories: the best reasons to spend money on security; top four areas of concern facing heads of security; top four areas of concern facing organizations; top five challenges facing security professionals in their efforts to provide security for the organization; top areas of responsibility for security directors; important factors to consider when making security product/service purchasing decisions; preferred security system components; important people involved in the decision-making for security systems; best reasons to integrate security; and the best targets for integration.

The author has decided not to list figures or percentages but instead will focus on security topics. Furthermore, the results will be listed in descending order of importance. For example, the best reasons to spend money on security include: lowering the incidence of crime/violence; improving operations; lowering liability and litigation; lessening loss/shrinkage; improving cus-

tomer confidence level; improving employee confidence level; achieving a return on investment; meeting mandates; lowering insurance premiums; improving business information; reducing staffing; and finally employing fewer security guards.

The top four areas of concern facing heads of security include employee theft, workplace violence, asset protection, and theft from outside sources. The top four areas of concern facing organizations include insurance and liability, asset protection, workplace violence, plus data and information security. The top five challenges facing security professionals in their efforts to provide security for the organization include issues related to money/budget/costs, management/employee support and education,technology issues/outdated equipment, finding/retaining good employees, and workplace violence/protecting employees.

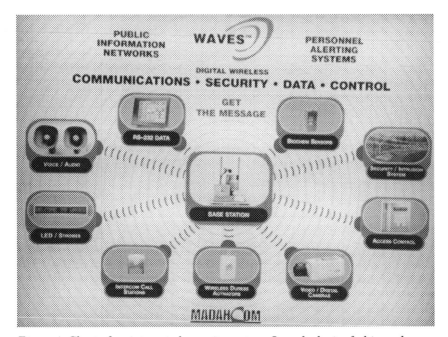

Figure 4. Chart of an integrated security system. In a clockwise fashion–alarms, security/intrusion systems, access control, video cameras, duress alarms, intercom call stations, LED strobes, voice/audio capabilities, security data–all tied into a central base station.

The top areas of responsibility for security directors include access control, perimeter security, electronic surveillance, fire detection/prevention, budgeting; information and data security, loss/shrinkage, employee tracking, and article identification. The important factors to consider when making security product/service purchasing decisions include product liability, service/support capabilities, ease of use, expansion/upgrade capabilities, meeting specifications, vendor reliability/experience, ease of servicing, and service costs. Preferred security system components include CCTV/surveillance, electronic access control, intrusion alarms, fire detection and alarms, electronic locks, photo ID/badging, perimeter security, contract guard services, intercoms/communications, and guard forces (in house).

The important people involved in the decision-making for security systems include the security manager/director, facilities manager, president/owner, human resources manager, other security titles, systems integrator, outside consultant, design engineer, dealer/distributor, and the outside installer. The best reasons to integrate security include centralized monitoring controlled by a central computer network, centralized management, to minimize redundant systems, ease of communications, shared databases and information, and single user interface. Finally, the best targets for integration include electronic access control, intrusion alarms, electronic locks, fire detection and alarms, CCTV/surveillance, photo ID/badging, computer network security, perimeter security, energy management, and intercoms/communications.

The broadest definition of security system integration is very simple: to allow multiple security subsystems to work together making the final master system more efficient. For example, a commonly integrated system includes access controls, alarm monitoring, and closed circuit televisions CCTV (as an access control is breached an alarm sounds and a CCTV system monitors and records the act). A key criterion in selecting and designing an integrated system is flexibility–having a system that meets both current and future needs. Making integrated systems work requires focusing on the solution not the technology.

School administrators and law enforcement agencies should collaborate when deciding what, if any, security technologies should be considered in the development of safe school strategies. Security technologies require thoughtful consideration, focusing not only on potential safety benefits but also the costs that schools may incur for capitol investments, school site modifications, additional staffing, training, and equipment maintenance and repair. The intent of this chapter is not to replace the use of appropriate expert advice or provide detailed instructions on installing equipment or making cost estimates. The intent is to offer practical guidance that should enable schools and law enforcement agencies to make better informed decisions on security technology.

Physical security controls are a vital component of a school security/protection systems; however, these controls are only one element in what should be a complete integrated protection program. Other measures, both physical and psychological, must be implemented to provide optimum protection. Indeed, physical controls, from a practical point of view, can be expected to act as psychological deterrents. Their purpose is to discourage the undetermined offender and delay the determined offender. Physical controls are usually designed to influence the movements, activities, or conduct of everyone located on the school campus. Finally, the design and use of physical security controls and security personnel should be focused on reinforcing school administration strategies.

School security is not simple and straightforward. At any particular school, security is affected by funding, facilities, building age, building layout, administrators, teachers, parents, students, campus order, security personnel, procedures, the neighborhood, policies, school boards, local law enforcement, fire codes, local government, politics, the community, and school reputation. Indeed, many schools have a number of common inherent problems; for example, schools do not usually have the funding for aggressive and complete security programs; schools generally lack the ability to procure effective security technology products and services at the lowest bid; many schools cannot afford to hire well-trained security personnel; school administrators and their staff rarely have training or experience in security technologies; schools have no infrastructure in place for maintaining or upgrading security devices (when something breaks, it is often difficult to have it repaired or replaced), and issues of privacy and potential civil rights lawsuits may prohibit or complicate the use of some available security technologies. Finally, no two schools will have identical and successful security programs, meaning, a security solution for one school cannot just be replicated at another school with complete success. The most effective way to find a security system and associated programs which will best fit the needs of a particular school is to perform a security survey.

Security Surveys

Unfortunately, many schools operate with little regard to security matters. Usually some security problem must surface before any action is taken to address security matters. The old philosophy arises: "it is cheaper and easier to be reactive in lieu of proactive." Of course, security experts realize the fallacy of this concept which include, compromised safety; damage or destruction of property, disruption or destruction of the school;s operation, personnel injury, loss of life, and negative public perception will likely outweigh any current monetary savings.

Quite often, only token security measures ("window dressing") are used in order to give the public the perception that students, school staff, and school property in question are secure, (dedicated adversaries will not be fooled by token security measures). In addition to "window dressing," more serious breeches in security arise when novices are placed in charge of security forces and/or other security-related operations. Novices may be assigned security management duties through politics and personal favors because many people believe that anyone can be a security officer or school resource officer. This belief is erroneous and leads to poor quality security forces, procedures, and protective measures.

To avoid "window dressing," any school facility concerned with security must complete a security survey. A security survey is designed to identify, by means of an on-site inspection, all requirements associated with the application of physical security personnel and equipment to counter one or more substantiated or perceived threats. Additional reasons to complete a security survey include regulatory requirements, insurance requirements, activation of a new site or facility, significant changes in a schools operation or layout, planned site upgrades, increased threat levels, or in response to a school violence crisis or attempted school violence crisis or other security incident.

When a security survey is desired, a

security survey process must be placed into motion. This process consists of gathering data necessary to conduct a thorough analysis of the physical and operational environment in which the security system must operate and the threat postulated against it. Considerations include the full range of events potentially confronting the site or assets to be protected, the consequences of loss or compromise, and what equipment, personnel and techniques would be necessary to deter or prevent such events. The scope and complexity of the security survey are flexible and determined on a case-by-case basis.

Factors influencing the scope of the survey include the size, mission, and complexity of the school; size and complexity of desired security systems; and the desired end results. To obtain specific end results, broad recommendations may be required; for example, site design changes, security expansion and upgrades, or the complete replacement of existing security systems. Remember, the desired end results must be decided upon and understood prior to commencement of the security survey.

For each specific school site, a security survey should contain the following: a description of the site to be protected to include any unique operational factors; description and evaluation of any existing security devices; description of any vulnerabilities; details of new protection recommendations; necessary upgrades or structural modifications; estimate of design and construction costs; and an evaluation of security force capabilities.

Security surveys can be conducted by in-house entities, security equipment suppliers, security consultants or security system integrators. Each of these options have their own limitations. For example, in-house personnel may possess a great deal of institutional knowledge, but may not have

the necessary expertise to conduct a full-scale site survey. Also, it is the author's experience that the purpose of in-house security surveys is almost always defeated by institutional politics; for example, survey personnel may be reluctant to point out problems, especially the ones located in their area of responsibility–how many people fail a self-assessment? Further, cost-saving bonuses may become the in-house goal in lieu of heightened security. To obtain a cost-saving bonus, in-house personnel may select substandard, inadequate, limited security systems which in the long run will perform poorly and require continuous maintenance. Finally, in-house surveys generally work best for small add-ons to existing security systems.

Security system equipment suppliers generally offer "free" security surveys to current or potential customers; however, the results often tend to be biased toward the suppliers products. Unnecessary or redundant equipment may also be recommended. This type of security survey should also be relegated to current security system add-on work.

Security consultants operating as independent operators can conduct security surveys, but they are only as good as their individual level of expertise. Security consultants may operate alone, in small teams, or sub-contract portions of the security survey to other security consultants. Sub-contracting involves one weakness–the dependence on a number of independent operators who may or may not perform to standard. However, efficient sub-contracting or teamwork concepts are indicators of quality consulting because few individuals possess all of the knowledge required for optimum performance in every area of a security survey.

Beware of the "know it all-done it all" security consultant. Full-time security consultants are usually a better choice than part-time security consultants because full-time security consultants are building and risking future job opportunities on each and every performance. They know that the security market will not bear many mediocre or even standard results. The best security consultants will have proven track records supported by a list of references. While some part-time security consultants are very good, many are not since they have other means of support, interest, and obligations which often interfere with security survey mechanics. "Let the buyer beware" many part-time security consultants are in the business for a "quick buck" operating under the philosophy "just give me one big score."

Security system integrators perform security surveys by using a number of security consultants operating in conjunction with a multidisciplined staff capable of delivering a total security survey package. These consultants often specialize in conducting large-scale security surveys, determining requirements, and integrating a wide variety of products and personnel into complete operating systems. The security system integration staff is determined by the project leader after the analysis of pre-security survey data. Like the survey itself, the make-up of the survey team is flexible and dependent on the individual circumstances of each school site.

Security surveys should be written in a professional and responsible manner in order to assist in motivating the recipient to take action to minimize security risks; provide an approach or plan that the recipient can use as a framework for taking action; validate or change the opinion of the recipient with regard to the level of threat potential within the surveyed environment; establish a channel of communications between involved parties to include law enforcement agencies and school administrations; and finally, provide the recipient with a benchmark or measuring device by which evaluation of the steps taken in attempting to secure the environment can be measured.

Initiating the Security Survey

There are generally four major headings in any effective security survey: introduction, identification of the school site, elements of the school site surveyed, and recommendations. The introduction should include the name, address, and telephone number of the target facility. The dates and times the security survey took place should also be included. The person or persons who conducted the security survey should be identified as well as a briefing-type format stating the reason the security survey was conducted, under what authority the security survey was made, and whether or not the security survey was an initial effort or a follow-up action.

The identification of the school site should include the location of the target site by street address, physical directions through the use of a recognizable landmark, and the types of facilities and/or residences located in proximity to the site. Elements of the site surveyed should include the types of risk potential beginning with the boundary and finishing with the interior of the school building(s). Each risk potential should be discussed in the security survey through the use of easy to understand terms.

Specific recommendations should be addressed and discussed in detail after each security element has been addressed. To accomplish this step, two levels of detail may be sought; for example, the site surveyor may describe the minimum steps to be taken to correct security hazards or second, the site surveyor may recommend the optimum steps to secure the site. Naturally, site surveyor(s) should present findings and recommendations as soon as possible upon completion of the site survey to the individual who requested or authorized the site survey.

Presurvey Planning Phase

The first step in conducting a security survey requires the completion of a pre-survey planning phase designed to capture the following information:

1. A master site map depicting all buildings and utilities, roadways, waterways, airstrips, neighboring population location, communication lines, electric lines and substations, and railroad tracks within approximately three miles of the job site. All of these places will be of interest to adversaries and may be used as avenues of approach or escape. Further, these areas will also be of interest to response personnel who may require the delivery of special operations items if a school violence crisis spirals into a protracted problem.

2. A topographic map depicting major terrain features, coastlines, forests, swamps, areas of erosion, creeks, lakes, and rivers. The terrain may assist or complicate site security and adversary activities.

3. Photographs and videotape of the site from as many angles as possible.

4. Information pertaining to important site characteristics.

5. Meteorological data. Are there certain times of the year which produce weather conditions conducive to adversary missions. Weather conditions may also effect response operations.

6. Documentation from prior site surveys. There is no need to completely "re-invent the wheel."

7. A prioritized list of assets or high-risk areas which require protection to include a description of their function and sensitivity. Photographs of the asset should include aerial and ground level photographs plus videotape. Blueprints, drawings, and proposed modifications should also be gathered.

8. All data concerning existing security systems.

9. Current and potential threat data.

10. Copies of all relevant security, safety, and fire regulations.

11. Security force data to include response capabilities.

12. Site access restrictions such as security identification, prohibited articles, searching requirements, and escort requirements.

13. A campus description focusing on primary and secondary missions including their sensitivity and criticality.

14. Data concerning planned upgrades or site modifications. These future activities can easily down-grade current security activities and even render them useless.

15. Number and type of employees including background checks.

Conduct of Events

A security survey should be conducted in an organized manner through the use of a defined conduct of events. An effective conduct of events should include an entrance briefing, site tour, validation of pre-survey data, survey of specific buildings or areas, survey of safes and vaults, survey of fence lines and perimeter terrain, evaluation of existing internal defense systems, survey of parking facilities, evaluation of site security forces, evaluation of site interface with local governments and population, survey of adjoining property, evaluation of site access controls, evaluation of lighting systems and requirements, survey of power supply systems, survey of telecommunication systems, and finally a survey of vulnerability countermeasures. Each one of these surveys or evaluations will now be discussed individually.

Entrance Briefing

The entrance briefing should be conducted on the first day of the survey. A designated team chief should brief school site personnel on the objectives of the survey, the information to be gathered, and the procedures to be followed. At this time, the school site representative should voice any special concerns, requirements or restrictions. Finally, logistical support questions should be addressed and resolved.

The School Site Tour

The school site tour should be conducted immediately after the entrance briefing and before the start of any detailed survey activity. This tour provides a "feel" for the overall school site layout and mission. A thorough school site tour should include as many angles and elevations as possible to include air assets, vehicle conveyed and foot propelled activities. Every floor of multi-storied buildings should be walked through as well as all underground areas and roof tops.

Presurvey Data

Presurvey data should be validated by identifying previously unidentified buildings or areas which require survey. Validation may disclose discrepancies in presurvey data and also identify any changes which may have occurred since the presurvey data was prepared. Remember, presurvey data is very time dependent, especially when dealing with rapidly expanding sites.

Performing the Security Survey

When surveying specific buildings, a description of the building, activity, priority, sensitivity, and existing security devices should be recorded. Physical and environmental conditions should also be recorded. Site personnel responsible for the building should be interviewed concerning operational considerations and planned structural modifications. Photographs should be made of the building to include aerial and ground level still photographs and videotapes plus blueprints and drawings should be gathered. A list of supporting utilities such as communication lines, electric lines, and water lines, plus their location should be recorded. The goal will be to identify proposed new security protection and any necessary structural modifications.

When surveying safes and vaults, the type and construction should be evaluated to include locking mechanisms; structure thickness; weight; attachment to the physical structure; suitability for the application of internal defense systems; tamper indication device use; utilization—opened daily, weekly, or infrequently; documentation of sign-offs and second party checks; and finally security officer checks and audits.

When surveying fence lines, age and condition should be considered. Rust, fabric tension, and material should be evaluated. Holes and the interface of the fence fabric to the ground should be noted. Interface should be evaluated by observing anchors, bottom railing, or wire design and the properties of the ground. The ground should be evaluated for washouts or other erosion. Concrete, gravel, and asphalt bases should be evaluated for strength and physical appearance. Fence attachment to support poles should be noted as well as the condition of gates. Top guard type and condition should be evaluated in addition to overall fence stability. Finally, the fence should be evaluated for proper lighting and existing internal defense systems such as sensors.

When surveying the perimeter terrain, the grade should be considered and typed as flat and level, rolling and hilly, or mountainous. The proximity of the perimeter to bodies of water, high vehicle traffic, pedestrian traffic, landing strips, and railways should be evaluated. Ground cover should be considered and typed as defoliated, rock/gravel, paved/asphalt surfaces, grassy, heavily foliated, or forested areas. Finally, soil composition should be broken down by type, compaction, stability, drainage, surface coloration, and reflection.

When evaluating internal defense systems, a record should be developed concerning the type, location (internal or external), specific components, age, condition, and effectiveness. Alarm annunciations should be tracked and recorded, paying particular attention to the amount, types, conditions, and results of physical assessments.

Parking facilities should be surveyed by considering the physical location, amount and type of vehicles parked, access requirements, lighting requirements, and existing internal defense systems. Site security forces should be evaluated by considering the size of the force, training level, equipment available, vehicle number and type, employee turnover, overtime worked, absenteeism, and morale.

An evaluation of site interface with local governments, military entities (military assistance to back-up response forces),

Figure 5. Razor wire, often not a good choice around school facilities.

general public (focusing on the local populace), local law enforcement agencies (especially the ability of local law enforcement agencies to assist internal response forces), and jurisdictional considerations.

A survey evaluating adjoining property should be conducted, focusing on neighboring industries, the economic climate of the surrounding area, and the potential for mutual aid programs with other nearby proprietary security forces.

Site access controls should be surveyed by evaluating badging and identification systems, vehicle access controls, electronic access control systems, the effective channeling of personnel to appropriate access control points, effective manning of access control points, and access control point capabilities.

Lighting systems and needs should be surveyed by considering area lighting, building perimeter lighting, fence, gates and access point lighting, parking lot and other structure lighting, and lighting in support of internal defense systems, especially close circuit televisions/cameras.

A survey should be conducted focusing on the power supply, distribution systems, and back-up systems. The focus should be placed on-site power and off-site power generation; power supply capacity; capacity for expansion; condition of power facilities;

Figure 6. Fence condition–surrounding vegetation has overgrown the fence concealing ingree and egress attempts. Vegetation may even aid a person in climbing the fence.

Figure 9. Fence condition–bottom guard intact, strong post support and good gravel base.

Figure 7. Fence condition–Fence fabric buckled and loose.

Figure 8. Fence condition–gate poorly secured; a person could easily slip between the gate posts.

Figure 10. Fence condition–bottom guard intact, strong post support and good concrete base.

and number, location, capacity, and condition of back-up power systems. Finally, the fuel supply for the power supply should be observed with a consideration placed on type, quantity, security, and location.

A survey should be conducted on existing telecommunication systems to include installation (above or below ground), capacity, potential for expansion, current assignments, condition, and type. A survey of vulnerability countermeasures should also be conducted focusing on barriers–natural, manmade, active or passive, command-activated, or intruder-activated. Finally a survey topic should be developed to fit any unusual considerations or sites.

Remember, while many of the aforementioned survey topics are generic, the survey is site specific and should be adjusted accordingly. The end product should contain

Figure 11. Fence condition–gate poorly secured to post and located too high from the ground. A person could easily slip into the campus from these areas. The gate is painted orange as a safety precaution.

Figure 12. Fence condition—surrounding vegetation has overgrown the fence concealing ingree and egress attempts. Vegetation may even aid a person in climbing the fence.

Figure 13. Fence condition—top guard unattached and hanging providing a person with a hand-hold for climbing.

Figure 14. Fence condition–top guard in good condition.

Figure 15. Lighting condition–good overlapping coverage.

Figure 16. Power supply protected by concrete vehicle barriers.

observed weaknesses and strengths and applicable recommendations for the enhancement of existing or additional internal defense systems, physical protection devices, and protective forces. Upon completion of the various survey topics, the information should be compiled into an appropriate format for presentation to the customer. A condensed oral briefing should also be prepared and presented as required.

In conclusion, security surveys are designed to find vulnerabilities or root causes to be corrected in order to neutralize or at a minimum decrease security threats. All school sites should invest the time and funds required to complete a security survey. It is amazing that many school sites continue to operate under the false assumption that "nothing has ever happened here and nothing ever will." This false assumption ignores the changing circumstances of politics, demographics, target criticality and vulnerability, and specific facility mission. The costs of major theft, pilferage, sabotage, bombing, arson, assassination or kidnaping of key personnel, destruction or disruption of operations, negative public perception, and the resulting embarrassment of these acts easily exceed the time and cost of a security survey.

Arguments Against Security Initiatives

Once a security survey has been completed and security initiatives are chosen to address security problems and/or weaknesses, it is not unusual for a variety of personnel to lodge arguments against proposed security initiatives. Indeed, many school systems are slow to implement physical security controls. School administrators may be reluctant to approve any changes they feel would detract from the open and friendly atmosphere of the school

campus and physical security controls may also be perceived as inhibiting the free flow of the campus population. However, the numerous types of security devices and reaction systems available today can go a long way in complimenting an open and friendly school atmosphere.

Specific arguments against the implementation of new security controls typically include statements such as: "We've never done it that way before." One can see the fallacy of this statement; times have changed and will continue to change and schools must evolve security strategies in order to keep up with these changing times. "This is a knee jerk reaction." A short-sighted view, many security solutions will be chosen to address immediate threats while longer-term programs are developed and put into place. "Our school will look like a prison." This may be true if security systems are designed in this manner; however, properly designed security systems will generate the look of a well-controlled facility. "Students rights may be infringed upon." Security operations and students rights can exist in harmony. Furthermore, students have a right to a safe and secure school environment.

Further arguments–"People will think we have a bad school." A faulty thought; the school may actually gain the reputation of being a "good school" as people recognize the fact that the school is taking proactive steps in controlling security/safety problems. "We may be sued." In the aftermath of any school violence incident, school officials will more than likely be sued if security systems were not developed and in place. Further, "security controls cost too much." As a rule of thumb, the cost of any physical security system should be compared to the value of the items being protected. In the case of school security, the highest value is placed on human life, which is priceless.

Additional common arguments–"there's

no way you can secure a school, look at the size of the building(s) and number of doors." This is inexperience talking; the number of security devices and supporting programs that can be implemented can provide a high degree of security even in very large structures. Of course, any security system can be penetrated; however, the idea is to make the school as secure as possible instead of throwing up ones hands and saying it can't be done. A ludicrous argument, "we're not doing anything different today than we were yesterday." This is pompous to say the least and falls into line with the many people who have said that they recognized and fully addressed school violence prior to the recent rash of school shootings. An organization operating under this philosophy will quickly be left behind by changing conditions such as demographics and security threats.

A final argument, "it's hands off unless you need us." School systems and law enforcement agencies operating under this philosophy will find out that "when you need us" will likely prove to be too late. This philosophy goes back to the age old reactive law enforcement operation. Further, this philosophy usually means that the school administration and law enforcement agency is not communicating when communications is central to the support of proactive school security efforts. In conclusion, the challenge is to apply security technologies in schools that are effective, affordable, and politically acceptable but still useful within a number of difficult constraints.

In conclusion, if a school is perceived as unsafe (it appears that no adult authority prevails on a campus), the school will often actually become unsafe. Security technologies may be instrumental in reducing crime or violence in schools. Indeed, security technologies may diminish a number of security infractions, eliminate or at least make crime and/or violence more

difficult to accomplish, and increase the likelihood of perpetrators being caught. Through technology, a school can introduce ways to collect information or enforce security procedures and rules that it would not normally be able to afford or rely on security personnel to perform.

School Security: A Comprehensive Program

The goal of school security is to create a learning environment that is perceived to be safe by all students and educational staff members; however, safety and security technology should only be viewed as one part of a comprehensive program that each school must develop in order to create a safe learning environment. Indeed, security technologies are not the answer to all school security problems. Thus, school administrators should never totally rely upon one type of physical security device, security/safety program, or security/safety action. One type of proactive measure will typically fall far short of an acceptable level of security (if one lone program fails the perpetrator has won).

To generate an acceptable level of security, a number of security systems should be placed into what is known as an integrated system. An integrated system ties a number of security devices and physical security operations together in such a way that if one device or procedure fails another will be present to act as a back-up. These integrated systems develop a security measure known as defense in depth. Finally, it should be noted that few school facilities can afford a security program that detects and protects personnel against all possible incidents. Here is where the concept of an integrated security system really shines. First, areas are carefully measured for risk by considering valuable assets and/or school threats. Then, using the integrated system concept, high threat areas may be protected by the most expensive systems, while areas of lesser concern are protected by more cost effective security methods. To clarify, security measures are driven by the characteristics of the school and its surroundings.

For example, schools may be experiencing a number of security problems such as outsiders on campus, fights on campus, vandalism and other malicious acts, theft, drugs, smoking, alcohol, weapons, parking lot problems, fence climbing, false fire alarms, bomb threats, bus problems, and teacher safety issues. Outsiders on campus may be effectively addressed by fencing-in campuses to include no trespassing signs; assigning security officers to man a main entry point; placing greeters in strategic locations; requiring students, visitors, and staff to wear identification cards or badges; requiring the display of parking stickers on vehicles; requiring school uniforms or the adherence to dress codes; locking exterior doors; utilizing a challenging procedure for anyone found out of class; placing security cameras in remote locations; and channeling all visitors through the front office.

Fights on campus may be reduced by the use of security cameras, duress alarms, and/or whistles. Vandalism may be reduced by the use of graffiti resistant sealers, glass-break sensors, assignment of school resource officers, eight-foot fencing, and the effective use of security lighting. Theft may be reduced by the use of intrusion detection systems, property marking, reinforced windows and doors, elimination of access points up to rooftops, security cameras, doors with hingepins on the secure side, bolting down computers and televisions, locating high-value assets in interior rooms, key control programs, and advanced alarm systems.

Drugs may be addressed by using drug detection swipes and other detection methods, drug dogs, removal of lockers, random searches, and vapor detection devices. Alcohol use on campus may be addressed by adopting a no open campus at lunch, no access to vehicle at lunch, no lockers, having breathalyser and saliva test kits on hands to test suspicious acting students, and the utilization of clear or mesh backpacks. If weapons are a problem, administrators may institute the use of walk-through metal detectors, hand-held metal detectors, vapor detectors, x-ray inspections, random searches, and crime stopper programs.

School officials may address parking lot problems by using security cameras, parking decal registrations, fencing, identification card systems for parking lot entry, parking lot sectioned off for different student schedules, motion sensors in parking lots that should have no access during the school day, walking patrols, and bike patrols. False fire alarms can be controlled by installing sophisticated alarm systems designed to assess alarms (cancel themselves out) before they become audible. Boxes may also be installed over the pull alarm that sounds a local alarm when activated.

Bomb threats may be addressed by installing caller I.D. on phone systems; offering rewards for information concerning bomb threats; recording all phone calls complete with a message regarding this fact at the beginning of each incoming call; routing all incoming calls through a district office; contacting the phone company for support; preventing the installment of pay phones on campus; developing a policy instituting strict/controlled use of school facility telephones; and finally, developing a policy to extend the school year when plagued with bomb threats and subsequent evacuations. Finally, teacher safety may be enhanced by issuing or installing duress alarms, instituting roving patrols, leaving classroom doors open during class, installing security cameras in classrooms, and instituting controlled access to classroom areas.

Of course, other options are certainly available and an integrated security system design is only limited by one's imagination. However, any application of a device, policy, or system should be researched and evaluated by the local legal organization and law enforcement agencies. It may be beneficial to check with other school systems in the area to see if they have already implemented any of the security measures under consideration. Finally, school staff members, the student council, the parent advisory group, and community leaders should be contacted for their opinions. It is true including these people will likely lengthen the decision-making process; however, invoking their participation may ensure their buy-in and the community will surely hear that the school is taking active security measures to develop a safe and secure learning environment.

In conclusion, a 1996-1997 report compiled by the U.S. Department of Education illustrates the percent of public schools using various types of security measures. They include: 96 percent use a visitor sign in process; 80 percent close the campus for most students during lunch; 53 percent control access to school buildings; 24 percent control access to school grounds; 19 percent perform drug sweeps; 4 percent use random metal-detector checks; and 1 percent require students to pass through metal detectors daily.

Physical Security Philosophy

There are three basic elements of physical security: control and monitor the access of persons or vehicles; prevent and detect unauthorized intrusions; and safeguard people, school assets, and campus buildings.

These elements are achieved by employing physical security controls, systems, processes, and procedures that deny unauthorized access; detering or discouraging attempts to gain unauthorized access; delaying those who attempt to gain unauthorized access; and detecting both criminal and non-criminal threats.

A school facility's protection system may be referred to as a series of perimeters or protective rings that goes far beyond the fringe of the school. Physical security controls are utilized at each of the three main perimeters or rings in an attempt to control or delay entry and in some cases to control and delay exiting. The main perimeters are referred to as the outer, middle, and inner protective rings.

An outer protective rings consist of physical controls such as: fences, barriers, lighting, warning signs, and alarms. These controls are generally designed to define the property line, channel personnel and vehicles through specified access points, and enable general surveillance of the activities occurring in these areas. A middle protective ring typically focuses on the exterior of campus buildings. This protective ring may include lighting, alarms, locks, window and door bars, warning signs, barriers such as fencing and walls, CCTV, and access control devices. The inner protective ring focuses on the interior of campus buildings. Like the middle protective ring, the inner protective ring may include lighting, alarms, locks, window and door bars, warning signs, barriers such as fencing and walls, CCTV, and access control devices.

Physical Barriers

Physical barriers may be used to define a physical area, prevent penetration, and/or control access to specified areas. The correct choice of barrier can enhance security to a significant degree; however, many physical barriers used in the world of high threat security operations are not suitable for educational facilities. Thus, only specific physical barriers deemed appropriate for a school campus will be discussed. Example physical barriers include walls, barbed wire, fences, obstacle systems, natural barriers, locked/blockaded entrances, and lock systems.

Security walls are generally used in a point protection role and may be used to cover doors, various openings, windows, other walls, and similar areas. Security walls are generally add-ons, meaning they are not part of the structural integrity of the building. Security walls may be constructed in various thicknesses and heights and from various materials such as wood, concrete, bricks, masonry, metal, rocks, sandbags, and/or plastic, etc.

Barbed wire is available in various designs and forms, for example, wire with knotted barbs, wire with razor-like barbs, string wire, and rolled wire/concertina. The use of barbed wire should be very limited in school environments. Barbed wire will often be viewed as adversarial by a number of people and thus generate negative comments. Plus, there could be liability issues directed toward the school system if a student is injured by structures or physical security barriers topped with barbed wire.

Fences represent one of the oldest forms of physical security devices and are typically used to define a particular area, preclude inadvertent or accidental entry into an area, prevent or delay unauthorized entry, and control pedestrian and vehicle traffic. Fencing is usually less costly than other types of construction materials and can be adapted to fit almost any security application. Fences may be constructed from a number of materials and in different designs and come complete with various means of fence

support. For example: Flat wood/picket fence; round wooden posts; wooden slats; chain link (metal); chicken wire (metal); iron grill/spiked metal; fabric/rope/material; soils plastic/vinyl; and rollable continuous–plastic expedient fencing. Finally, the protection offered by fencing is in direct proportion to its height. For example, a short fence is basically a psychological deterrent whereas a high fence with barbed wire outriggers is a physical deterrent.

Some general suggestions concerning fences include the following: chain link fences should be constructed of 16 gauge wire or stronger gauges to avoid being easily cut; fencing should consist of a two-inch opening per link (fine mesh can be hard to see through and wide openings can provide intruders with hand and toe holds for climbing); fences should be eight feet tall or higher with a minimal number of entrances and exits, and fence materials should be installed under the ground and covered to prevent intruders from tunneling or crawling underneath. Further, barbed wire, concertina wire, or razor ribbon may be attached to the top of the fence to discourage intruders from climbing over the top. Additionally, fences should be positioned where there are no physical or organic obstructions nearby which could afford intruders ways to scale or otherwise breach the fence. Vehicles and machinery should be prohibited from parking or otherwise be located within ten feet of any fence. These devices may afford an offender the opportunity to scale the vehicle or machinery and jump over the fence. Of course, security personnel should periodically check the fence for damage or signs of unauthorized access.

Additional fencing concerns include the following: gates, alarms, surveillance systems, security personnel, and dogs. Gates should be few in number and placed in strategic, easily observed, well illuminated locations. Further, gates should be secured with heavy chains, padlocks and/or a closable locking bar. Of course, gates may also be electronically controlled by card-keys, security guards, or push-button codes. Alarms and surveillance systems may be incorporated into fences to serve as additional protection. Finally, fences may be periodically patrolled by security personnel and/or canines.

Obstacle systems accomplish their purpose by providing various types of obstacles, blockades, and hinderences to access certain areas. Possible types of materials and designs include the following: planted trees, shrubs, bushes, hedges, and plants; felled or partially felled trees, shrubs, and bushes; wooden, concrete, or metal blocks partially embedded into the ground; bricks, rocks or stones, and road spikes. For example, trees and shrubs may be used to create physical barriers or to enhance other barriers. Bushes with thorns are an effective physical barrier by themselves or can be planted in front of a wall or fence. While trees and shrubs are used effectively as part of a security protection system, they can create security vulnerabilities. For example, trees and shrubs permitted to grow out of control can conceal persons trying to penetrate the area or provide a convenient place to store contraband or stolen property. Mechanical devices may also be used as obstacles. These mechanical devices are typically vertically or horizontally hinged, and are often capable of being remotely opened to allow traffic, when desired, through a point of entry. Mechanical systems may also include door/gate entry systems.

Natural barriers may be considered in the original plan of design to accomplish various objectives. Essentially, these types of barriers are those which are naturally located in an area. For example: hills, ridges, canyons, valleys, bodies of water, forests, plateaus, and plains. Although some of these natural areas are not necessarily barriers in the colloquial sense of the word, such as plateaus or plains, they can enhance the physical security of an area by allowing a greater degree of observability of the surrounding area.

Locked/barricaded entrances often use barriers which can be removed intentionally to allow access and entrance into a certain area. For example, doors and windows, which by design are meant to open and close, are included in this category since they are meant to be opened at times. School administrators should develop policies mandating that windows remain closed and locked to avoid avenues of accessibility by unauthorized personnel or the introduction of contraband into the campus buildings. Further, aside from being locked and closed, entrances must also be designed with sufficient strength to resist forced entry. Forced entry protection may also be required in the following areas: roofs, ceilings, floors, walls, and dividing barriers (expensive locking and alarm systems mean nothing if one can easily enter through one of these areas).

Of course, windows and doors will prove to be the most vulnerable to unauthorized entry so a few additional concerns will be noted. Hinges should be located on the inside of the area protected to prevent an outsider from removing the hinges pins and the entire door. Further, doors and windows may be purchased that have hinges located within the confines of the door/window itself or they may be constructed using a pinless design. Glass may be protected by using impact resistant glazing, or the attachment of bars/grills/fences which are secured to the structure itself and locked in place. Finally, the strength of many doors and windows is sometimes a function of the strength of screws which hold them in place. Long strong screws should be used in these areas. Also, to avoid tampering and or removal of screws in areas where screw heads are exposed, one way screws may be used. One way screws allow the turning of the screw with a conventional screwdriver only in the tightening direction. A regular screwdriver cannot be used to remove these screws. Of course, where possible, screws should be situated in such a way that they cannot be removed from the outside.

Protective Lighting

Protective lighting provides a means of continuing, during hours of darkness, a degree of protection comparable to that maintained during daylight hours. The major purpose of protective lighting is to enhance safety during operating hours, create a psychological deterrent to intruders, and to enable intruder detection. Generally, protective lighting is the least expensive and perhaps most effective security measure a school facility can employ. Of course, lighting should be positioned to prevent glare and silhouetting. The placement of lights and the style of lighting fixtures must be considered if closed circuit television (CCTV) equipment is being used. **Note**: See the full explanation of CCTV and protective lighting concerns described later in this chapter. Additionally, protective lighting enables security systems to continue operations during hours of darkness. Finally, effective protective lighting makes the task of an intruder difficult. Indeed, protective lighting is an essential element of any integrated physical security system.

A number of lighting types are typically in use on school campuses; they include: incandescent, fluorescent, and high-intensity discharge. Incandescent lighting in the most expensive to operate and includes the flood or quartz lights that are commonly used for exterior home security applications. Most fluorescent lighting is used indoors for office and work area lighting. High-intensity discharge lighting is the least expensive to operate (more light is produced with less power consumption) and is the least common for commercial exterior lighting applications. High-intensity lighting includes high-pressure sodium and low-pressure sodium lighting. A disadvantage of high-intensity discharge lighting is the restrike time. If a momentary power outage occurs, these lights will go out and can take up to several minutes to return to full brightness. Low-pressure sodium lighting is somewhat more efficient to operate than high-pressure sodium due to its ability to provide a fairly uniform light pattern.

There are generally five basic types of lighting systems; they are as follows: continuous lighting, controlled lighting, area or entry lighting, stationary or portable lighting, and emergency lighting. Continuous lighting is the most common protective lighting system and is used to continuously light a specific area. Standard design usually consist of a light fixture mounted on a pole or building. Controlled lighting is typically used when there is a need to limit the area of illumination, for example, avoiding the illumination of adjoining property.

Area or entry lighting is normally used to illuminate perimeter doors and/or entrance ways. Stationary or portable lighting is normally used to supplement continuous lighting by using flood lights or searchlights. These light systems are usually moveable and capable of directing a beam of light on a specific area or object. Finally, emergency lighting is primarily used as a back-up lighting source in the event of a power failure that effects a facility's continuous lighting. Emergency lighting can usually be employed to duplicate any lighting system.

Some common types of perimeter lights include: floodlights, streetlights, fresnal units, and searchlights. Floodlights form a beam of concentrated light and are often used to illuminate boundaries, structure exteriors, and other areas. Floodlights may be positioned to produce glare for intruders trying to look into certain areas. Streetlights usually cast a diffused, low-intensity light in an even pattern, over a certain area, for example, parking lots and storage areas. Fresnal units provide a long, narrow, horizontal beam of light in areas where glare is undesirable. Finally, searchlights may be used that are either portable or fixed. Searchlights provide a highly focused light beam that can be aimed in any direction. These lights are ideal for emergencies requiring additional lighting in a specific area. All of these lights can be identified as timed, manually operated, motion activated, sound activated, or photoelectric.

There are also several types of lamps used in protective lighting systems. Some of the more common lamps include: incandescent, mercury vapor, sodium vapor (high and low pressure), fluorescent, and metal halide. Mercury vapor lamps can be distinguished by their strong, bluish light. Sodium vapor lamps emit a soft yellow light. The low pressure sodium lamp is perhaps the most cost-effective and is an ideal lamp for outside protective lighting.

There are also some non-traditional lighting systems that may be encountered; they include, infrared (IR) or near infrared lighting. The spectrum for this lighting is just below red and is not visible to the human eye. Commercial IR light sources include incandescent and light emitting diodes (LED). The incandescent IR type typically uses a 300-500 watt lamp, a visible light cut filter, and will provide more illumination than an LED type. IR lights are expensive to purchase, operate, and maintain. The LED type emits light in the IR and is also expensive to purchase but uses less power and has a much longer life expectancy than IR lights. With either type of IR light, more light fixtures will be required to illuminate an area than with standard visible lighting.

Lights must be evaluated for effectiveness by observing their functioning at night, noting times of operation, brightness, area covered, and ease of access to wires and bulbs. Lights beams may be designed to overlap one-another in a continuous arc or designed to highlight specific areas. All dark areas should be noted and evaluated for attractiveness as an ingress/egress point. Naturally, possible ingress/egress points should be covered with effective lighting schemes. Lighting systems should also be periodically checked for operation. Any malfunctioning lights should be noted and replaced as soon as possible (perpetrators hate lights and may telegraph intentions by breaking or removing light bulbs a few days prior to an attack). Finally, lights should be evaluated for any interference caused by foliage such as weeds, shrubs, bushes, and trees. Foliage must be trimmed or removed if it is causing shadows or completely blocking light beams.

Finally, any protective lighting installation must take into consideration the vandalism problem associated with light fixtures. Proper design and location of fixtures can reduce the probability of malicious destruction; for example, break-resistant cover guards may be used or the fixture design should be such that the failure of a single lamp will not leave the area unprotected. Of course, periodic inspections should be conducted in order to evaluate lighting efficiency and to discover any malfunctioning lights (discrepancies should be addressed as soon as possible).

Mechanically/Manually Operated Lock Systems

Locks represent one of the oldest forms of security and their function is to deter or deny access from unauthorized personnel. Lock systems come in many shapes, sizes, capabilities, and kinds which may be categorized into two types of lock and key systems: mechanically/manually operated and electrically operated. Mechanically/manually operated systems generally entail a locking mechanism with a key and/or manually operated opening and closing mechanism. At times, the locking unit may be spring-actuated allowing an automatic locking capability. Other systems entail a design which has the locking unit being the same as the opening and closing mechanism. Generally, mechanically/manually operated locks are the most common and easy to operate locking systems available.

The following is a list of some common mechanically or manually operated lock and key systems and accompanying components: cylinder locks–barrel bolts, barricade bolts, cylinder straight deadlocks, and cylinder guards, key-in-knob locks, mortise locks, night latches, panic hardware, pivot bolts, police bolts/braces, straight bolts, vertical interlocking deadbolts, vertical swing bolt locks, multidirectional door-frame interlocking systems, air lock systems, bar locks, channel locks, hook bolts, and combination locks.

Barrel bolts are an inexpensive type of deadbolt that do not allow the use of a key from the exterior. Barrel bolts consist of a cylindrical rod that is free to move in a metal housing attached to a flat plate. These locks are frequently used for fences or gates and are sometimes used on windows. Barricade bolts consist of a massive metal bar that is attached to large strikes on both sides of a door. Barricade bolts are available with

locking devices and are completely removed from the door when not in use.

Cylinder straight deadlocks consist of a type of deadbolt that is controlled by a key-operated cylinder lock. Essentially, the working mechanism of most of these locks consist of a series of pins which are pushed in some direction by the properly designed key so as to allow the cylinder to turn, thereby allowing the actual locking unit to enter either the locked or open position.

However, there are many cylinder designs each of which functions in a different way. Some of these designs require straight keys with grooves cut in them which fit the working mechanism of the particular lock being used, others have round cylindrical keys. Some cylinder designs have the grooves cut straight in a vertical fashion, and some have the grooves cut at various angles to the plane of the key. Some keys have no grooves and are magnetically coded.

Some cylinder designs are easy to pick while others are very hard to pick or otherwise defeat. Any cylinder lock can be defeated by various types of physical attack if the cylinder is unprotected. For example, the use of cylinder guards prevents the cylinder from being wrenched or pried away from the door. Two examples of cylinder guards consist of a steel plate that is fastened over the cylinder and another is a ring that is mounted around the cylinder. Finally, lock manufacturers have different policies for duplicating keys for certain locks. For example, some manufacturers allow the use of standard key duplicating equipment found in many hardware stores, others require specialized equipment, and still others require the serial number of the lock be sent to the company so that the manufacturer can provide directly, based on the information on file, keys for the lock.

Key-in-knob locks consist of locks installed in a door as part of the door knob.

These locks are available with spring latch bolts or dead locking latch bolts. The outside knob is locked against movement when a push-button or thumb-turn located on the inside of the door is actuated. Key-in-knob locks should not be used as the only door lock unless it has a dead locking latch bolt because spring latch bolts can often be moved out of the locking position by physically forcing the bolt.

Mortise locks are inserted into a rectangular cavity cut into the edge of a door or into a cavity fabricated in a metal door at the time of manufacture. These locks are available in a number of operational configurations. Mortise locks should not be used in a wooden door unless the door is specifically designed for such use because the rectangular cavity will severely weaken most wooden doors. Vertical swing bolt locks are a type of mortise lock designed for use in thin doors with small frames. These locks use a bolt designed to swing up from the lock, rather than project horizontally.

Night latches are typically rim locks that are attached to the inside surface of a door and cannot be operated from the outside. The latch is projected into a strike box that is surface mounted to the door jamb. Some night latches incorporate a dead-locking latch bolt. Many of these locks are unsuitable for serious security efforts.

Panic hardware is often used on doors which are secured from outside entry but provide rapid interior access in case of emergency evacuation. Panic hardware usually consists of a massive lock and strike and a horizontal rod across the door. When the horizontal rod is pushed, the door is unlocked and opened at the same time.

Pivot bolts are keyless locks whose resistance increases as the amount of force against it increases. These bolts are basically a cam which moves in and out of place by swinging on a pivot. Pivot bolts lock automatically when the door is closed and are released by manual action from the inside.

Police bolts/braces commonly use bars which are braced between the inside surface of a door and the floor; however, some of these bars are simply wedged beneath the door knob. Some of these bolts/braces have a key locking mechanism attached to the door allowing the brace to be locked. Straight bolts consist of a metal bar attached to a door which is manually moved into a strike located on the door jamb.

Vertical interlocking deadbolts are attached to the inside surface of a door in the same manner as the night latch. This lock uses a bolt system in which the strike has two or more metal rings which are aligned vertically and extend out from a metal attaching plate. These rings mesh with similar rings on the edge of the lock when the door is closed. Each lock ring contains a bolt which is basically a vertical rod positioned on the end of a lever. When the unit is locked, the rods are moved vertically into the strike rings. These locks have the advantage of restricting lateral movement making jimmying efforts more difficult.

Multidirectional, door-frame interlocking systems generally consist of a door mounted key/knob and lock system which, when locked, projects one or more bolts/rods into the door frame at various locations (top, bottom, center, left, and/or right). This system provides a very powerful door locking capability. Another locking system, known as air lock systems, uses pneumatic and air pressure mechanisms to provide for the locking and unlocking procedures.

Bar locks consist of a rigid bar that is extended between the center edge of a sliding glass door and the opposite jamb. Some bar locks have keyed locking devices, may be permanently mounted on the door, and are often pivoted at one end so the device can be moved out of the way into a stored position when not in use. Another lock, called channel locks, are placed so that the device butts against the edge of a sliding glass door or window and fastens to the adjacent channel, or track in which the door or window slides. In some cases, the side of the channel is drilled in a number of places so that the door/window can be either locked or opened to one of these positions, with the lock being bolted through the appropriate channel hole. In other cases, the lock is held in place by being clamped to the channel. Finally, a channel lock may be completely manual or include a keyed lock.

An additional mechanical or manually operated lock to be discussed is called a hook bolt. A hook bolt is often used as the primary lock in sliding glass doors. This lock is mounted inside the door frame, and can be manually or key operated. The bolt has a hook on its end and swings downward from the inside of the lock front, hooking into the strike hole to prevent the door from being moved laterally.

A final mechanical or manually operated lock to be discussed is called a combination lock (push button and dial) which consist of a number of tumblers which must be matched to open the lock. These locks are often more effective than key operated locks in the sense that they do not allow intruders the opportunity to gain access into the inner workings of the lock. These locks do have the disadvantage of requiring a number of operators to memorize a code in order to operate the lock.

Electrically Operated Lock Systems

Electrically operated systems may use the same basic locking mechanism designs as the mechanically or manually operated systems. However, their opening and/or closing mechanisms are connected to electrical

sensing systems. The following is a list of some common electrically and/or electronically related locking systems: card reader locking mechanisms; electric strikes; fingerprint access mechanisms; physical attribute access mechanisms; and push-button locking mechanisms.

Card reader locking mechanisms open a lock, when an authorized card is inserted into the card reader. Cards are scanned either optically or magnetically and some systems will retain unauthorized cards and/or sound an alarm. Some computer operated systems allow authorization codes to be changed as required. Another type of card reader, called proximity readers, scan cards with radio waves, infrared waves, through magnetic means and/or use other non-contact methods.

Another system called electric strikes uses a button to electrically move the strike away from the locking mechanism so that the door can be opened. The door is also capable of being operated in a normal fashion with a key. Electric strike systems may be used in conjunction with an intercom (voice identification), by line-of-sight (visual identification), or closed circuit television cameras (visual electronic identification).

Fingerprint access mechanisms use holographic (three-dimensional photographic) techniques to examine fingerprints by comparing a fingerprint stored on an access card with a control system or an actual fingerprint may be compared with a file stored in a control system. Another system operating along these lines is called physical attribute access mechanisms. These mechanisms control access by comparing an individual's physical attributes (hand shape, retinal signature, voice signature, palm print, written signature, body weight, and similar aspects) with measurements stored on file in the system.

A final electrically-operated locking

system to be discussed is called a push-button locking mechanism (also known as cipher locks). These devices employ a keyboard or push buttons mounted in a protected housing adjacent to the locked door. When the buttons are pushed in the proper coded sequence, the electronic circuit actuates the door bolt or electronic strike to permit access. These devices may also operate on a mechanical basis to allow for manually opening the locking mechanism and manually locking it, when desired.

In conclusion, there are many different types of locking systems which provide various levels of security oriented design. The combination of properties needed or desired should be properly analyzed so that the optimum design is chosen and implemented. Finally, any lock and key system will only be as good as an accompanying control system. For example, all keys should be assigned to specific personnel, should be accounted for during periodic security inspections, personnel should be prohibited from loaning their keys to anyone, all personnel should be prohibited from making copies of keys, lost keys should be reported immediately and compromised locks should be replaced; finally, a master key (a key that will fit all of the locks of a specific type installed in a school) should be provided to a responsible law enforcement official. A master key will quicken law enforcement response (enable key entry without fumbling around with numerous keys) and lessen damage (ramming doors or breaking down doors or breaking windows) to the building during school crisis response missions. Some facilities use what is known as a "Knox Box"–a steel container accessible by a special key. The Knox Box is mounted in a strategic location and contains a master key which operates through an encoder and decoder system. Using this system, the master key is irretrievable until a dispatcher

or other authorized person enters a release code.

Seals and Seal Presses

Locked or otherwise secured areas may be enhanced by the use of seals and/or seal presses also known as Tamper Indicating Devices (TIDs). TIDs may be color coded for specific security area use and/or display a serial number or other identity method. Seals are primarily used to identify whether an area, building, or other protected area has been entered or exited. Seals may be constructed from steel, brass, lead, wire, plastic, paper, or other materials. When affixing seals, security officers or SROs must correctly thread the seal through the object to be sealed and connect the seal insuring the integral locking mechanism engages. The seal should then be physically inspected for correct affixing. To clarify the use of seals, the following description is provided: a locked door would have a seal affixed through the locking mechanism, and once an alarm or periodic inspection takes place, the broken or unbroken seal will visually flag the security officer as to whether the door had been opened. If the seal is intact, the door has not been used, if the seal is broken, the door has been accessed and unauthorized ingress or egress has taken place. Of course, a broken seal may also mean security systems have been circumvented and contraband has been passed into the school facility. For ultimate protection, seal issue and use must be controlled and recorded.

Security System Technologies

Like physical barriers, security screening technologies are numerous, varied, and have many different applications. A comprehensive discussion concerning each technology would go beyond the intent of this book.

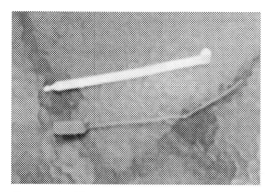

Figure 17. Two types of tamper indicating devices (TID). The top TID is a band type and the bottom TID is a string type. Once affixed, these devices cannot be opened without breaking the device.

However, in order to fully present the reader with a general knowledge base concerning these technologies a large number of security systems will be discussed in an overview fashion. Next, a number of security systems deemed as particularly applicable to school security will be discussed in detail. The intent is to provide the reader with enough information to streamline research efforts, when considering security systems/devices for the needs of any particular school campus. The discussion will begin with alarms and accompanying reaction systems will be discussed at the end of the next section.

Alarms

The function of an alarm is to provide notification of physical condition changes. Alarm systems may be implemented in school facilities to detect unauthorized entry or exit, breaking and entering, smoke, fire, water spillage, equipment malfunctions, changes in temperature (hot or cold), humidity, and the presence of various substances (toxins for example) in a room or area.

Security officers must be thoroughly familiar with alarm locations, operations, and procedures at the campus they are assigned to protect before their efforts will be efficient and effective. The following is, in part, a listing and discussion of some of the sensing, detector, triggering components, and reaction systems. For example, alarm glass (detector) consists of glass containing small wires (sensing) molded in the glass which (trigger) an alarm if the glass is broken or cut. Sensing mechanisms may use point (such as the alarm glass described above), area (a doorway), or volume sensors (a large room) which sense a triggering occurrence either at specific points or in large encompassing areas.

Generally, there are four types of alarm systems; they are as follows: local alarms consisting of units which produce a loud audible sound intended to alert nearby individuals that a breach or attempted breach of security has or is occurring; proprietary alarms focusing on in-house operations using alarm boxes; on-site central station alarms monitored by contracting security agencies, and off-site police connection systems which are monitored at police stations.

The devices to be discussed include: alarm glass, alarm screens, capacitance proximity detectors, duress buttons/switches/alarms, metallic foil, photoelectric controls, photoelectric detectors, pressure mat switches, pull/trip trap switches, stress detectors, and switch sensors. Vibration detectors, infrared motion detectors, microwave motion detectors, sound monitoring systems, sound sensing units, ultrasonic motion detectors, video motion detectors, laser system detectors, personal alarm transmitters, door/window alarms–self-contained, portable audible alarm devices, vehicle alarms, and wafer switches will also be discussed.

Figure 18. Motion detector.

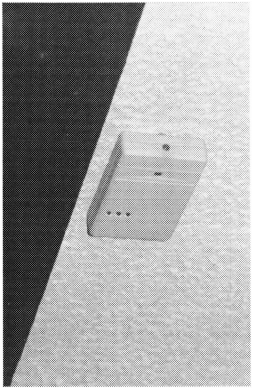

Figure 20. Sound and impact sensor.

Figure 19. Contact switch, located at the bottom of the door.

Figure 21. Local alarm with magnetic switch.

Figure 22. Control pad used to set or deactivate alarms.

Alarm glass typically includes small wires molded into the glass which triggers an alarm if the glass is cut or broken. Alarm screens which are usually placed in front of windows or other areas contain thin metal wires that activate an alarm if the screen is cut or broken. Capacitance proximity detectors respond to a change in the electrical capacitance of a protected metallic item or area caused by the approach of an intruder. They can be used in conjunction with metallic screens, doors, safes, and similar items. Emergency buttons/switches/bars are activated manually and can alert security personnel to a particular situation or trigger a reaction such as the locking of ingress/egress points.

Metallic foil may be used on glass or other breakable materials. The thin foil is designed to break with the glass or other breakable material thereby activating an alarm. Photoelectric controls sense a change in available light and may be used to turn lights on or off or to detect any individual, vehicle, or object coming between the light source and the sensor, thereby triggering an alarm.

Photoelectric sensors consist of a light beam, often an invisible infrared light beam, and a corresponding receiving unit. The detector is triggered when an object or person interrupts the beam by passing through it.

Pressure mat switches are often placed under carpets or similar materials and are triggered when pressure is placed on the device, for example, stepping or setting an item on the device. Pull/trip trap switches are mechanical switches that respond to the pulling of wire connected to the device. Typically, the thin wire is placed across a particular area and as an intruder walks into the wire or otherwise pulls the wire, an alarm is sounded. Of course, this device may be installed in a number of places; all that is required is a pulling motion. Stress detectors are very sensitive instruments which are usually connected to a floor area, steps, or other structural components. These devices activate an alarm upon sensing stress placed on the particular structural component.

Switch sensors are normally used to detect the opening of doors or windows. The switch itself detects the actual movement and in turn activates an alarm. Switch sensors are usually found in one of three types: magnetic switches–the switch opens and closes in response to movement; mechanical switches–the switch opens and closes by spring action; and mercury switches–the switch opens and closes when moved or tilted.

Vibration detectors detect the vibration of structural components of a building, wall, or other structure, caused by the force of an attempted forced entry. Infrared motion detectors sense a source of heat which has moved into the field of sensitivity. Microwave motion detectors use microwaves such as radar waves to detect motion within a given area. Sound monitoring devices automatically respond to unusual, unwarranted or different sounds or

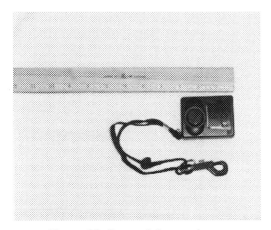

Figure 23. Personal duress alarm.

noises typically associated with a break-in. Some of these units incorporate a device which allows various noises (such as equipment starting or running) to proceed without triggering the alarm system. Also, various combinations of sound sensors and sound monitoring systems are possible.

Ultrasonic motion detectors generate a high frequency sound that is above the normal hearing range of humans. A microphone monitors the sound and triggers an alarm response, if motion within the protected area modifies the constant sound the device has been set to receive. Video motion detectors monitor a stationary scene on the video transmission field/sector/screen. Any change in the transmission field caused by motion will be detected implementing a response system. Laser system detectors are similar to photoelectric detectors (described above), except that these devices use laser beams in lieu of regular light.

Personal alarm transmitters are actually portable panic switches. These devices are low power radio transmitters which allow a person carrying one to actuate an alarm by pushing a button or pulling a lanyard. The response system reacts to the received radio signal and implements whatever response has been previously arranged. Further, these

devices operate on batteries, and depending on the power available, have varied ranges and capabilities.

Self contained door/window alarms are usually battery powered and include an integral audible alarm. Generally, they can be controlled only from inside the protected area; however, some systems include a radio signal and accompanying control box which allows the device to be turned on or off from outside the protected area. These devices are typically used on doors and windows or other entrances and sense the opening of the supporting structure, sounding the alarm.

Portable audible alarm devices are self-contained and are carried by a person. When activated, they emit a loud alarm which can be used at any location to summon assistance or to deter a transgressor. These devices are usually powered by compressed air, compressed gas, or batteries. Vehicle alarms are designed to sound an alarm if someone tries to gain unauthorized access into a school vehicle. These devices are normally powered by the vehicles own power supply; however, back-up power units are available. Most systems provide only a local audible alarm, some systems may provide only a remote signal alarm, and some systems may provide both types of alarms. Some vehicle alarms sense the opening of various entrance points through mechanical means or through a change in a vehicle's electrical system equilibrium. Finally, some vehicle alarms sense any significant movement of the vehicle, including the shaking or vibrating of the vehicle in one or more directions.

Wafer switches are essentially miniature pressure switches. However, instead of signaling an alarm when pressure is applied, these switches operate when the pressure is released. For example, when an item of a certain weight is placed on the switch, the contacts close completing the alarm circuit.

When the item is removed, the contacts open and the alarm system is activated. For example, these switches are easily concealed and do not interfere with the attractiveness of a display.

Reaction Systems

Reaction systems are tied into alarms and serve the purpose of visually or audibly notifying personnel that a security situation is or has occurred. Like alarm systems, reaction systems are numerous, varied, and have many different applications. Various reaction systems include sirens; horns; buzzers; bells; flashing lights; strobe lights; continuous beam lights; mechanical spraying of water, dyes, or other materials; camera activation; telephone dialer units; automatic locking of certain ingress/egress points; and central alarm station notification. The reactions may be local (within the vicinity of the triggering occurrence) or remote (notification of a central monitoring station) or a combination of the two (local and remote). Reaction systems should be chosen to meet various individual campus requirements.

Audible reaction systems (sirens, horns, buzzers, or bells,) may be chosen for two reasons: first, to shock an intruder with the noise of the alarm and with the fact that the intrusion did not go unnoticed, and second, to alert various individuals that an intrusion or attempted intrusion has occurred. Visible/light alarms, also known as alerting annunciator lights (flashing lights–colored or standard beam, strobe lights, and continuous beam lights), may be used in addition to and/or instead of audible reaction systems. Visible/light alarms usually employ sudden flashes or continuous beams of light to deter the intruder and to alert personnel in the area that an intrusion or attempted intrusion

has occurred. These units may be particularly useful in noisy areas where it might be difficult to differentiate the noise produced by a local audible alarm from that of surrounding sounds.

Telephone dialer units, upon activation by an alarm unit, automatically dial one or more telephone numbers and relay a recorded message to those on the other side of the line. They may be used to dial the police, security personnel, school administrators, and/or others. The mechanical spraying of water, dyes, or other materials; camera activation; and the automatic locking of certain ingress/egress points are examples of "other response mechanisms." Of course, there are a vast number of response mechanisms that could be added to this list.

Finally, central alarm station notification involves contacting proprietary security personnel that an intrusion or attempted intrusion has occurred. These units are basically receivers of data, captured either through wireless transmissions, telephone line transmissions, or cable transmissions. The data received is then coded or identified in a manner which relates to the particular location of the triggered alarm. Upon notification, the personnel attending the central alarm station employ their specific alarm response procedures.

Popular School Security Systems

For the purpose of this book, the following security systems are deemed as particularly applicable to school security will be discussed in detail: hand-held and walk-through metal detectors, explosives/narcotics detectors, video surveillance, blast mitigation systems, intrusion detection systems, x-ray devices, duress alarms, and robotic devices.

Hand-held Metal Detectors

Metal detection is not an exact science and no guarantee has been or can be made as to the results obtained when using these devices. The success of metal detection will depend upon speed of movement, the distance the metal detector is from the metal object, and other factors. A metal detector actually detects any conducive material (anything that will conduct an electrical current). Counter to popular belief, the mass of a particular object is not significant in metal detection. The size, shape, electrical conductivity, and magnetic properties are the important aspects. Indeed, metal detectors are considered a mature technology and can accurately detect the presence of most types of firearms and knives. When a questionable item or material is detected by these devices, the detector produces an alarm signal which may be audible, visible (lights), or both audible and visual.

Hand-held metal detectors are usually battery operated (9-volt or rechargeable Nicad) and are moved around a person's body in a set pattern to search for conducive materials (metal) on or in a person's body. When a suspect object is discovered the detector will sound an alarm, display a light, or sound an alarm and display a light at the same time. Unfortunately, a metal detector alone cannot distinguish between a firearm and a large metal belt buckle. Thus, trained personnel are required to make these determinations. However, metal detectors work poorly if the operator is untrained or lacks attention to detail. Indeed, a metal detector is only as good as the operator overseeing its use. Further, metal detectors are usually not effective when used on purses, bookbags, briefcases, or suitcases due to the large number of different conductive items they contain or the materials used in their

Figure 24. Garrett hand-held metal detector.

construction. These items will typically require a physical hands-on inspection.

Hand-held metal detectors should have the following desirable features: a long detection paddle (at least ten inches long in order to reduce the amount of passes necessary across a person's body); a warning light or beeping system (distinguishable from the alarm tone) that warns the operator that the battery is running low; and an audible feedback alarm that alarms louder or changes alarm pitch for larger suspicious items and softer for less suspicious items. If not accidentally or intentionally abused, most hand-held detectors will require no maintenance. The only in-house maintenance that is required is to provide for the replacement or recharging of batteries each night (a new or freshly recharged battery will last for approximately one hour of constant screening). Therefore, hand-held metal detectors should be turned off when not in

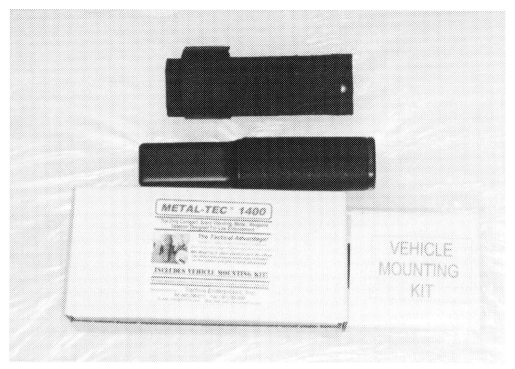

Figure 25. Metal-Tec hand-held metal detector.

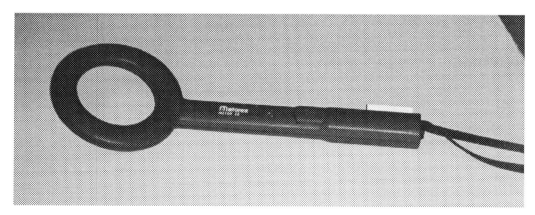

Figure 26. Metorex hand-held metal detector.

use. A supply of fresh batteries should always be on hand. Hand-held metal detectors should have a useful lifespan of about 5 years and much longer if used infrequently. Finally, smaller compact metal detectors may be purchased and carried on the belt of specific personnel at all times in order to supplement the metal detection program.

The use of hand-held metal detectors requires less space and they are not as sensitive to their surroundings as walk-through metal detectors. However, there are space requirements such a waiting area, a 6' x 6' scanning area, and space for a table used to support hand carried items and people as they lift their feet for scanning. Finally, the area should be in plain view of everyone in order to avoid possible misconduct, accusations of misconduct, or a confrontation with a student. The exception to this rule may occur if a student is suspected of hiding some type of contraband on or in a private area of the body.

Though hand-held metal detectors are affordable, it would be unusual for a school of any size to effectively scan people for contraband by solely using hand-operated metal detectors. Manpower would be the major cost of such an endeavor. Plus, using a through-put (scanning) rate of approximately two students per minute, a school would need one operator for a full hour for every 120 students. Of course, this example through-put rate assumes the students' arrival rate is evenly spread across a 1 hour time period, which is not likely. **Note**: The through-put rate will be discussed at greater length in the walk-through metal detector section. Indeed, hand-held detectors are most frequently used in conjunction with walk-through metal detectors. For example, hand-held scanners are usually required for use on people who have triggered an alarm while walking through a portal type detector

and the operator cannot determine what object has caused the alarm.

Although hand-held metal detectors work well, when properly operated, written procedures will need to be developed, followed, and enforced to maintain an acceptable level of performance. A disinterested or unmotivated operator can negate much of the benefit that could be derived from a school's metal detection program. While it is not difficult to learn to use a hand-held metal detector correctly, school administrators should not underestimate the value of periodic training for their operators. Training sessions should also include selected members of the school staff that may be called upon to serve as back-up or supplemental operators.

To support any metal detection program, standard operating procedures (SOPs) should be written to describe operating procedures and to support the use of metal detectors. For example, it must be clearly established in written form that in order to ensure the integrity of any metal detection program, everyone must be subjected to the screening process. This SOP should include students, teachers, parents, school support staff, school administrators, and visitors. This SOP may grant an exception to law enforcement personnel who are armed and emergency response personnel who are responding to an emergency. However, granting an excessive number of exceptions will prove counterproductive and may be viewed as prejudicial.

Guidelines should also be developed for procedures concerning how many times a person may try to pass through the walk-through portal, when hand-held metal detectors and other support scanning devices will be used, procedures in response to discovered contraband, and processes for calling local law enforcement support. A school may also consider having both male and female operators to perform scans on students of both genders as the hand-held process is a bit more personal than other scanning methods. An option to this procedure is to perform the hand-held scan in front of a recording CCTV system. Further, it may be a good idea to post signs notifying people that metal detectors are in use and the fact that if anyone refuses to be screened, they will be denied access. This sign may also include a list of items designated as contraband within the school community.

While these metal detectors are seen nearly everyday, there have been advances in technology which are worth noting. For example, many hand-held metal detectors can now be adjusted for sensitivity by external switches and/or internal adjustments. This allows a security entity to adjust screening efforts to fit current threat levels. Some detectors now provide proportional audible and visual alarms in reference to the size, distance, and location of an object. Another new feature is the ability to use earplugs or headphones; these help the operator hear and prevent an alarm annunciation from being heard by the subject being scanned. Other new features concern good battery/low battery indicators and operating strengths calibrated to avoid endangering pacemaker wearers or damaging magnetic tapes. Finally, hand-held metal detectors are becoming smaller and lighter (8.6 oz.) or less, enabling security personnel to easily carry the detector through the use of built-in belt clips.

For example, two compact hand-held metal detectors include the Metal-Tec 1400 and the Garrett Enforcer G-2. The Metal-Tec 1400 is designed to be used as an enhancement of the officer's hand during searches and is not intended to be used as the sole means of searching for weapons. The Metal-Tec 1400 is designed to be used in close

contact with the subject and should be used in conjunction with the officer's hands, while conducting a search for weapons.

Metal-Tec 1400

The Metal-Tec 1400 was designed to be used as an enhancement of the hand during searches. Furthermore, the Metal-Tec 1400 requires only one hand for operation, leaving the other hand available for more important tasks. For example, this device can be held between the fore finger and the thumb freeing up the other fingers so that they can be used during a search or frisking of the subject. The Metal-Tec 1400 can find a metal object and pinpoint its location without the need for a constant sweeping motion. Once detected, the operator can easily determine the object's size by the vibration signature. This pinpoint accuracy capability is very important for discovering metal objects which may have been otherwise overlooked.

The Metal-Tec 1400 has two advanced features: (1) A vibration signature which can reportedly determine the approximate physical shape (length and width) of a metal object being detected. This is done by turning the Metal-Tec 1400 on end to observe where the vibration starts and ends while moving the unit over a suspicious object. (2) A density discrimination capability which can help the officer determine the threat level of an object based upon its size. For example, large objects such as handguns can be detected approximately three to four inches away, smaller objects such as razor blades can be detected approximately one to two inches away, and metal foil (which may contain drugs) can be detected approximately one-eighth inch to one inch away based on the amount of foil. The Metal-Tec 1400 contains a triaxial sensor which detects in all directions simultaneously regardless of the position relative to the subject.

The Metal-Tec 1400 has only one switch, the power push-on/push-off switch which is embedded in the handle and protected by a water resistant non-slip metal grip. The Metal-Tec 1400 is reportedly the only unit on the market with "silent vibration" which gives the operator a tactical advantage by not warning the subject when metal is detected. The Metal-Tec 1400 can be used in up to 2,000 searches using one nine-volt battery and includes a low battery indicator designed to notify the user that the battery has been depleted to a level which no longer meets operating specifications. The low battery indicator causes the unit to constantly vibrate which notifies the user to replace the battery. This feature removes the possibility of the unit being used with a weak battery which may give incorrect detection results. Furthermore, the battery is housed in a separate watertight compartment and can be inserted into the unit in either direction (a non-polarity capability) making battery replacement in the field easy and uncomplicated.

The Metal-Tec 1400 is a single piece design and is constructed of high impact ABS plastic which has a tensile strength of 6,800 PSI for maximum durability. The Metal-Tec 1400 is 7.9 inches long, 1.75 inches wide, 1.30 inches high, and weighs approximately 8.8 ounces. The device is factory set for sensitivity and should never need adjustment in the field. The unit is self-calibrating and will automatically adjust itself for temperature changes between -15 to +30 degrees F.

The unit comes complete with a heavy Nylon web holster which includes a Velcro strap for easy device deployment. The holster also includes a metal snap to allow easy removal of the holster from the duty belt and also serves as a trigger to indicate if the unit is left on when it is returned to the holster (the device will start to vibrate in the holster if left on). Finally, there are five other holster types which may be chosen to match existing gear and a vehicle mounting unit for those personnel who do not want to constantly wear the device.

Garrett Enforcer G-2

The Garrett Enforcer G-2 operates by using a transmitter/receiver with automatic instant retune (no adjustments are necessary). The Garrett Enforcer G-2 is 6.3 inches long, 3.25 inches wide, 1.1 inches thick, weighs 8 ounces and is powered by a standard nine-volt battery. A speaker in the unit automatically sounds an audible alert when metal is detected. The sound can be heard in the ambient atmosphere or directed through an optional earphone assembly. The alert tone can also be used to indicate battery condition (when approximately 10% battery life remains, the sound emitted when metal is detected changes from a warble to a steady tone).

The Garrett Enforcer G-2 also has a red light located atop the unit which illuminates whenever metal is detected. This light appears whether the earplug is in place or the detector's speaker is sounding. When the power control switch is depressed and held, the unit will detect metal; when the switch is released, the unit automatically ceases to operate.

Walk-through Metal Detectors

The typical pulsed-field walk-through metal detector generates electromagnetic pulses that produce very small electrical currents in conductive metal objects within the portal archway which, in turn, generate their own magnetic field. The receiver portion of a portal metal detector can detect

Figure 27. Metorex walk-through metal detector.

this rapidly decaying magnetic field during the time between the transmitted pulses. This detection method is called "active" because it generates a magnetic field that actively looks for suspicious materials or objects.

Some people fear the use of metal detectors on themselves because of the possible side effects of being subjected to the magnetic field. This fear has proven to be unfounded; metal detectors emit an extremely weak magnetic field that is of no concern to anyone including heart patients who are using pacemaker type devices. For comparison, an electric hair dryer subjects the user to a much stronger field than would be received by a person walking through a metal detection device.

The portal metal detector, perhaps better known as a walk-through detector, is a stand-alone structure that resembles a deep door frame. These devices will typically take up a space on the floor about three feet across, two feet deep, and seven feet high. Weight can vary from approximately 60 pounds to 150 pounds. Portals are generally free-standing and are rarely attached to the floor or surrounding structure. Power requirements are generally a one plug system leading to a 110-volt wall outlet.

One of the problems associated with walk-through detectors located in schools is the fact that the entire school population will arrive to be monitored over a short period of time. Thus, school administrators must decide how many detectors will be required to scan the school population and anticipated population. The logistics concerned here may prove problematic; for example, most screening processes will occur indoors so space will be required for people waiting to be scanned (school personnel will have to monitor this area to control foot traffic and prevent any potential problems from occurring as numerous students mill about in a constricted area); each device will require one operator; at least one other person will have to be on hand to hand-scan people who fail to pass the portal scan, and at least one other person may be required to physically search hand-carried items or operate other types of scanning equipment.

Furthermore, to avoid sending conflicting signals to the detector, the person waiting in line to use the portal should be kept back at least three feet from the current user walking through the portal. Additionally, operators of the equipment and people who have already walked through the device need to be at least three feet from the portal in all directions before the next person enters. Further, if more than one portal metal detector is being used, each device needs to be located at least ten feet from the other device unless the devices have been professionally synchronized.

Finally, it is very important that there be neither space nor opportunity for people to walk around the detection system. Definite boundaries must be established to prevent circumvention of the system and prevent the pass-back of contraband (handing prohibited items from outside the screening area to those who have already successfully cleared the scanning process). Of course, some of these problems may be alleviated by staggering reporting times, staggering class times, locating the staging/scanning area further within the school facility, or by developing several multiple entry setups.

Some schools have experimented with random spot checks in lieu of a full-scale, every-morning, every-person effort. However, it is very difficult to perform truly random checks with any hope of locating weapons. There is almost always a small but distinct group of students that a school administration is most concerned about possibly carrying a weapon. These high-risk students often object when they are searched more frequently than other students and once this pattern is set, they may solicit the help or force another student to carry their weapon onto the campus. Perhaps, a more successful approach to the random spot check is for the school administration to choose an entire classroom(s) at a time and scan every person (including the teacher) in the room.

A well-trained and motivated operator should be able to process between 15 and 25 people per minute through a portal type metal detector; however, this does not include investigation of alarms or intentional/unintentional delays generated by the student population. Thus, the through-put (scanning rate) is generally driven by several circumstances: the number of metal detectors in use; the rate at which students arrive; the motivation of the students to cooperate and move through the system quickly (school staff members will normally have to make certain students move along at a quick pace); the breakdown and subsequent troubleshooting of equipment; the familiarity and training of personnel operating the equipment; and the arrival of visitors not familiar with the scanning process. **Note**: To address these issues, school systems may purchase back-up equipment, borrow or rent back-up equipment from a vendor, or enter into a pooling arrangement where spare equipment is shared within a certain school district. Indeed, the pooling of equipment will often generate a mass purchase of equipment which will in turn lower the cost per unit.

In general, for a complete, full-scale metal detection program to be conducted every morning, for every member of a school, approximately one to two weeks will be needed for students to acclimate themselves to the screening process. The first week of any metal-detection program will likely be chaotic. However, as students and school personnel become familiar with the scanning process, they will avoid taking prohibited items with them into the facility, avoid taking items with them that will sound an alarm, avoid wearing clothing that is suspect, and add an additional few minutes to their schedule in order to clear the process in time to attend classes. Students may be assisted in learning the scanning procedure by being issued handouts and attending verbal presentations describing required steps. Signs may also be posted at entry areas which provide proper scanning instructions.

In designing the layout of the metal detection system, the composition of surrounding walls, furniture, flooring, near-by electromagnetic equipment (such as an elevator), near-by plumbing in the walls, and even metal trash cans must be taken into account. Indeed, the optimal effectiveness of a portal metal detector can be downgraded by a poor location.

Like hand-held metal detectors, walk-through metal detectors are seen nearly everyday, and there have also been advances in this technology which are worth noting. To effectively organize this discussion walk-through metal detectors will be placed into categories; for example, base level high sensitivity types, multi-zone types, weatherproof types, and high discrimination types.

High sensitivity types now offer uniform detection sensitivity over the entire walk-through area from top to bottom. Magnetic fields are now capable of detecting all metal objects regardless of orientation in the detector. New technology has coupled high sensitivity with lower false alarm rates which enhances security efforts while generating an optimum traffic flow. New technology includes the following list of advances:

1. Microprocessor technology possessing multiple programs and the ability to select 100 or more sensitivity levels.
2. Uncomplicated mechanical construction.
3. Self-diagnostics used to continuously monitor unit operation.
4. Automatic sensitivity for easy calibration.
5. Programmable reset times.
6. External noise displays complete with volume and tone controls.
7. Visual displays which indicate the area of alarm.
8. Adjacent detector identification through the use of variable tones.
9. Manual and automatic reset capabilities.
10. Easy maintenance procedures.
11. Portability enhancing the ready use of spare/reserve units, the building of integrated systems, and the ability to move the device at will.
12. Finally, these metal detectors are designed to be safe for the monitoring of cardiac pacemaker wearers and magnetic recording materials.

Multizone type, walk-trough metal detectors possess many of the same technological advances listed above; however, these detectors have numerous additional unique characteristics:

1. Uniform detection may be provided by eight or more separate overlapping detectors which eliminate weak points found in older models.
2. The ability to recognize the presence of several innocuous metal items without combining them into a single item causing subsequent false alarm responses.
3. The ability to display all metal detected at each designated level whenever the signal exceeds the threshold level for that particular zone.
4. The ability to use the metal detector above a metal floor or near other areas of local disturbance by adjusting the sensitivity to provide uniform performance.
5. The availability of integrated construction systems which afford easy installation and dismantlement.
6. Enhanced maintenance abilities assisted by self-testing diagnostics.
7. The ability to detect all metals including mixed alloys.
8. The development of continuously active capabilities meaning that at no time is it possible to toss, pass, or slide a weapon through the system without detection.
9. The development of enhanced through put capabilities made available through the use of fast reset functions.
10. Finally, the availability of adjustable speed responses designed to cover a wide range of velocities or object speed.

Weatherproof, walk-through metal detectors also possess many of the same technological advances listed above; however, these detectors possess unique characteristics designed to offer full weather-proofing protecting the unit in harsh climates ranging from sever winter conditions to tropical environments. Finally, high discrimination, walk-through metal detectors also possess many of the same technological advances listed above; however, these detectors have some additional unique characteristics designed to offer high discrimination factors; for example, improved discrimination of metal objects reducing false alarm rates to less than 5 percent; improved interference rejection; enhanced uniformity of detection in high traffic areas; improved reset speeds for optimum traffic flow and minimum alarm times; and the availability of preset programs designed to meet the requirements set by leading security organizations.

An additional technological development concerning walk-through metal detectors can be found in the area of monitoring networks. These computerized networks provide for the development of remote security monitoring systems. For example, one central PC can be programmed to monitor and adjust numerous walk-through detectors in an instant. Various preset security levels can be applied at any single detector, group of detectors, or a whole network of detectors. Indeed, a specified detector can be set independently of existing security levels if required. These networks control the detectors settings and alarms if deviations arise. In case of emergency situations or detector malfunctioning, both a signal and a printed message are sent to the PC operator. Furthermore, the operator will also receive a message if a detector's setting is altered at its physical location. Finally, the network is protected by multilevel pass-

words in order to prevent unauthorized access.

In conclusion, to make any metal detection program effective, school access during the rest of the school day, during off-hours, and during special activities needs to be tightly controlled. A motivated student can defeat a lax system. Lax systems, improperly operated systems, or poorly designed systems will be a waste of precious security resources and school funds. Finally, a successful metal detection program cannot be poorly funded or run by a school administration that is reticent to make major changes to school policies and procedures.

Intrusion Detection Systems (IDS)

Exterior security at many educational facilities, especially the perimeter, is often given only cursory consideration. This lapse of security can often be attributed to an unfamiliarity concerning basic perimeter security systems. The root cause of this unfamiliarity can often be traced to the lack of a basic understanding of the principles of sensor technology and confusion involving the real threat compared to a perceived threat. To begin any satisfactory discussion concerning exterior security, the four parts of an effective security system (Detection, Delay, Assessment, and Response), must be considered. To clarify, effective exterior alarm systems must detect an intrusion; provide a delaying effect while the intruder('s) attempt to defeat the system; allow time for both remote and on-the-ground assessments, and provide security forces with the information needed to choose an appropriate response. It must be understood that no intrusion detection system (IDS) is 100 percent perfect; some degree of successful penetration is inherent in all security systems. Thus, it is important to study an applicable intruder profile (for example, juvenile vandal) in order to choose an IDS barrier that has the highest probability of defeating or thwarting the efforts of the profiled intruder.

Designing an IDS

To design an exterior IDS, the following aspects must be considered: the physical configuration, the site, the sensors, probability of detection, nuisance alarm rates, and vulnerability to defeat. Proper physical configurations generally consist of the following three parts: a sector, a detection zone, and a clear zone or isolation zone. A sector is defined as a segment of a perimeter sensor system with a specified length, usually 100 meters. A detection zone is defined as the volume of space in which an intrusion sensor is expected to detect the presence of an intruder. A clear zone or isolation zone is usually defined by two parallel fences between which all obstructions to visibility have been removed. These three configurations are required for the generation of perimeter intrusion detection goals—detection, delay, assessment, and response.

When evaluating the site, particular attention must be focused on the condition of existing physical barriers, for example, walls or fences, etc. A solid physical barrier is critical because it acts as an initial deterrent against human intrusion, protects sensors from environmentally-caused nuisance alarms (wind blown debris or stray animals), and the barrier may be chosen as a platform for a sensor system. Of course, the perimeter must be well illuminated, visible (free of obstacles and vegetation), and well maintained. Remember, the perimeter is only as strong as its weakest point (areas that might afford an easy means of system bypass; for example, storm culverts, overhead utilities, adjacent light poles or trees, close building structures, equipment parked next to the perimeter, etc.).

Today's exterior IDS sensors have improved greatly over the past several years and are reliable if they are properly applied according to the installation recommendations of the manufacturer. However, it must be understood that exterior IDS sensors have a lower probability of detecting intruders and a higher false alarm rate than their internal counterparts. This is attributed largely to many uncontrollable factors such as wind, rain, ice, standing water, blowing debris, stray animals, random human activity, vehicle traffic, and other sources to include electronic interference. Keeping these factors in mind, IDS sensors must be evaluated by considering three standards: probability of detection, nuisance alarm rate, and their vulnerability to defeat (all discussed in detail below). Of course, sensors must be adequately maintained and routinely tested.

IDS Types

There are a great number of security intrusion detection systems on the market today. Some are applicable to interior applications only, exterior applications only, and a combination of the two applications. The reader will soon understand that a complete description of each IDS is far beyond the scope of this chapter, thus, in the interest of brevity, a listing of technology available has been compiled minus extensive technological descriptions. IDS sensors include microwave, bi-static and monostatic microwave, exterior active infrared, dual-technology passive infrared/microwave, fence vibration, electric field, capacitance, strain sensitive cable, fiber optic fence, taut wire, in-ground fiber optic, ported coax buried line, balanced buried pressure, buried geophone, video motion detection, radar, and acoustic detection (air turbulence). Additional IDS fall into a category other than sensors, which include CCTV's, night vision surveillance systems, and wide area thermal imaging systems. Even this list is not inclusive of all exterior IDS due to the plethora of new or improved equipment being continually developed and introduced into the market place.

IDS Sensors

Sensors are generally classified into five different types, passive or active, covert or visible, line of sight or terrain following, and volumetric or line detection. Passive sensors are non-radiating and detect some type of energy that radiates from the target, or change in a natural field caused by the movement of the target, for example, passive infrared, seismic or magnetic, fence disturbance, sensor fences, or video motion detection. One advantage of a passive sensor is its difficulty of being intruder-identified. Active sensors use a radiated energy to create a detection field which is disturbed by the intruder; examples include microwave, active infrared, and RF buried, or surface mounted sensors. Active sensors have the advantage of offering more data for advanced signal processing and are more difficult to defeat by spoofing.

Covert or visible sensors include the plethora of IDS listed above. Visible sensors may act as good intruder deterrents while at the same time offering easier installation and maintenance. Covert sensors do not reveal (to the layman) any form of IDS on the perimeter; however, covert systems are much more expensive to install and more difficult to maintain than visible sensors.

Line of sight sensors require an unobstructed view from the origin of detection field to its termination point; examples include bi-static (an active intrusion detection sensor in which the transmitting and receiving devices have separate locations), monostatic (an active intrusion detection sensor in which the transmitter and the receiver devices are either the same or in the same location) microwave, and active and passive infrared. Line of sight sensors are easy to install and service but may require a great deal of site preparation. Furthermore, detection zones are readily identified by potential intruders. Terrain following sensors are mounted on platforms conforming to the existing terrain–up and down, twists and turns, etc. While terrain following sensors solve the problem of site preparation, they are often more expensive to purchase, maintain, and install. Examples of terrain following sensors include buried sensors, sensor fences, fence-mounted sensors, and RF electric field sensors.

Volumetric sensors have a three-dimensional detection field, or a wide area of detection (the wider the detection pattern, the more difficult the system is to defeat). Examples of volumetric sensors include microwave, passive infrared, electric field, video motion, and buried ported coax. These sensors offer a high degree of probability of detection plus require a great deal of real estate. Line detection sensors detect along a finite line or point. These sensors require less real estate, require a great deal of maintenance, and are easy to defeat by bypassing efforts since they require physical contact by an intruder. Examples of line detectors include fence-mounted sensors, strain sensitive sensors, and sensor fences.

Probability of Detection

The probability of detection may be broken down into the following six factors: amount and pattern of emitted energy (the more definitive the energy pattern the better); size of the object (the larger the object, the greater the chance of detection); distance to the object (the shorter the distance to the sensor the greater the probability of detection); speed of the object (the faster the movement of an object the greater the probability of detection); direction of movement (lateral movement has a higher probability of detection than straight-on movement), and reflection/absorption characteristics of the energy waves by the intruder and the environment (the greater the contrast between an object and the overall reflection/characteristics of the area under surveillance, the greater the probability of detection).

False Alarms/Nuisance Alarms

For the purpose of this book, the term false alarm rate will encompass both false alarms and nuisance alarms. False alarms may be defined as an alarm where the cause is unknown and an intrusion is therefore possible, but a determination after the fact indicates no intrusion was attempted. Nuisance alarms may be defined as an alarm event in which the reason is known or suspected (e.g., animal movement/electric disturbance) and therefore probably not caused by an intruder. False alarm rates are of great concern; multiple false IDS alarms equate to multiple assessments and responses which after awhile may be ignored and/or generate inadequate responses. Remember, many intruders don't intend to defeat security sensors, but attack poorly designed assessment and response procedures. Therefore, a system without effective assessment and response is dangerous and at the very least almost worthless. To effectively address false alarm rates, a maximum number of false alarms should be established; once this number is reached, delineated compensatory measures, recording and reporting procedures, and

maintenance guidelines should be initiated.

Any discussion of alarm types would not be complete without covering two additional alarms–intrusion alarms and tamper alarms. Intrusion alarms are defined as alarms which are actually caused by an intruder(s). Tamper alarms are defined as alarms generated when access doors to sensor electronics or wire connections are opened or when the sensor detects a spoofing attempt.

Vulnerability to Defeat

Vulnerability to defeat is accomplished by either bypassing the system or by spoofing (causing numerous repeated alarms at various places along the perimeter over short periods of time). Spoofing generates assessment methodology frustration, security force confusion, and overloads alarm monitoring personnel and equipment. Vulnerability to defeat can be reduced by designing sensor coverage using multiple units of the same sensor, and/or co-locating more than one type of sensor to provide mutual sensor protection and overlapping coverage (defense-in-depth) of the area. The major goal of a security planner is to choose and field an integrated IDS that exhibits a low false alarm rate, possesses a high probability of detection, and is not susceptible to defeat. Technology will certainly make these goals more achievable in the future, as sensors become "smarter" through the use of advanced digital signaling processing.

Explosives/Narcotics Detection

There are a variety of new explosives/narcotics detection devices available which will certainly prove valuable in many integrated security systems. Indeed, chemical trace detection and identification systems may provide substantial improvement in security against the threat of explosives or the introduction of contraband drugs into educational facilities. These systems strengthen essential elements of physical security programs such as access control points and enable the development of more efficient preplanned responses to suspected or actual explosives/illegal drug discovery.

Intelligent Detection Systems

Some of the newest explosive/drug detection systems operate around the principle of trace detection devices manufactured by Intelligent Detection Systems (IDS). IDS allows the operator to detect what can't be seen by the human eye, for example, minute traces of organic compounds. This trace detection technology incorporates both gas chromatography (GC) and ion mobility spectrometry (IMS). This resulting GC/IMS dual technology enables operators to simultaneously sample and analyze vapors and particles generated from explosives and narcotics. This compounding of technology reportedly delivers the highest level of chemical accuracy (a combination of high probability of detection coupled with low false alarm rates) available on the market today.

Chemical Trace Detection Systems

Cutting edge chemical trace detection systems should deliver accuracy, plus effectiveness and enable the following critical system aspects to be realized: high throughput, sensitivity, low false alarms, ease of use, portability, integration, adaptability, low maintenance, and cost-of-ownership effective. High throughput capabilities means trace detection scanning can be effectively performed in high-volume areas. Sensitivity focuses on the ability of the system to detect minute traces of organic compounds (nanograms to picograms for particles and parts per million for vapors) and the ability to detect and identify specific compounds among varying background levels of other substances.

Low false alarm rates are possible due to dual technology use (false alarm rates enhance operator confidence that alarms are real and actionable). Ease of use is especially important for new personnel who are inexperienced and have minimal training. These individuals must be able to learn to use the equipment and be able to interpret test results quickly and efficiently. The system must be user friendly in order to facilitate its use at facilities with high personnel turnover. Portability (lightweight hand-held devices to stationary yet mobile devices) is often important for effective field operations. Integration is important to achieve efficient security-in-depth operations, for example, chemical trace detection systems integrated with x-ray tomography and/or K-9 units.

Adaptability is necessary for application engineers to tailor chemical trace detection systems to the users needs, specifications, and operations. Low maintenance and cost-effectiveness can be enhanced by a well-designed support program. Indeed, a support program should be negotiated in any contract and should include technological advice and guidance given online, by telephone, and through on-site visits. Support programs should also include full documentation of related activities and the training of operators. All of the aforementioned chemical trace detection system aspects are necessary for fast, accurate, clear, and dependable results, while being safe, cost-effective, and convenient to use.

There are a variety of chemical trace detection systems on the market today. One of the most comprehensive lines is offered by IDS; for example, the Orion system, an automated stand-alone one-step sampling and analysis explosives detection system; the OrionPlus explosives detection system that simultaneously detects explosives and ICAO-mandated taggants; the Ariel stand-alone stationary system that detects a wide range of drugs, including cocaine, heroin, amphetamines, and hallucinogens; the Sirius system which is reportedly the only commercially available system in the world capable of simultaneously detecting both explosives and drugs; and the Northstar one-step, lightweight, hand-held GC/IMS drug detection system. IDS also offers some custom systems such as the Orion walk-through system and V-BEDS–fully automated systems designed respectively to inspect personnel and vehicle traffic based on the OrionPlus architecture.

Another line of chemical trace detection systems is available from Ion Track Instruments (ITI). ITI manufacturers the ITEMISER and the VaporTracer. The ITEMISER desktop contraband detector is a dual function detection and identification system, ideally suited for detecting trace quantities of narcotics and explosives. For example, the ITEMISER is designed to detect all common explosives such as C4, RDX, PETN, TNT, EGDN/NG, dynamite, Semtex, and ammonium nitrate. Furthermore, the ITEMISER is also designed to detect all common narcotics such as heroin, speed, THC, LSD, morphine, amphetamines, PCP, and cocaine. The ITEMISER can be easily programmed to screen and search for approximately 40 types of narcotics and explosives.

The ITEMISER can be used to successfully screen and search for the trace quantities of contraband that inevitably contaminate the surfaces of baggage, vehicles, cargo pallets, and all types of containers in which contraband may be hidden. Any surface where contraband has been present including walls and floors, furniture, and even people can be tested. The ITEMISER switches instantly from a narcotics detector to an explosives detector making the system ideal for circumstances where the search mission concentrates on both substances.

The ITEMISER works by first trapping traces of vapors or particles given off or left behind by explosives and/or narcotics. These trapped samples are evaporated and drawn into the detection system where they are analyzed by a new technology detection system which provides almost one hundred times more sensitivity than any previous detector (as reported by ITI). The detection technique is known as Ion Trap Mobility Spectrometry (ITMS) and operates by ionizing the target vapors and then subsequently measuring the mobility of the ions in an electric field. The mobility of each target ion differs sufficiently so that each is uniquely identified. The whole detection process can take less than three seconds to complete.

Sample collection is accomplished either by wiping a surface with a paper filter (sample trap) or by the use of a battery-operated hand vacuum that uses a sample trap. In either case, the trap containing the sample is simply dropped into the ITEMISER sample inlet, automatically triggering the analysis. The ITEMISER confirms the presence or absence of the contraband within five seconds, allowing numerous samples to be processed each day. When contraband is detected, the ITEMISER's alarm panel flashes, the substance is identified, and an audible alarm sounds. A bar graph display changes colors to indicate the strength of the alarm, or for a more detailed analysis, an ion signature spectrum known as a plasmagram can be

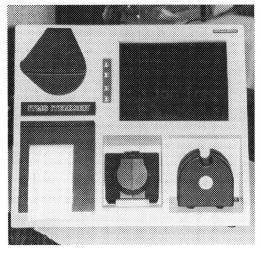

Figure 28. ITI Itemiser.

Figure 29. Vapor tracer.

selected. The ITEMISER can be set to automatically print out the plasmagram or alarm, or it can be stored on computer disk. The stored data which includes the time and date of the alarm and any notes entered at the time of the alarm may be recalled for printout or display at any time.

Ion Track Instruments (ITI) also markets a portable contraband detector called the Ion Trap Mobility Spectrometer–ITMS VaporTracer Portable Contraband Detector. The Vapor Tracer is a battery-powered (110/220 current, 90 minute fast recharge battery or a six hour battery pack) portable device which uses ITEMISER (see above) technology. This instrument is 16 inches long, five inches wide, nine inches tall, weighs seven pounds, and is capable of detecting and identifying extremely small quantities of narcotics or explosives. The system works by drawing a sample of the vapor into the detector where it is heated, ionized, and then identified by its unique plasmagram. Furthermore, this device is easy to operate through the use of a five-button keypad and LCD display. Indeed, the instrument requires little operator training and is internally calibrated with the touch of

a single button. Finally, the VaporTracer can be connected to the ITEMISER contraband detector for analysis and access to the touch screen display and on-board printer.

Video Surveillance (CCTV)

Perhaps the best thing about cameras is the deterrence factor they introduce both to outsiders who do not belong on campus and to students and employees who do belong on campus. An important aspect of security and response involves knowledge of what's happening, or what has happened around or in a specific area. One of the most efficient methods to obtain this information is through the use of cameras. There are many types available, each serving a particular need. Closed circuit television (CCTV) has two basic security uses, access control and general surveillance. These systems are very useful in observing perpetrators in the act allowing real time intervention or for recording evidence on tape. From a cost standpoint, the use of CCTV in public areas on school grounds can free-up manpower. Finally, the solid documentation that a video recording provides can be invaluable in situations involving liability claims.

Of course, CCTV systems are not without their down side. CCTV systems may be very expensive to install and logistically difficult to service. Additionally, choosing the correct camera equipment requires some technical knowledge. Typically, a single camera is often limited to viewing smaller areas than originally thought requiring many cameras, equipment and expense than is normally expected. Further, cameras can be stolen or vandalized and ongoing maintenance and/or operational support are often required. Some applications or areas will not avail themselves to CCTV use and some individuals or even communities will challenge the legality of using cameras. Additionally, CCTV's may be circumvented or once the location of cameras becomes common knowledge, students may move their misbehavior to uncovered areas. Finally, someone has to monitor the camera; if not, who will see the crime happen and take action to stop the action? Otherwise all the school has is a recording of a crime that has already happened.

The hard evidence made available in the form of a video recording can more than make up for the cost of a recording system. Indeed, quite often, when a suspected student is shown a recording of himself or herself, he or she is likely to admit to a role in the incident even though there may not be enough detail on tape for a positive identification. Additionally, doubting parents often quickly accept their child's role in an incident when shown a video tape of the event. Ease of prosecution and the likely prevention of future incidents are additional benefits. Further, color cameras are probably more helpful for most school applications than black-and-white cameras. While color cameras are more expensive, require brighter and more evenly distributed lighting, and are not as defined as black-and-

white cameras, they typically produce much more information concerning the scene (color of hair, clothes, and color of car) , than black-and-white cameras.

Two types of camera configurations are available on the market: the fixed camera and the pan-tilt-zoom camera. Fixed cameras are mounted in a stationary position and will view the same scene until they are physically relocated. Of course, these cameras may be mounted on a mobile platform such as a patrol car. The scene is typically recorded but may also be viewed simultaneously on a monitor by security personnel.

Some school systems are using remote viewing services provided by emergency services with the intent of achieving immediate response to real-time campus crises. However, the real-time viewing of video monitors has typically produced inconsequential results. Security studies reveal that after 20 minutes of watching and evaluating monitor screens, the attention of most individuals degenerates well below acceptable levels. Indeed, monitoring video screens is both boring and mesmerizing due to a lack of intellectually engaging stimuli. The task of trying to watch multiple monitors will generally exacerbate the situation. A practical real-time security application concerning fixed cameras is to point them at a specific target (a locked door) and tie in a video alarm that will sound if the area is disturbed. Of course, the use of cameras and a real-time display unit without the benefit of a recorder is not recommended. Finally, new technology may achieve a heightened measure of real-time response as computer operated CCTV systems enable operators to control live video and live audio (two-way conversation may be possible).

Pan-tilt-zoom cameras can operate in one of two modes. The mode for which these cameras are most useful allows the scene that is viewed to be controlled by an operator sitting at a video monitor. The operator controls the direction and angle of the camera as necessary and the zoom option allows the operator to focus in on parts of a scene. The second mode is an automatic mode. The automatic mode allows the camera to automatically scan back and forth over a certain range. Normally, these cameras are protected and shielded from view by opaque enclosures such as domes so that it is difficult for a would-be perpetrator to ascertain where the camera is actually pointed. Pan-tilt-zoom cameras may be effective if they are employed during a fixed portion of the day (lunch periods), if an operator is available to watch and track suspects with this type of camera. Finally, a few pan-tilt-zoom cameras may be placed in certain areas in order to supplement fixed cameras and foster a defense-in-depth posture.

However, most applications in schools are better served by fixed cameras. One consideration is that pan-tilt-zoom cameras costs much more than fixed cameras. More important is the fact that pan-tilt-zoom cameras, when run by an operator, consume the time of a security staff member which may be better spent on roving patrol. When run on the automatic mode, the chance of a pan-tilt-zoom camera looking and recording in the direction where an incident is occurring is much less likely than the chance that it will be looking in the wrong direction. Pan-tilt-zoom cameras also introduce a mechanical component to the system that will require additional maintenance. Finally, it will normally be more cost effective and more reliable to capture incidents using multiple fixed cameras looking in different areas from a single point than to use a single pan-tilt-zoom camera.

CCTV Terminology and Operating Requirements

Before purchasing a CCTV security system, school administrators should become familiar with basic terminology and operating requirements. This information is important in selecting a CCTV system which will provide the most efficient and effective security requirements for the money spent. School administrators cannot afford to waste precious funds on non-essential or inadequate CCTV equipment.

A basic CCTV system consists of four elements or subsystems and function in the following manner: the camera lens collects light and forms an image on a sensitized camera chip and this image is then electrically transmitted over a transmission link to a monitor which translates the signal back to a visible image. A fifth subsystem would be to incorporate a recording device, otherwise known as a video tape recorder (VTR), for preserving the image.

Basic terminology and operating requirements include formats, resolution, pixels, lens focal length, field of view, lighting, shadowing, camera aiming, and camera sensitivity. Formats, resolution, pixels, and lens focal length are the camera-specific part of what determines if a camera scene will be useful for a particular security application. Camera format relates to the size of the cameras imaging device. The sizes may be 1/2, 1/3, 2/3, or 1/4 inch. The current trend is to make camera formats smaller as picture element densities increase.

Resolution is the ability to resolve or see small details in an image. Resolution is usually specified in terms of horizontal lines per inch. Higher resolution equates to higher image quality. Typical color security cameras produce approximately 300 to 400 lines of horizontal resolution, while black-and-white cameras range from 500 to 700 lines of resolution. Higher resolution cameras can be used to distinguish objects farther away than a lower resolution camera. Typically, fewer higher resolution cameras will be needed than low-resolution cameras in some interior and many exterior applications. Of course, higher resolution cameras will typically cost more than lower resolution cameras.

Pixels refer to active picture elements and are directly related to horizontal lines of resolution. Pixels are the actual number of light sensitive elements that are in the camera imaging device. Pixels are expressed in a horizontal number and a vertical number. For example, a camera specified with 768H by 494V picture elements has 494 rows of picture elements vertically, with each row having 768 elements horizontally.

The lens focal length describes the relative magnification of the lens. Similar to the camera imager format, there is a formal size for lenses. The most common sizes are 4.8mm, 5.6mm, 8mm, 12mm, 16mm, 25mm, and 35mm. A 35mm lens has the longest range with the narrowest field of view (the size of the area that a camera will see at a specific distance from the camera). The 4.8mm lens can see much shorter distances but will have a much wider field of view. Most lens sizes can be used in exterior applications, depending on the view desired. However, shorter focal length lenses are typical for interior applications due to the shorter distances involved. Further, the lens format size should be matched to the camera imager format size. Mismatched format sizes can result in the focused image being too large or too small for the camera imaging device.

Lighting, shadowing, camera aiming, and camera sensitivity will correspond to the effects of blooming, streaking, and glare which will wash out the video image. Exterior cameras should be mounted below lighting sources and aimed downward to shun direct sunlight, especially that occurring during sunrise and sunset. Most schools generally will not attempt to use exterior CCTV cameras at night due to the high levels of lighting that are required. Important items to consider for nighttime camera lighting are illumination level, camera sensitivity, lens type, light-to-dark ratios, area of illumination in the camera field of view, and lighting position.

Illumination level must be high enough for the camera to produce a useable image. The light level required will depend on camera sensitivity and lens type and quality. Black-and-white cameras generally have more light sensitivity than color cameras and are thus recommended for most nighttime applications. The light-to-dark ratio is generally set at 6 to 1 (as measured on a horizontal plane 1 foot off the ground). This ratio applies to the entire area of interest that the camera is viewing. The idea is to prevent areas that are so dark or so bright that a person or object would be obscured. Furthermore, a minimum illumination of 70 percent of the camera field of view is normally recommended. A camera is an averaging device (if too little of the field of view is illuminated, the camera will average between the illuminated areas and the nonilluminated areas, resulting in blooming and loss of picture detail in the illuminated area).

The position of lighting in relation to the camera field of view is also important. As much as possible, lighting sources must be kept out of the camera's field of view. Lights that are illuminating a camera scene should be mounted higher than the cameras. Of course, extraneous light sources (other structure or area lights that will be in the cameras view) must be considered since they may cause blooming or streaking. **Note**: Distant light sources that are relatively dim are usually not a problem.

There are a few special lights which may be used with security cameras, these include infrared (IR) or near infrared and light emitting diodes (LED). The spectrum for this lighting is just below red and is not visible to the human eye. Most black-and-white cameras have sensitivity into the infrared range; however, security cameras must be specifically designed to make use of IR lighting. These lights are mentioned for information purposes only, as few schools if any will use this type of lighting.

Additionally, there are a few types of security cameras that can see at night without the use of artificial lights; they include intensified cameras and thermal cameras. Intensified cameras can produce a picture in conditions ranging from moonlight to starlight. Thermal cameras use the thermal energy radiated by objects in order to produce a picture. Like the lights mentioned above, these cameras are mentioned for information purposes only because they are probably cost prohibitive for most school systems.

Cameras should always be mounted on solid surfaces to prevent movement caused by the wind and vibrations. Furthermore, in the interior environment, cameras cannot be mounted higher than the ceiling so it may be easy for an intruder out-of-view of the camera to vandalize or otherwise tamper with them. This situation may be mitigated if the scene viewed by two cameras includes the other camera; for example, cameras mounted at each end of a hallway or room should be aimed to include a view of the other camera.

Covert Cameras

There is a special purpose camera which should be discussed due to the fact that it may be used in specific instances. These special cameras are known as covert cameras which are designed to be used when it is suspected or known that unlawful events or security lapses are occurring on campus in a certain area. However, laws concerning privacy issues and civil rights may vary widely, so before any electronic surveillance program is initiated, legal council should be sought. There are some generalities concerning electronic surveillance which are fairly consistent across the country; they include that cameras may not be used in any area where there is a reasonable expectation of privacy (bathrooms, gym changing areas, and some private offices).

Normally, school security cameras are mounted in plain view; however, covert cameras are hidden from view. Of course, conventional size cameras may be installed in a hidden location such as behind an air duct, but covert cameras are very tiny and may be placed virtually anywhere. Covert cameras may even be disguised as nearly any common object and are available with a wide range of lenses and capabilities such as infrared operation.

Further, covert cameras come in black-and-white or color and often include microphones (caution must be exercised, when using microphones, due to state laws intended to protect private conversations). Audio recording is often considered to be a greater legal concern than video recordings in most states. The recording of conversations is viewed as more of an invasion of privacy, as conversations often take place where the participants do not expect to be overheard. Finally, while the use of covert cameras can be extremely effective in providing evidence for prosecution, most schools are more interested in deterrence. Thus, not all school boards or school districts will support the use of covert cameras.

Dummy Cameras

Some schools have been known to use dummy cameras in an attempt to fool people into thinking they are under electronic surveillance. This is generally not a good idea because some states have ruled that a person may be misled into believing they will be rescued if attacked. Of course, dummy cameras are not the same as the "black boxes" installed on buses which may or may not have a camera installed at any time. While fake or dummy cameras can create a temporary deterrent to some security incidents, the potential liability it creates due to a victim's impression of being rescued quickly is considered unacceptable.

In conclusion, a camera scene is useful only if an object can be distinguished in the scene. Camera resolution, camera format size, lens focal length, lighting, shadowing, camera aiming, and camera sensitivity all play a role in being able to distinguish objects. Resolution and performance of other components such as TV monitors, recorders, and signal transmission equipment must also be considered.

Video Recording Equipment (VCR)

The video cassette recorder (VCR) is considered to be the weakest link in electronic surveillance systems due to their mechanical nature. VCRs, which typically operate at temperatures between 32 degrees Fahrenheit and 104 degrees Fahrenheit, need to be placed indoors in a well ventilated area where the relative humidity is less than 80 percent and the air is free of noncondensing moisture. If a video recorder must be placed in a dirty environment, a housing complete with a fan, vent holes, and filters should be used.

Further, probably the most ignored maintenance task in most school security departments is the regular servicing and cleaning of VCRs. A maintenance schedule should be developed to include the cleaning of the VCR heads after every 100 hours of use (about every four days of constant recording). The entire VCR unit should be serviced every 2,400 hours, or about every three months of constant use. If well-serviced, a typical VCR will last about four to five years with constant use.

Finally, the VCR should be set up in a secure, protected area. VCRs are attractive targets for thieves, but even more importantly, tapes can be stolen or destroyed if there is an illegal incident to be covered up. VCRs should be placed in a strong lockable cabinet within a locked room. Only the school principle and appropriate security personnel should have the keys to the cabinet.

Multiplexers

Multiplexers can be used to combine two or more individual video camera signals and send them to a single recorder. This is often referred to as timeshare multiplexing and allows up to 16 video camera signals to be recorded on a single half-inch videocassette simultaneously and played back as individual pictures or combinations of pictures upon command. A multiplexer can either be a simplex multiplexer or a duplex multiplexer. The simplex multiplexer can only display a full-screen image of one selected camera or a sequence of selected cameras while recording. A duplex multiplexer can also display multiscreen images while still recording. Essentially, a multiscreen display consists of a split screen that allows for the viewing of all camera images on the system simultaneously.

A duplex multiplexer costs more than a simplex multiplexer and is best utilized when someone is watching or operating the system while it is recording. A more cost effective simplex multiplexer is best used in school applications where the system is unmanned. Most multiplexers feature camera titling for recording and a permanent time/date stamp on each frame of recorded video. Another feature is compensation for camera synchronization. Multiplexers are equipped with an alarm input for each camera. When activated, these can be used to generate an output to the VCR to place both the multiplexer and VCR into the two-hour recording mode (real time) for a predetermined period of time. Some multiplexers allow only images from the alarm camera to be recorded, but others allow a choice of interleaving (every other field). On-screen programming of the multiplexer allows for simpler programming and review of settings. Programming features should display VCR tables because it is important to synchronize the multiplexer to the particular model and brand of VCR to avoid missing crucial information.

Time-Lapse Recorders

There are also time-lapse recorders which have the ability to incrementally record at specific time intervals, recording a single field or frame of video information with each increment. In other words, a time-lapse recorder can provide a continuous flow of recorded information that can span long periods of time in a very small, storable format.

Event Recorders

Another recorder choice includes event recorders. Event recorders may be designed to interface (viewing the area where an alarm is occurring) with intrusion detection systems or other types of alarms. Upon alarm, this interface signals the recorder to turn itself on to record the alarm event. This

feature allows a tape to be used for very long periods of time as no recording is being done during uneventful times. Additionally, event-recorders are generally cheaper than time-lapse recorders.

Digital Recorders

Digital recorders are capable of recording full-motion video. Digital storing and recording have many advantages over a time-lapse or event recorder. The most important advantage is probably the fact that digital recorders require no human intervention, which means no maintenance and no cleaning. This technology is new and is continuing to advance; however, its cost will preclude most schools from using this technology for the foreseeable future.

VCR Tapes and Recording Plans

Premium quality VCR tapes are recommended for the constant use experienced by most school applications. Their expected quality lifespan is about 25 recordings. Recording over the same tape indefinitely is not recommended because this practice introduces several logistical problems. For example, some incidents are reported several days after they occur, thus the video of the incident has already been recorded over. A good recording plan should be developed and should include six new tapes every fall and spring (by replacing the tapes every spring and fall, the tape quality is not compromised). Tapes should be labeled Monday through Friday, and weekend. Each morning, the appropriate tape is put into the VCR and when an incident occurs, that particular tape should be pulled and labeled as "removed," along with the date it was last used. A new tape labeled with that day of the week should replace the original. This recording plan should be adequate for most schools.

CCTV Warning Signs

It is recommended that the installment of CCTV systems also include the posting of very visible and hard-to-miss signs at the entrances to a school campus and at major entrances leading into school buildings. These signs may provide an effective front-line deterrence informing the public and the school occupants that certain security measures are in force. Additionally, liability issues may be avoided or minimized through the use of signs. Finally, covert approaches to security can sometimes be open to contention, especially by someone who is caught in this way. Thus, signs may reduce contention.

Soliciting Bids for CCTV Systems

School administrators should follow a number of common sense approaches, when soliciting bids for purchasing any security system. For the purpose of this book and the avoidance of providing redundant information, the bidding process will be discussed in terms of selecting a CCTV system. First, administrators should identify an acceptance criteria very clearly in the request for proposal (RFP). Second, administrators should not accept or pay for a CCTV system until it has been installed and is demonstrated to operate according to the RFP specifications. Third, it is often beneficial to request two different camera layouts and their associated costs. One layout should provide the exact capability requested to meet the schools requirements and the second layout would include the best possible configuration within a specified dollar amount. These two layouts may then be used by the administrator to approach the school board or other approving entity in order to request the funding necessary to meet the goals of the required security system. This is especially important if set funding requires the installation of a security system that will perform substantially below the school's requirements.

Finally, administrators should pay particular attention to factory and/or installer warranty language and time lines. A person should be assigned the responsibility of regularly checking equipment functioning and immediately remove any failing components in order to return them to the manufacturer within the warranty period. Of course, it is best for the installing vendor to respond to problems in a reasonable amount of time. Indeed, a maintenance contract is an attractive option and should, if possible, be included in the RFP.

Video Intercom Systems

Video intercom systems are finding extensive applications in school security systems because they offer advantages far beyond typical intercom systems. First, the CCTV capability allows individuals within the protected area to observe individuals outside the protected area. Second, these systems allow the entry door to an area to remain locked at all times and allows operators to selectively grant access onto the premises. Finally, the intercom allows communication from the entry door to the control unit inside the premises. Multiple video intercom systems allow for multiple door coverage, multiple interior stations, and communications between both door to interior station as well as between interior stations. Video intercom systems range from simple door answering units to sophisticated video entry security systems using complex microprocessor-based commercial systems.

Blast Mitigation

Schools are often subjected to bomb threats and there is a distinct possibility that perpetrators may use conventional or unconventional explosive devices during a school violence crisis. Due to this possibility and the fact that most injuries and deaths attributed to explosive devices come from fragmentation (normally glass), school administrators should consider blast mitigation efforts. In relation to blast mitigation, school administrators generally have three choices: requiring new structures to have blast resistant windows; replacing in-use windows with new blast resistant windows; or requiring the use of blast curtains or blast coating. Naturally, choosing new blast resistant windows is the best choice. However, many school will not be able to pursue this option. With this thought in mind, only blast curtains and blast coatings will be discussed.

Blast curtains come in a variety of materials, shapes, and designs. Some are easily identified as blast curtains, while others are more subdued having the appearance of conventional curtains. Basically, blast curtains work by capturing blast propelled glass into a special material which bunches these secondary projectiles together, slows their velocity, and drops the pieces directly to the floor. In many cases, blast curtains may be seen as too "adversarial or high profile" for many schools. Plus, the number of blast mitigating curtains a school may require will generally be very expensive. Additionally, blast curtains may interfere with law enforcement officers attempts to surveil the inside of an area during a school violence crisis response operation. Of course, schools may decide only a select area(s) require this type of protection.

Blast coating is typically a 15 mil. thick maximum security film which is custom installed right over the existing window glass. This security film is actually a specially blended biaxially-oriented, polyester laminate capable of providing a measure of protection from bomb blast, severe storm damage, smash and grab crimes, and some bullets. The security film is coated on one side with a resilient, scratch-resistant substance and the other side is covered with an acrylic adhesive so powerful it reportedly forms a molecular bond with the glass. The film may be transparent or ordered in bronze, gray, or silver tinting. When a window treated with this security film is subjected to a heavy impact, instead of merely breaking as in the case of a normal window pane, the treated glass cracks similar to a shatterproof car windshield, preventing secondary glass projectiles from sailing into a room. If hit hard enough, the coated glass may simply part from the window frame and fall in a contained lump to the floor.

Blast coating may be the best choice for many schools for a number of reasons. First, the coating is undetectable until needed. Second, blast coating is cost effective (approximately $6.00 per square foot installed) when numerous windows require this type of protection. Third, the coating is quickly installed; standard size windows can be protected in just a few minutes. Fourth, any size window can be custom fitted with the coating material. Finally, the treated glass may be cleaned in the same manner as conventional window glass.

Window Protection

Over 50 percent of all break-ins are said to occur through glass windows. A number of glass and plastic products have security applications designed to reduce this vulnerability. Some of the most commonly used products include laminated glass, bullet-resisting glass, wired glass, acrylic glazing material, and polycarbonate glazing material.

Laminated glass is composed of two sheets of ordinary glass bonded to an intervening layer of resilient plastic material. Laminated glass is often strong enough to withstand the force repeated blows. Bullet-resisting glass is also made of laminated glass. This type of glass protection typically consist of multiple plies of glass and plastic, and is manufactured in a variety of thicknesses ranging from 3/4 inch to 3 inches. Wired glass consist of glass containing wire mesh and is designed to provide resistance to the impact of large objects. However, there is a risk of injury from the glass shattering. Wired glass has a limited applicability for aesthetic reasons.

Glazing materials are designed to strengthen glass and may be added to standard glass panes at any time. For example, acrylic glazing materials are actually clear plastics which are seventeen times more resistant to breakage than glass. Finally, polycarbonate glazing materials are usually blue or gray tinted plastics having 300 times the impact resistance of glass and twenty to thirty times more impact resistance than acrylics.

Security Robots

Technology has reached the point that robots are now being used by a number of blue-chip corporations and government agencies to provide physical security in certain areas. Some school systems that have a large tax base or who have been successful in obtaining a number of the larger government grants may also be interested in procuring this exciting security technology.

These robots are used in conjunction with computers and video cameras to provide a unique form of security in depth. This technology is moving forward at such a pace

that the U.S. Army predicts fully operational security robots such as the Mobile Detection Assessment Response Systems (MDARS) to be in use by the latter part of this year. Many robots such as Cybermotions Cyberguard SR2/ESP, SR3/ESP, NavMaster III, Cybermotion CyberGuard Security Robot, CyberClean Vacuuming Robot, and the ARIES Nuclear Waste Inspection Robot are currently being fielded.

Most robots are designed around two major components: a navigational system designed to enhance movement, and an array of sensors designed to detect a range of hazards. Examples include ultrasonic intrusion detectors, intrusion threat assessment logic, optical flame detectors, passive infrared arrays, microwave intrusion radar, smoke sensors, gas sensors, temperature sensors, humidity sensors, ambient light sensors, video transmitters, oxygen sensors, optical pyrometers, inventory tag readers, and high speed automatic cameras complete with zoom lenses, to name just a few.

The typical robot will operate on its own "random patrol" chosen from a library of preestablished path segments during computer programmed periods–hours of darkness or during the close of business, etc., unless an intruder, fire, chemical spills or imbalances, radiation releases, or other unusual event is encountered. Under these circumstances, an audio/visual alarm is registered in the control room; officers manning the control room may choose to observe the robot as it automatically follows preselected routes to the alarmed area or dispatch the robot using destination commands. Control room officers may even direct the robot to follow perpetrators anywhere in the protected facility, even if an intruder(s) attempts to evade on foot. Furthermore, control room operators can issue verbal challenges or other commands through the robot. Thus, alarms can be immediately assessed and some adversary contact can be initiated with no physical risk to security personnel. Most robots are capable of operating from eight to twenty hours and may cover more then 50 miles before requiring recharging.

Some robots also have the ability to conduct an inventory of more than 60,000 specified items while on patrol. This inventory is conducted as the robot reads inexpensive radio frequency (RF) tags affixed to selected controlled items, high-dollar items, sensitive items, easily pilfered items, or special-interest items, etc. Using its RF tag reading capabilities in combination with its navigation system, these robots offer near real-time notification of the presence (or absence) of RF-tagged items and their respective locations. Inventory data can be downloaded at the end of the robots patrol or immediately reported, if desired.

Many robots are equipped with low light cameras designed to maintain surveillance of an area in total darkness. Some robots have an active near-infrared light source which illuminates the area at an optical wave length humans can't see but which the robots camera can see. This is an important concept, by providing real-time surveillance, security personnel will no longer have to take the risk of blindly entering dangerous situations. Control room officers may monitor the robots camera and then feed responding officers information by radio. Security officers may also enter these situations wearing night vision devices (NVD) which will pick up the robots near-infrared light source in areas which normally would have been too dark for some NVD's to operate. These security robots can even be used in conjunction with traditional security forces for searching facilities for intruders or for setting up passive blocking positions.

While moving, some robots use sophisti-

cated sensors to check their current location and to make necessary course adjustments. All autonomous robots have collision avoidance systems consisting of navigation sensors which will detect an imminent collision with an obstacle, even if the unit is being operated by tele-operation. In such cases, the robot will take over the navigation mechanics and either stop or maneuver around the obstacle. If the robot cannot plan and execute a path around an obstacle, it will notify the operating console and request instructions. The controlling officer then has the option of tele-operating the robot around the obstacle. Today's indoor security robots ride on platforms propelled by wheels engineered to deal with rough surfaces, minimize slippage and to climb very low obstacles. Older systems and systems designed for bomb disposal or outdoor activities are propelled by high maintenance tracks. Treaded operation is designed to overcome very rough terrain, climb obstacles, or even push down obstacles, thus these robots can be very destructive indoors.

During traditional duty hours robots may be stationed at an ingress/egress point to monitor pedestrian traffic through the use of the closed circuit camera and/or monitor the movement of RF tagged items. Typically, robots used in static locations record data for approximately one hour, erase video tape if that period was uneventful, then continue recording for another hour, and start the process again. Of course, there are time lapse tapes available which provide 48 hours of recording time and these tapes are excellent tools for organizations requiring the archiving of events (remember, events may not seem important at the time of occurrence, only future investigations may reveal the importance of an event). Robots may even be programmed to monitor certain employee identification badges in order to ascertain authorization to certain areas. There is no need to be concerned that robots will run into personnel or equipment as many of these robots track nearby personnel or objects to avoid collisions, plus possess wall navigation and circumnavigation instructions.

A robot's strong points are as follows: robots do not suffer from human foibles and therefore perform duties with exacting consistency, accuracy, and completeness. Furthermore, robots often come complete with a team of experts who work with the purchaser to define the robot's responsibilities and duties; configure the robot to the purchaser's specifications; test and verify the robot's operation; train security personnel to program the robot's functions; provide troubleshooting services, and provide maintenance and service programs. Finally, robots do not require a vacation, pay increases, or benefits, and never go on strike. Indeed, robots will often pay for themselves in a short period of time (operating costs may be as low as $1.50 an hour). The author believes that security robots are a viable addition to the sound security principle of strengthening security in depth.

Security efforts will surely be revolutionized as technology advances are applied to future robots. In the future, security robots may be armed with a variety of weapons which range from lethal platforms to less-than-lethal devices. Presently, robots represent excellent systems for providing enhanced security and product assessment within warehouses, educational facilities, office buildings, hospitals, prisons, and other enclosed structures where people or property need protection.

Mobile and Static
X-ray Equipment

X-ray equipment best suited for school applications are known as single-energy units. Single-energy units use a vacuum tube to emit x-rays on and through hand carried items. These x-rays come from inside the top of the unit and scan downward in a pencil-thin beam of radiation that generally moves back-and-forth across baggage that is automatically moved through the equipment. Sensors collect the magnitude of the signals that make it through scanned items. For example, items made of a low Z-number material allow more energy through scanned items and material with a high Z-number allow less energy through scanned items. The resulting images are transferred to a TV monitor (black-and-white or color) where an operator carefully examines each image for evidence of firearms or knives. Infrared (IR) beams automatically start and stop the x-ray beam source so that the x-rays are not operational when there is not a piece of baggage located in the imaging position. Shielding has also been added to x-ray machines to protect the operator and the general public. Indeed, today's x-ray machines are safe and are of negligible health risk. About the only potential health risk from an x-ray baggage screening machine would be if someone rode the conveyor belt through the equipment, which would still result in substantially less radiation exposure than would be gained from a medical x-ray.

X-ray equipment is a valued addition to any metal detection program. X-ray systems are ideal for scanning bookbags, purses, briefcases, and other hand carried items. However, x-ray equipment will require additional space. An x-ray machine will typically require a space of four feet by four feet plus an eight foot conveyor belt which would add about two feet on either side of the detector itself. Smaller desktop x-ray units are available, but these are used primarily for screening letters and mailed parcels. X-ray scanners are not sensitive to their surroundings so virtually no clearance is required around other types of equipment or utilities. Extra space may be needed for the scannee to place parcels on the x-ray machine, room to place pocket items in a special pass-through container, room to pick up scanned items, and space to turnaround in order to walk through the portal device a

Figure 30. X-ray looking into a vehicle.

Figure 31. X-ray looking into a briefcase.

second time if necessary.

The expected throughput of an x-ray scanner will normally depend upon two things: the efficiency of the operator and the amount of clutter in a typical hand carried bag. Clutter can also affect the speed of the operator. Purses and bookbags may contain many high Z-material items such as metal rulers, screwdrivers or other tools, foil-wrapped items, etc., which can significantly slow down an operator who is examining each piece of baggage. This clutter may necessitate the bag being pulled from the conveyer and manually searched. Generally, 10 to 20 items can be scanned per minute and as many as 30 items may be scanned if they contain predominantly benign items.

Adequately staffing an x-ray machine may be a problem for many schools. These devices require a number of tasks which may require distribution among a number of personnel, for example, placement of bags on the conveyor belt, operating machine controls, viewing the monitor, making a judgement regarding each bag, and performing physical searches of parcels as required. Of course, security personnel or SRO's may be assisted by using trained school staff members. The challenging part of operating x-ray equipment is knowing what to look for (the recognition of contraband or dangerous items).

Most x-ray scanners will last ten years or more. Indeed, technological advancements are more likely than device failure to render x-ray machines less useful. Thus, there is little regular maintenance required for this equipment.

Great efforts have been made all over the world to develop a system or process designed to automatically and reliably detect weapons, explosives, or drugs hidden in mail, luggage, freight, or vehicles. The nearest systems, to date, which begin to achieve these lofty goals concern the use of mobile and static x-rays machines. Indeed, present technological advances have been made which enable x-ray machines to perform a 100 percent non-invasive inspection of parcels, freight or cargo, and vehicles to a degree unheard of in the past.

X-ray inspection systems are now

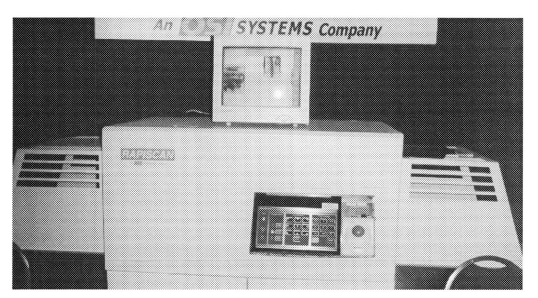

Figure 32. X-ray looking into a notebook and parcel.

designed to meet a list of essential requirements, for example:

1. The system should be compact and reliable, while at the same time be affordable and economic to operate.
2. Allow integration into existing logistical requirements and security systems.
3. Optimize image representation by furnishing all information relevant to security operations.
4. Maximize inspection quality while expending minimum inspection time.
5. Possess a very high image resolution in order to distinguish very fine structures and differences in density so that wires or hidden items in manipulated luggage or other containers can be easily recognized.
6. Possess image recall capabilities and image manipulation functions for review purposes.
7. Possess loss-free digital recording capabilities for playback requirements.
8. Have the capability to penetrate up to 25mm of steel.
9. Finally, be completely harmless to system operators and personnel located in the immediate area (the x-ray source should generate extremely low radiation dose "integrated exposure" levels outside the direct source beam, allowing operation in confined spaces with insignificant radiation exposure).

Granted, it can be difficult for operators to recognize certain types and configurations of explosives or drugs, especially when using some of the more antiquated systems on the market today. The author considers two of the greatest improvements in x-ray technology today to be the ability of x-ray machines to code material information by means of pseudo-color or color mapping such as the system developed by Heimann Systems, and the ability of some systems to visually highlight drugs and explosives.

Pseudo color representation works by placing different materials on a continuous color scale according to the atomic number Z of the elements. The color scale comprises colors from orange for elements of low atomic number ($Z<10$), i.e., elements which can be found in organic material, to green for elements of medium atomic number ($10<Z<18$) and up to blue for elements of higher atomic number ($Z>18$). The information concerning material thickness, respectively, the absorption factor is furnished by means of the brightness degree of the color signal so that items composed of the same material which are, however, different in thickness, show the same color while differing in brightness. Material which cannot be classified because of too much thickness is represented in grey. The advantage of a continuous color scale becomes evident when considering overlapping materials: in systems with abrupt color switch-over between organic and non-organic materials, even thin layers of overlapping materials such as steel, copper, or plastic will lead to organic materials being classified incorrectly as non-organic materials. The continuous color scale provides a mixed color representation depending on the degree of the mixture of materials which can be distinguished from the color of the overlapping materials. In conclusion, ergonomic color representation presents the operator with additional material information, does not overtax the operator, and supports the operator in making a decision by reducing the confusion many older black/white systems generate.

Perhaps one of the most exciting developments in x-ray inspection systems can be found in Heimann Systems X-ACT inspection technology. X-ACT provides real time image evaluation functions by marking drugs or explosives with a red frame for explosives or a green frame for drugs–the red or green frame will appear at the same time as the image is produced. Thus, the operator is instantly presented with the data required to make a decision without any additional manipulation of the image.

There are a few x-ray inspection systems which are very portable such as the RTR-4 portable digital x-ray imaging system designed and manufactured by Science Applications International Corporation (SAIC). The RTR-4 is a rugged, portable, fully digital x-ray imaging system that can be used by explosive ordnance personnel, law enforcement, security personnel, postal inspection personnel, and industrial quality assurance inspectors in a variety of situations. The flexibility of this system can be seen by considering the RTR-4's ability to penetrate a wide variety of materials from woods and plastics to concrete and steel, while still retaining the ability to detect the thinnest of wires. For example, ordnance disposal personnel may use the RTR-4 to evaluate unexploded ordnance in order to determine a fusing type, function, or condition. It can also be used by a corporate security staff to perform mail room inspections or point-of-ingress examination of personal belongings. Customs personnel use the RTR-4 for investigation of vehicle panels and tires, when searching for hidden contraband, and even quality assurance inspectors may use the RTR-4 for evaluating manufacturing process control standards.

The RTR-4 was specifically designed to facilitate rapid image acquisition, and provide image enhancement and measurement tools for the evaluation of the content of small objects or packages. The system, powered by 110 or 220 volt AC internal battery or 12 volt DC vehicle battery, is easy to assemble and operate (by one person in less than five minutes), and requires minimal maintenance. The compact size of the x-ray source and imager make it possible for the system to be installed around a fixed target,

or situated so that the objects can be placed in front of the imager's screen. Once the system has been assembled, images can be acquired and viewed immediately. Operators may acquire and evaluate images from several hundred feet away by using wireless connections. RTR-4 images are achieved digitally and can be transmitted via modem or floppy disk to other computers for off-site evaluation. Furthermore, these stored images can be used to compile a database for consultation, future comparison, and evidence for prosecution.

Field deployment of the RTR-4 is simplified and made convenient by a variety of custom features. The self-contained control unit, which is housed in a lightweight aluminum case, is designed to operate over broad temperature and humidity ranges. For added protection, the entire system is stored and transported in two foam-lined, weatherproof transport cases constructed to withstand the roughest abuse.

Other types of inspection equipment include cargo screening systems such as SAIC's VACIS vehicle inspection system. The VACIS system uses a highly penetrative gamma ray to non-intrusively inspect freight contained on pallets and in trucks, cargo containers, railcars, and passenger vehicles. Operators viewing the gamma-ray images on a video monitor can quickly and efficiently identify voids, false walls or ceilings, and other secret compartments typically associated with the transportation of drugs, explosives, and weapons. Operators searching for stolen or smuggled goods can use the images to determine whether the cargo is consistent with the declared manifest.

The VACIS gamma-ray based system eliminates the large accelerator-based x-ray source, its accompanying power and control systems, and the conveyor system for the truck or container. This makes the gamma-ray systems far smaller than their x-ray counterparts. The VACIS system can be disassembled, transported, and reassembled in one to three days depending on the configuration. SAIC representatives report that their VACIS-II, Stolen Vehicle Recovery System (STAR) SENTRY-Auto, Truck & Cargo Inspection System, Sentinel-Railroad Inspection System, and Recon-Mobile Inspection System packages are faster, safer, more reliable, and simpler to operate than other x-ray systems.

Of course, some of these cargo x-ray inspection systems are static and quite large due to their mission, e.g., full cargo x-rays. For example, some cargo x-ray systems designed by EG&G and SAIC allow a fast, detailed inspection of fully loaded trucks– 20-foot and 40-foot containers may be effectively searched without opening the container. This is an important concept especially for organizations which forbid security personnel from breaking seals on containers during routine security inspections. In addition to the cargo, the vehicle structure, cab, and engine compartment are seen in great detail. Images are obtained less than three minutes after each vehicle enters the system. Such a detailed inspection by manual methods would take many hours for just one truck or container, possibly causing damage to the contents. False compartments and smuggled goods such as arms, ammunition, drugs, and fraudulently manifested goods (to avoid payment of duty) are readily revealed, even if hidden in dense cargo. Various image processing functions, which are quick and easy to use, make the examination completely effective. With a minimum amount of training, many of these systems can be operated by customs officers or security personnel.

Like other security systems, x-ray inspection systems are only as effective as the operator–thus, many x-ray inspection system manufacturers offer operator training courses. Any agency intending to purchase or which has already fielded an x-ray inspection system(s) should consider pursuing this training for all system operators.

In conclusion, x-ray machines enable a high degree of security to be obtained. Indeed, x-ray machines make 100 percent visual security check of parcels, freight, or cargo, and vehicles to a degree unheard of in the past; offer a broad field of application, for example, enable image evaluation to be carried out in a centralized manner; and finally, offer high throughput capabilities which enable airports and other high security areas to automatically inspect while simultaneously helping to improve operational efficiency. Indeed, x-ray inspection systems protect against a complete range of threats including explosives, weapons, and contraband. Finally, x-ray inspection systems provide a valuable security service designed to enhance security at government buildings, courthouses, corporate offices, and many other high profile or sensitive areas or facilities.

Entry Control Philosophy

A number of security technologies and procedures are valuable for preventing unauthorized personnel from accessing campus buildings. These trespassers may include suspended or expelled students, students from rival schools, parents seeking revenge against a student or school employee, active shooters, gang members, and drug dealers. All of these people, clearly represent a threat to the security of the campus. In other words, these technologies and procedures should focus on the controlling of who enters the facility, when people enter a facility, what items individuals take into a facility, who exits a facility, and what items individuals take out of a facility.

Logically, entry control methods and equipment should focus to a large extent on the discovery of contraband items. Further, it is very important for security officers or SROs to recognize contraband articles and take necessary actions when they are discovered. Of course, certain types of prohibited articles pose no danger to the school population and these items may be confiscated and held for administrative investigation, or released to the owner for subsequent removal from the school campus. These items are varied and are deemed contraband in direct correlation to a school system's rules and regulations, for example, radios, hand-held televisions, hand-held video games, telephone pagers, cigarette lighters, head-phones, and cell phones, etc.

In instances where dangerous or illegal prohibited articles are found, the security officer or SRO must be able to recognize the articles and handle the item according to school campus procedures. Certain prohibited articles do pose a danger to the school population and immediate action must be taken to prevent an accident or threat to the school inhabitants. Illegal prohibited articles will normally require confiscation and the probable involvement of law enforcement and/or medical personnel. These items include firearms, ammunition, explosives, incendiary devices, alcohol, controlled substances, illegal drugs, and related paraphernalia, etc.

Finally, officers must remain alert to potential danger and/or threat and use all of the detection equipment at their disposal. Officers must apply knowledge, skill, and ability to control the situation and follow post orders, procedures, safety rules, and regulations. When confiscating and holding prohibited articles for evidence, officers must follow chain-of-custody procedures. Finally, officers must complete a full written report concerning any actual or attempted security breach.

Entry Control Operations

Entry control solutions begin with determining specific requirements. If site specific requirements are ignored, systems may be chosen which do not meet the needs of the school, thus money, resources, and time will often be wasted. As the reader has already observed and will continue to observe, schools share many characteristics with other type occupancies; however, they are also, in many ways, unique. Entry control can be tailored to "report personnel who get in that belong in," and/or "report the ones who get in, that belong out."

Entry control may be broken down into four levels of security, which are open areas, controlled areas, limited areas, and exclusion areas. Open areas are areas where there is no control over who enters (e.g., perimeter grounds). A controlled area is an area with a minimum amount of control over who enters (e.g., an area where individuals must sign in to gain access or sign out when departing). A limited area is an area where only certain classifications of individuals are allowed to enter (e.g., teachers). Finally, an exclusion area is an area where only a few individuals may have access (e.g., administrators). Of course, each of these areas requires different levels of security personnel and devices corresponding to their classification.

There are a number of entry-control technologies in use today; some are more technical than others. Of course, advanced technology does not necessarily equate to high security and lesser technology does not necessarily equate to low security. The best technology in the world will not help anyone if it is not used. Thus, it is imperative that access control systems be easy to use, reliable, and require low maintenance. Some of the lesser technological approaches to deterring unauthorized entry include posted signs warning that trespassers are subject to arrest, signs that inform all visitors that vehicles brought onto campus are subject to search by school officials, security officers checking identification at the main entrance gate to the campus, the development of written protocol for after hours building entry, and vehicle parking stickers used to identify unauthorized vehicles which are in turn ticketed and towed (this would not include a monitored visitor lot).

Additional lesser technology approaches include school uniforms which make outsiders readily identifiable; policies prohibiting exposed tattoos; and prohibiting the wearing of hats, droopy pants, and t-shirts with alcohol, drug, violence, and/or gang affiliation messages. More of these approaches include stationing greeters at all entrances to the school (these can be parent volunteers); establishing a minimal number of entrances to the campus and school buildings (superfluous exterior doors should be locked to prevent entry from the outside and labeled on the inside): "For emergency exit only—alarm will sound."

Some final approaches include anyone walking around campus during classtime should be challenged and asked for a pass and/or a student ID (suspicious students may be searched or scanned with a metal detector to be checked for weapons and/or drugs); the main student parking lot may be closed off and locked during the day (this would not include monitored visitor and work-study student lots); if possible, channel entry to the school building during the school day directly through the front office; install fencing around the campus area to discourage casual intruders and to define school property; and finally, confiscate a student's ID when he or she is expelled or

suspended as well as presenting the SRO with a picture of the student and a do-not-admit notice.

Additional discussion is required in reference to student IDs or badging systems. A personnel badge identification system is typically used to control access to a school campus as well as access to specific areas within the campus area. Every person desiring admittance to a school facility should be required to wear an identification badge; this includes all school officials, visitors and vendors. A temporary badging system may be developed for visitors, vendors, or for personnel who are awaiting the issuance of a permanent badge. IDs may be physically checked as personnel drive their personal vehicles up to a main entry point controlled by a security officer, checked for admittance to school system vehicles and/or checked for admittance to school buildings. Identification badges should be worn on the outermost garment above the waist on the torso.

All school officials should challenge any person failing to properly display a badge. All campus residents, including school officials, must release their badge for physical inspection when entering the school campus area or when challenged. A physical inspection includes taking the badge and comparing the face of the individual with the face on the badge; checking other identification such as markings, area access numbers, expiration date, etc. located on the badge; the composition, weight, condition, and facility markings should also be examined to determine counterfeiting efforts. People with broken or damaged badges should be directed or escorted to the badge office for a new badge. Further, if a picture does not reflect current appearance (changes in the length of hair, beards, mustaches, scars, disfigurements, etc.) direct or escort the individual to the badging office for a new badge.

Personnel who do not have a badge (missing or lost) must be escorted to the badging office for positive identification. A disciplinary program should be developed to address individuals who constantly improperly wear, lose, forget, tamper with, or damage their badge. Lost or stolen badges must be reported to security personnel immediately. Finally, any student, employee, or vendor who is banned from entry to the school campus should have his or her badge confiscated and his or her picture should be distributed to all security personnel. These pictures are typically housed in a do-not-admit book which is subsequently located at school campus entry points.

Limiting entry/exit points is an important aspect of current security needs. Indeed, to best control a school building and/or campus, the number of entryways into the building or onto the campus must be severely limited. Further, restricting normal entrance to only one or two locations can greatly reduce the number of security personnel or security devices that must be supported.

A logging in and out procedure may be established at entry/exit points to include parking areas. All visitors, vendors and personnel requesting admittance after specified hours may be required to sign in/out on a daily log containing the following information: name and address of the individual requesting admittance; destination; contact person to include their telephone number; reason for admittance; time in, and time out. The school facility may require a printed name and signature of the person requiring admittance; the person conducting the logging procedure; and the escort or person being visited, if applicable. Finally, the person requesting admittance may be required to remain in a specified waiting area while the contact individual is notified and verification of the visiting person(s) need to enter and identification is ascertained. The visitor may now be permitted to enter, wait for the physical presence of the contact person, or be escorted to the desired destination by a security officer or other designated school official.

Some schools, especially those which do not have a campus per se (buildings that sit directly on the street), may need to use fences to control entry onto the school grounds. Of course, schools with campuses can also use fences to discourage unauthorized entrance onto the campus grounds. Fencing does not have to be unattractive and razor tape or barbed wire are rarely appropriate for a school setting. Wrought iron fencing may be used to discourage unauthorized admittance while at the same time being attractive. Chain link fencing is common and less expensive than wrought iron and provides an excellent barrier. However, chain link fencing should be at least eight foot high and have a small mesh (1-inch to 11/20-inch), to thwart a person trying to pull themselves upward or to prevent gaining a toehold. A robust fence defines property boundaries and forces a person to consciously trespass rather than allowing idle wandering onto a campus that has no fencing. The goal of fencing is to deter the casual or unmotivated trespasser. No fence can keep out someone determined to enter the campus or who is motivated and comes prepared to breach the fence.

Once entrances to a school facility are limited in number, the process of allowing or denying access is generally accomplished through one of four approaches. The first is manpower intensive, and the remaining three employ technology devices. These four approaches include: a security guard-controlled entry point; a special ID card/badge with automatic readers; a personal identification number (PIN) use in conjunction with a keyboard, and a biometric device for feature recognition. Security guard control is self-explanatory. However, if security guards become bored or complacent, they may easily miss properly identifying a person or may miss the identification of bogus or modified identification cards. Finally, while a security person can do far more than check ID cards, in the long run, they cost far more than technology systems.

ID cards using automatic readers require the identification to be validated by an electronic reader before a lock will be electronically opened. Viable card technologies for school systems include bar codes or magnetic strips used in conjunction with card-swipe devices. Some school systems may choose active radio frequency (RF) cards in conjunction with proximity readers. These card readers may be attractive since no manpower is required; however, in some circumstances more than one person can enter upon one tripping of the lock (called cabusing) if the authorized operator is acting under duress or possible collusion. Finally, the cost of these devices including installation, maintenance, and support systems may be too expensive for many schools to purchase.

Personal identification numbers (PIN) are normally used in conjunction with an ID card and accompanying reader. Using a PIN system in a stand-alone fashion is usually weak due to the fact that onlookers can easily gain knowledge of the pin code. When used in conjunction with a card reader, one can easily understand the importance of redundant or back-up security systems. Some high-end PIN systems use scramble keypads that allow only the user to view the cipher numbers. Of course, these devices cost more.

Biometric identification uses an electronic device to verify the identification of a person through the use of a personal attribute such as hand or finger shape (hand geometry), fingerprint, voiceprint, signature dynamics, retinal pattern, or iris pattern. Biometric identification devices are very accurate, identification methods cannot be loaned, lock and key control programs may be reduced, and there is nothing for a person to remember such as an ID card or PIN number. However, biometric devices may not be user friendly, devices are subject to vandalism, and they may be very expensive.

Duress Alarm Devices

Modern duress alarms are generally electronic devices found in one of three types. The first type is the panic-button alarm (a push-button mounted in a fixed location). The second type is the identification alarm (a portable device that identifies the owner of the device), and the third is an identification/location alarm (a portable device that identifies, locates, and tracks the person who activated the duress alarm).

The panic button is by far the more common type of duress alarm presently found in schools. The simplest application uses a strategically placed button that, when initiated, forwards a signal through a dedicated telephone line. A prerecorded message specifying the school, its location, and the urgency is sent to several locations, such as the police department. Some push-button duress devices are designed to use wiring which transmits a signal (flagging the alarm location) to a location where a visible and/or audio alarm is activated. A final push-button duress system includes the use of public address (PA) systems. When initiated, the PA system speakers can be used in a two-way communication mode. In conclusion, while push button duress systems are cost effective and valuable in many ways, they suffer from some weaknesses. For example, the person in duress may be separated from the area where the push-button is located, mischievous students may trigger the alarm, and the alarm does not identify the person in distress–only the location of the alarm may be ascertained.

The second type of duress alarm, the identification alarm, is a portable device that identifies the owner of the device. These systems incorporate a page-like device that are worn by school personnel. When the built in panic button is pushed, a wireless alarm signal is sent to the closest installed wireless sensing unit which then sends the signal on to an alarm console. The console operator will receive a coded number which corresponds to a specific teacher. A major limiting factor for this system is the fact that the device must have a clear line of sight to the nearest sensing unit for an accurate transmission. Walls, glass, roofs, floors, etc. will degenerate the transmitted signal which decreases the precision of identifying the individual under duress. An improved version of this system incorporates a two-way radio into the pager device that allows communication between the console operator and person under duress.

The third and final type of duress alarm, the identification/location alarm, is a smarter version of the identification duress alarm described above. This type of duress alarm operates in essentially the same manner as the identification alarm but has the added capability of identifying, locating, and tracking the person who activated the duress alarm.

Supporting Physical Security Systems

The physical security systems described above will help generate a safe school environment in a stand-alone fashion; however, these devices can provide additional levels of safety when they are supported by a number of physical security operations. For example:

1. Physically supervising access to school buildings and grounds.
2. Reducing class size and school size.
3. Adjusting schedules to minimize time in the hallways or other potentially dangerous locations. Areas of congestion should be controlled by developing traffic flow patterns, for example, designated up and down staircases. The idea is to limit the potential for conflicts or altercations.
4. Conducting a building safety audit in consultation with school security personnel and/or law enforcement personnel. However, these individuals must be true security professionals or a security consultant should be retained.
5. Closing school campuses during lunch periods.
6. Adopting a school policy on uniforms or at the very least dress codes.
7. Arranging supervision at critical times (for example, in hallways between classes) and having a response plan to deploy supervisory staff to areas where incidents are likely to occur.
8. Prohibiting students from congregating in areas where they are likely to engage in rule breaking or intimidating and aggressive behaviors.
9. Having adults visibly present throughout the school building.
10. Staggering dismissal times and lunch periods.
11. Monitoring the surrounding school grounds to include landscaping, parking lots, and bus stops.
12. Coordinating with local police to assure that there are safe routes to and from school.
13. Safe areas should be established where school staff and children can go in the event of a crisis.

14. Finally, School buildings should be kept clean, temperature controlled, free from graffiti, fully repaired and sanitary. Studies reveal that the physical condition of a school building can have an impact on student attitude, behavior, and motivation.

New School Designs

Most school buildings in the United States have been constructed to achieve an inviting and open-to-the-community feeling, using multiple buildings with big windows, multiple entrances and exits, and many opportunities for privacy. These layouts are not conducive to many security requirements. The designs of new schools should include the participation of security experts whose goal will be to minimize security vulnerabilities. Plus, there are architectural firms that specialize in schools that incorporate good security principles. Security conscious designs can actually help compensate in the long term for tight security budgets, fewer security personnel, and less sophisticated security equipment.

Some security-oriented suggestions to be incorporated into the building of new schools include the following: limit the number of buildings (one building is best); minimize the number of entrances to buildings; allow enough room at the main entry point for a security screening area and accompanying security equipment; alarm all exits and relegate them for emergency use only; and minimize the line of sight into traditional student gathering areas from off-campus areas.

Also, design parking lots conducive to the posting of security personnel who may effectively challenge each vehicle (one lane ingress and egress is best); provide a drop off/pickup lane for buses only; and minimize the number of driveways or parking lots that

students will have to walk across to get to the school building. Additionally, a separate parking area should be designed for work-study students or those who will be leaving during the school day.

Additionally, build a number of single-stall restrooms to mitigate restroom confrontations and other problems; use fences to enclose the entire campus area; design the school building and classroom areas so that they can be closed and locked off from the gym and other facilities used during off hours. Further, minimize secluded hiding places; reduce the number of windows and place them in strategic locations (secure skylights may be used to let light in while being less vulnerable then traditional buildings); maximize the line of sight within buildings, and use large wide spaces especially in hallways and commons areas.

Consider installing student lockers in classrooms or other areas easy to monitor; install numerous receivers and transmitters throughout the structure to allow for dependable two-way radio and cellular phone use in order to defeat dead space; construct buildings at least 50 feet away from streets, driveways, and parking areas. Furthermore, a basic security alarm system should be installed throughout all hallways, administrative offices, and rooms containing high-value property, such as computers, VCRs, shop equipment, laboratory supplies, and musical instruments. Finally, ample lighting should be sufficient to cover all areas of concern.

Security Guards

Security may be defined as "a stable, relatively predictable environment in which an individual or group may pursue its ends without disruption or harm, and without fear of such disturbance or injury." Thus, in relation to school security, security guards should be tasked with providing the sum total of those preventative and protective efforts designed to generate security as defined above.

There are two types of security services known as proprietary security and contract security. Proprietary security is in-house, directly hired and controlled by the school system or campus. Contract security is provided by outside individuals or organizations. Either of these security services should be directed to provide a broad spectrum of activities designed to eliminate or reduce a full range of potential hazards. These activities include, but are not limited to, the following: personnel protection; building and perimeter protection; intrusion and access control; alarm and surveillance systems; fire prevention and control; emergency and disaster planning; prevention of theft; accident prevention and safety; and enforcement of campus rules, regulations, and policies.

Further, there are three main categories of security personnel tasking which include stationary, patrolling, and alert-response security officers. Stationary security officers usually have a basic function of guarding a particular location. Aside from screening people and materials, or observing various areas, these personnel may be used to provide other services such as providing information and directions, and locating in-house personnel when needed.

Effective patrol is the backbone of any good security and safety program. This tasking affords the opportunity to monitor the entire environment; prevent problems from occurring; correct problems as they emerge; and generate a feeling of personal safety on the part of the staff, students, and visitors. There are several different ways or methods to patrol a school campus and they can be used in conjunction with each other.

Patrolling methods include foot patrol, vehicle patrol (automobile, bicycle, moped, motorcycle and/or golf cart), conspicuous patrol, inconspicuous patrol, general patrol, selective patrol, stake out, indoor patrol, and outdoor patrol.

Roving or patrolling security officers may be used to prevent, deter, and repress crime; prevent accidents; detect and apprehend perpetrators; regulate noncriminal conduct; recover property; and perform miscellaneous services. Miscellaneous services include checking the condition of various ingress and egress points, performing security checks in certain areas, accomplishing routine and surprise security inspections, and responding to alarms and alerts or other emergency situations.

The third tasking, known as alert-response, may require security officers to be dedicated to the function of being ready and available to respond to all alert, alarm, and emergency situations as practical. Their responsibilities may be geared toward a particular type of security category or more interdisciplinary targeting functions involving various security categories.

One of the main problems associated with security personnel is a lack of training. Thus, there is a gap between commissioned law enforcement officers who have typically received many hours of training and the security officer who may not have received any training. This lack of training is amazing when one considers the fact that these personnel are dealing with civil and criminal law, not to mention the weight of their duties in protecting school staff members and students. Another interesting fact was reported in a National Institute for Occupational Safety and Health study of on-the-job homicides covering the period of 1980 to 1989. This study listed security guards as having the fifth riskiest job in the country with a homicide rate of 3.6 per

100,000 persons.

Regardless of these facts, many states still do not require security personnel to possess any authorizing authority or registration requirements such as bonding, finger-printing, criminal record checks, and/or formal training. Indeed, state licensing and regulation may not exist (as of 1996 only 23 states required some form of security guard training and out of those 23 only 14 states required any training for unarmed guards). Further, the amount of state-mandated training, in 1996, varied between four and 40 hours, depending on whether the guard is armed or unarmed. Thus, training may be left to the discretion of the security company. In these cases, it is highly unlikely that penurious security companies will spend funds in the furtherance of professionalism.

In many cases, security officers are paid minimum wages while the security company keeps a large part of the fees paid by school systems. Two Rand Corporation reports, one conducted in 1981 and the other in 1989, revealed that low pay, lack of promotional opportunities, and lack of training attract marginal security guard personnel which in turn leads to ineffectual performance and an average annual turnover ratio of 121 percent. It will do little good for a school system to purchase expensive security systems and pay installment, maintenance, and service fees, while being operated by underscreened, undertrained, undersupervised, underpaid security personnel.

Security officers must understand the physical control systems used in their facility. Recognizing that a system exists and how that system works will prepare the officer to understand the importance of his role in monitoring and supporting the system. The central idea is to use physical security controls to enhance both security and safety for the school's people and property. Thus, all physical security pro-

grams are dependent upon qualified and trained personnel to operate them or these systems will be rendered ineffective.

Security education and training are a vital determinate of job performance. The responsibilities assumed by security personnel in the protection of students, school staff, other personnel, equipment, and other physical assets mandates proper and effective training. Further, legal issues demand that the security officer of today remain well versed in the changing laws. Additionally, the problems addressed by security personnel are becoming increasingly complex. Plus, there is a great dependence on technology and information systems. Indeed, security operations will certainly continue to make greater use of innovations and technology. In conclusion, the inadequate protection of personnel and assets plus costly negligence judgements will often be the result of little or no training.

Another topic of vital importance is the proper screening and investigation of the capabilities, character, personality, moral values, allegiance, dedication, and similar factors of candidate security personnel. All security personnel should go through a back-ground check and preemployment screening prior to employment. During pre-employment screening, a number of applicants will typically be denied employment due to falsification of applications, poor employment background, and even felony convictions. Other applicants will require further investigation targeting significant problems which must be clarified, often through investigative tech-niques, prior to any job offer. This statement can be made in reference to the fact that security personnel are entrusted with the security, protection, and safety, of students and school staff.

The implied accomplishment of these particular job functions is directly related to the security personnel themselves. Thus, optimum guidelines should be set forth. These guidelines should include proper training designed to meet the requirement of professionalism, proper and respectful modes of conduct and communication, restraint when called for, and appropriate action when needed. Retraining and refresher courses should be given on a regular basis to maintain optimum job performance.

Furthermore, security officers should, at a minimum, be briefed and trained on a clearly delineated code of conduct. This code of conduct should contain the following topics: mission statement (authority and intent), specific duties (job description), special campus requirements, job qualifications, standard policies and procedures, security specific policies and procedures (for example, use-of-force), performance requirements, personal conduct, attendance, working hours, performance appraisals, personnel files, conflicts of interest, safety, release of personal information, sexual harassment, ethics, smoking, uniform and grooming standards, training, and required paper work. To reiterate, a school's security efforts will only be as good as the security officer's implementing the program.

School Resource Officer (SRO)

School resource officers (SROs) are not security officers; they are sworn law enforcement officers with the same arrest power and duties as other peace officers. SROs are law enforcement officers assigned to a school or a number of schools for a two-fold objective. First, the SRO is responsible for the safety and security of the school, students, staff, and visitors. Second, the SRO is tasked with interacting with students, staff, and at times parents, offering opportunities to present classes designed to acquaint these individuals with laws, safety and security matters.

School resource officers should attend training specific to the job assignment. This training will typically require 40 to 80 hours to complete. A school resources officer training program should contain at a minimum the following topics.

1. Definition of duties.
2. How students are affected by school violence.
3. The causes of violence in schools.
4. The drug culture at school.
5. Special education issues.
6. School security and safety issues.
7. Crime prevention.
8. Emergency management.
9. Juvenile legal issues.
10. Student counseling.
11. Child abuse.
12. Protective custody.
13. Gang activity.
14. Identification of violent or troubled youths.
15. Intervention techniques.

The increase in a police presence in schools will frequently have a positive effect, when it comes to students and school officials feeling safe. Many people will find the presence of a police officer on campus reassuring in dealing with all levels of school violence. Indeed, a September 1999 poll taken by the Associated Press revealed that two out of three Americans support having uniformed law enforcement officers patrolling the nation's schools. Furthermore, 65 percent of those polled also stated that they thought stationing officers in schools would reduce violence.

Keeping these statistics in mind, it should be clear that the SRO must be chosen carefully. This person should be qualified as a police officer and have expertise in the security field. Further, this person must have an interest in and like to interact with young people. Additionally, it takes a dedicated professional to perform what may be termed as routine security functions. SRO turnover may be great, if this person cannot accept performing mundane tasks, find repetitious tasks boring, or perceive that a school administration has neglected to identify anti-social behaviors complete with unwavering enforcement and serious consequences. High turnover rates will eventually make locating qualified people difficult, increase manpower costs, and weaken an otherwise effective security program.

Canine Operations

Canines often provide a very useful function in a security program. These functions include patrol/guard duty, explosives sensing, drugs/chemicals sensing, general searching, sound monitoring, and attack/protective modes. When used for patrol/guard duty, canines most often function in coordination with security personnel. However, under certain special circumstances, canines may be left on their own. When used for explosives sensing, canines use their acute sense of smell to pick up vapors emitting from the explosive. Canines are very accurate when searching for explosives and often enhance the safety of personnel who might otherwise be required to manually search for an explosive device. Indeed, dogs have abilities that can't be matched by humans or by scientific instruments. A dog's sense of smell is approximately three thousand times more sensitive than the average human being. Most dogs have such as acute sense of smell that they can detect minute odors that even sensitive scientific instruments cannot identify. Finally, it has been reported that some dogs can identify 19,000 different compounds.

As with explosives, canines are often used to assist in searching for certain types of drugs, chemicals, or other substances. Dogs may also be used to assist in the task of searching for people. Canines, with their powerful sense of hearing, can also be used to monitor an area for sound and noise, and can be trained to differentiate between various categories of noise. At times, dogs may also be used to supplement security personnel by having the capability to attack. Of course, dogs used in this manner must be highly trained to obey both active and passive commands. Further, there are generally two types of dogs: active and passive. Passive dogs will alert but will not otherwise interact with the subject. Active dogs may bite, scratch, jump, etc..., upon alerting and these acts are sometimes considered as a use-of-force. Passive dogs are probably the best overall choice for use in schools.

Canines used in scent detection operations typically involve "dog sniffs" in public areas and are not considered searches and therefore don't require reasonable suspicion, probable cause, or warrants (U.S. v. Place, Supreme Court). Further, dog alerts can be used for probable cause. However, the use of dogs "on people" is very sensitive legally and should be done only if specific affirmative legal advice is obtained.

Integrating a K-9 program into a security force does not come without a price. As with any other specialized unit, there are costs for training, maintenance, and special equipment. Specific costs include purchase of the dog, training dog and handler, food, veterinary care, grooming, vehicle modification, officer compensation, canine protective vests, boarding, and liability insurance. However, canines are well worth the price when one considers the valuable role they play in securing school campuses.

Addressing Cost Issues

Yes, it is true that all of these discussed security measures and support programs may be expensive. However, school safety and security is a great political topic and elected officials at every level of the government are increasing their involvement in this issue. The government is addressing this issue by increasing funding in fiscal year 2001 for the school safety budget. This increase reportedly includes $247 million for the Safe Schools/Healthy Students initiative, a $100 million increase over the fiscal year 2000 budget. Furthermore, in fiscal year 2000, the Justice Department's Safe Schools initiative totals $200 million, including $15 million from the community policing budget slated to be transferred to the National Institute of Justice to develop school safety technologies, $180 million for school resource officers, and $30 million for school safety partnerships.

The Safe Schools/Healthy Students initiative was launched in 1998 to help communities develop and implement community-wide responses to school and youth violence including technologies to keep schools safe. The biggest problems with these programs is the lack of information on where grants are located, the process required for application, and the guidelines for grant award. For example, in September 1999, more than $100 million in grants under the the Safe Schools/Healthy Students initiative were awarded to 54 school districts. This may sound impressive on the surface but quickly pales when one considers the number of existing school districts which exist throughout the United States. Of the many school officials the author has contacted in the past two years, none had any idea that grant money was available for countering school violence, where the finds were located and/or how to apply for grant money.

To seek grants, probably the most effective step concerns involving local, city and state political leaders in the process. The next important step is to articulate the fact that the grant money will be spent on a formal community-based effort involving the local law enforcement agency, mental health authority, and school district. Of course, the more community organizations that are involved, the better the chances that a grant will be awarded to the grantee.

It will also be helpful to understand a few terms connected to the grant process. Readers pursuing grants will find the following terms helpful. There are generally four types of grants: discretionary grants, earmarked funds, formula grants, and initiatives. Discretionary grants are sometimes referred to as "project grants," which are often designed to support research, evaluation, and demonstration projects or service projects. Discretionary funds are awarded for specific periods of time often covering one to five years.

Earmarked funds are legislative directives in the appropriations laws (as distinct from authorization acts). Earmarked funds normally dictate how to spend certain portions of funds appropriated within larger funding programs. Earmarks may be termed as "hard" or "soft." Hard earmarks are written into legislation, usually with specific amounts to be spent and the specific recipient of the finding identified. Soft earmarks are based upon conference reports. Earmarks occur in a specific fiscal year and may not be continued to the next fiscal year. Earmarked funds are by far the most likely type of grant process school administrators will encounter. Due to fiscal constraint and the possibility of non-renewal, school administrators should aggressively apply for these funds at the beginning of the fiscal year.

Formula grants are usually based on population, unemployment levels, census data, or other demographic indicators. Most formula grants go directly to state agencies for on-going services through block grants or categorical programs. Finally, initiatives are special efforts by federal departments and tend to focus on specific issues.

Developing and writing grant proposals is a learned discipline and only the most effectively prepared proposals will generate positive action. Grant writing may be broken down into two parts. The first part concerns preparation, developing an idea for a proposal, community support, identification of funding resources, getting organized to write the proposal, review, and mailing. The second part concerns basic components, an outline of project goals, presenting a credible applicant or organization, stating the purpose at hand, stating project objectives, delineating a plan of action, evaluating a product and process analysis, long-term project planning, and planning a budget.

Preparation begins with researching all pertinent criteria related to the grant. Pertinent information includes a point of contact; the availability of funds; deadlines, if they exist, the process used by the grantor agency for accepting applications; basic requirements; application forms; and any required information and procedures. These topics of pertinent information frequently vary with the federal agency making the grant award. Further, many entities send a specific person to grantmanship workshops to learn the grant writing process and actually staff a grant writing position on a daily or frequent basis.

When developing an idea for a proposal, it is important to determine if the idea has been considered in the applicant's locality or state. A careful check should be made with legislators and area government agencies and related public and private agencies

which may currently have grant awards or contracts to do similar work. Federal agencies are required to report funding information as funds are approved, increased, or decreased among projects within a given state. If a similar program already exists, the applicant may need to reconsider submitting the proposed project, particularly if duplication of efforts are perceived. If significant differences, unique circumstances, and/or improvements in the proposed project's goals can be clearly established, it may be worthwhile to pursue federal assistance.

Community support for most proposals is essential. Groups representing academic, political, professional, local government organizations, public officials, and lay organizations should be solicited for support of the proposal. Statement of support should be represented in writing if possible. Numerous letters of support, letters of endorsement, and/or affiliation agreements detailing exact areas of project sanction and commitment may be requested as part of a proposal. Even if statements of support are not a requirement, they can be persuasive to a grantor agency. A useful method of generating community support may be to hold meetings with the top decision makers in the community who would be concerned with the subject matter of the proposal. The forum for discussion may include a query into the merits of the proposal, development of a contract of support for the proposal, to generate data in support of the proposal, or development of a strategy to create proposal support from a large number of community groups. Finally, type and caliber of community support are often critical in the initial and subsequent review phases.

Naturally, the identification of funding resources is a must; however, applicants should also peruse related programs as potential resources. Common sense dictates that the applicant and the grantor agency should have the same interests, intentions, and needs if a proposal is to be considered an acceptable candidate for funding. Furthermore, applicants should review the Federal Budget for the current and fiscal years to determine proposed dollar amounts for particular budget functions.

Once a potential grantor agency is identified, a point of contact (POC) should be located and a grant application kit should be requested, if applicable. The POC should also be used to solicit eligibility requirements suggestions, criticisms, advice, review, and comments concerning the proposed project. If possible, an applicant may conduct a personal visit to the grantor's regional office or headquarters. A visit may establish a favorable face-to-face contact, bring out some essential details concerning the proposal, and/or help secure support literature and references from the agency's library. The more agency personnel know about the proposal, the better the chance of support and of an eventual favorable decision. If the proposal review is unfavorable and differences cannot be resolved, the examining agency POC may be asked to suggest another department or agency which may be interested in the proposal.

The actual developing and writing grant proposals concerns eight basic components: (1) the proposal summary, (2) introduction to organization, (3) the problem statement, (4) project objectives, (5) project methods or design, (6) project evaluation, (7) future funding, and (8) the project budget.

The proposal summary represents an outline of project goals and should appear at the beginning of the proposal. It could be in the form of a cover letter or a separate page, but should definitely be brief–no longer than two or three paragraphs. The summary would be most useful if it were prepared after the proposal has been developed in order to

encompass all of the key summary points necessary to communicate the objectives of the project. It is this document that becomes the cornerstone of the proposal, and the initial impression it gives will be critical to the success of the venture. In many cases, the summary will be the first part of the proposal package seen by agency officials and could be the only part of the package that is carefully reviewed before the decision is made to consider the project any further.

The applicant must select a fundable project which can be supported in view of the local need. Alternatives, in the absence of federal support, should be pointed out. The influence of the project both during and after the project period should be explained. The consequences of the project as a result of funding should be highlighted.

The introduction presents a credible applicant or organization. The applicant should gather data about its organization from all available sources. Most proposals require a description of an applicant's organization to describe its past and present operations. Some features to consider are a brief biography of board members and key staff members and the organization's goals, philosophy, track record with other grantors, and any success stories. The data should be relevant to the goals of the federal grantor agency and should establish the applicant's credibility.

The problem statement focuses on the purpose at hand. The problem statement (or needs assessment) is a key element of a proposal that makes a clear, concise, and well-supported statement of the problem to be addressed. The best way to collect information about the problem is to conduct and document both a formal and informal needs assessment for a program in the target or service area. The information provided should be both factual and directly related to the problem addressed by the proposal.

Areas to document include the purpose for developing the proposal; the beneficiaries– who are they and how will they benefit; the social and economic costs to be affected; the nature of the problem (provide as much hard evidence as possible); how the applicant organization came to realize the problem exists and what is currently being done about the problem; the remaining alternatives available when funding has been exhausted (explain what will happen to the project and the impending implications); and most importantly, describe the specific manner through which problems might be solved, including a review of the resources needed, considering how they will be used and to what end.

There is a considerable body of literature on the exact assessment techniques to be used. Any local, regional, or state government planning office, or local university offering course work in planning and evaluation techniques should be able to provide excellent background references. Types of data that may be collected include historical, geographic, quantitative, factual, statistical, and philosophical information, as well as studies completed by colleges, and literature searches from public or university libraries. Local colleges or universities which have a department or section related to the proposal topic may help determine if there is interest in developing a student or faculty project to conduct a needs assessment. It may be helpful to include examples of the findings for highlighting in the proposal.

Project objectives cover goals and desired outcomes referring to specific activities in a proposal. It is necessary to identify all objectives related to the goals to be reached, and the methods to be employed to achieve the stated objectives. Applicants should consider quantities or things measurable and refer to a problem statement and the outcome of proposed activities when developing objectives which will probably be used to evaluate program progress.

Program methods and program design delineate a plan of action. The program design refers to how the project is expected to work and solve the stated problem. Applicants should sketch out the following topics: the activities to occur, along with the related resources and staff needed to operate the project (inputs); a flow chart of the organization features of the project; a description of how the parts interrelate; where personnel will be needed, and what they are expected to do; the kinds of facilities, transportation, and support services required; what will be achieved plan for measurable results,;project staff which may be required to produce evidence of program performance through an examination of stated objectives during either a site visit by the federal grantor agency and/or grant reviews which may involve peer review committees.

It may be useful to devise a diagram of the program design. For example, draw a three-column block. Each column is headed by one of the parts (inputs, throughputs, and outputs), and on the left (next to the first column), specific program features would be identified (i.e., implementation, staffing, procurement, and systems development). In the grid, specify something about the program design; for example, assume the first column is labeled inputs and the first row is labeled staff. On the grid, one might specify under inputs five nurses to operate a child care unit. The throughput might be to maintain charts, counsel the children, and set up a daily routine; outputs might be to discharge 25 healthy children per week. This type of procedure will help to conceptualize both the scope and detail of the project.

Wherever possible, applicants should justify, in the narrative, the course of action taken. The most economical method should be used that does not compromise or sacrifice project quality. The financial expenses associated with performance of the project will later become points of negotiation with the federal program staff. If everything is not carefully justified in writing, in the proposal, after negotiation with the federal grantor agencies, the approved project may resemble less of the original concept. Carefully consider the pressures of the proposed implementation, that is, the time and money needed to acquire each part of the plan. A Program Evaluation and Review Technique (PERT) chart could be useful and supportive in justifying some proposals.

Applicants should also highlight the innovative features of the proposal which could be considered distinct from other proposals under consideration. Finally, applicants should, whenever possible, use appendices to provide details, supplementary data, references, and information requiring in-depth analysis. These types of data, although supportive of the proposal, if included in the body of the design, could detract from its readability. Appendices provide the proposal reader with immediate access to details, if and when clarification of an idea, sequence or conclusion is required. Timetables, work plans, schedules, activities, methodologies, legal papers, personal vitae, letters of support, and endorsements are examples of appendices.

Evaluation includes a product and process analysis. The evaluation component is twofold: (1) product evaluation and (2) process evaluation. Product evaluation addresses results that can be attributed to the project, as well as the extent to which the project has satisfied its desired objectives. Process evaluation addresses how the project was conducted, in terms of consistency with the stated plan of action and the effectiveness of the various activities with the plan.ÃMost

federal agencies now require some form of program evaluation among grantees. The requirements of the proposed project should be explored carefully. Evaluations may be conducted by an internal staff member, an evaluation firm, or both. The applicant should state the amount of time needed to evaluate, how the feedback will be distributed among the proposed staff, and a schedule for review, and comment for this type of communication. Evaluation designs may start at the beginning, middle, or end of a project, but the applicant should specify a start-up time. It is practical to submit an evaluation design at the start of a project for two reasons: (1) convincing evaluations require the collection of appropriate data before and during program operations, and (2) if the evaluation design cannot be prepared at the outset, then a critical review of the program design may be advisable.

Even if the evaluation design has to be revised as the project progresses, it is much easier and cheaper to modify a good design. If the problem is not well-defined and carefully analyzed for cause and effect relationships, then a good evaluation design may be difficult to achieve. Sometimes a pilot study is needed to begin the identification of facts and relationships. Often a thorough literature search may be sufficient.

Evaluation requires both coordination and agreement among program decision makers (if known). Above all, the federal grantor agency's requirements should be highlighted in the evaluation design. Also, federal grantor agencies may require specific evaluation techniques such as designated data formats (an existing information collection system) or they may offer financial inducements for voluntary participation in a national evaluation study. The applicant should ask specifically about these points. Also, consult the Criteria for Selecting Proposals section of the Catalog program descripting to determine the exact evaluation methods to be required for the program if funded.

Future funding includes long-term project planning. Applicants should describe a plan for continuation beyond the grant period, and/or the availability of other resources necessary to implement the grant. Additionally, applicants should discuss maintenance and future program funding if the program is for construction activity. Furthermore, applicants should account for other needed expenditures if the program includes purchase of equipment.

Finally, the proposal should include the planning of a budget. Funding levels in federal assistance programs change yearly. Thus, it is useful to review the appropriations over the past several years to try to project future funding levels. However, it is safer to never anticipate that the income from the grant will be the sole support for the project. This consideration should be given to the overall budget requirements, and in particular, to budget line items most subject to inflationary pressures. Restraint is important in determining inflationary cost projections (avoid padding budget line items), but attempt to anticipate possible future increases.

Some vulnerable budget areas are utilities, rental of buildings and equipment, salary increases, food, telephones, insurance, and transportation. Budget adjustments are sometimes made after the grant award, but this can be a lengthy process. Be certain that implementation, continuation, and phase-down costs can be met. Consider costs associated with leases, evaluation systems, hard/soft match requirements, audits, development, implementation and maintenance of information and accounting systems, and other long-term financial commitments.

A well-prepared budget justifies all expenses and is consistent with the proposal narrative. Some areas in need of an evaluation for consistency are (1) the salaries in the proposal in relation to those of the applicant organization should be similar; (2) if new staff persons are being hired, additional space and equipment should be considered, as necessary; (3) if the budget calls for an equipment purchase, it should be the type allowed by the grantor agency; (4) if additional space is rented, the increase in insurance should be supported; (5) if an indirect cost rate applies to the proposal, the division between direct and indirect costs should not be in conflict, and the aggregate budget totals should ideally refer directly to the approved formula, and (6) if matching costs are required, the contributions to the matching fund should be taken out of the budget unless otherwise specified in the application instructions.

It is very important for applicants to become familiar with government-wide circular requirements. The applicant should thoroughly review the appropriate circulars since they are essential in determining items such as cost principles and conforming with government guidelines for federal domestic assistance.

Lastly, the review and mailing process concerns the elements of criticism, signature block, neatness, and mailing. At some point in the writing process, perhaps after the completion of a second draft, a neutral third party should review the proposal working draft for continuity, clarity, and reasoning. The idea is to gain constructive criticism rather than wait for the federal grantor agency to volunteer this information during the review cycle. As most proposals are made to institutions rather than individuals, the signatures of chief administrative officials will be required. Thus, these signatures must be included in the proposal where appropriate. The proposal should be typed, collated, copied, and packaged correctly and neatly (according to agency instructions, if any). Each package should be inspected to ensure uniformity from cover to cover. A neat, organized, and attractive proposal package can leave a positive impression, with the reader, about the proposal contents.

Concluding Remarks

In conclusion, with so many security options available, school administrators must do their homework to determine which choice is most adaptable to their facilities, student population and staff. Additionally, it must be understood that physical security controls are only one component of a school system's security protection program. They are not intended to be the sole means of protecting the school; instead, their mission is to complement and enhance other security measures such as security staffing. All physical security measures are dependent upon trained people to operate or otherwise render them effective. Further, unless the proper security equipment is specified and professionally installed, little positive effect will be realized in relation to reducing crime and saving lives.

Many citizens have been taken aback by recent revelations that many school security structures are very weak. In some instances, critical protection postures and capabilities can be easily evaded or defeated. Indeed, some school systems rely totally upon security officers as a compensatory measure for aging physical security systems or the complete lack of security systems. The decline or lack of a safeguards and security program readiness and capability represents a disturbing trend, especially when one considers the fact that while funding for safeguards and security programs has fallen significantly, program requirements have not. In fact, requirements are growing, meaning these systems no longer provide

the necessary level of protection required in today's threat environment. There are numerous real-world security threats which many school systems continue to ignore or decide to employ "half measures" to thwart.

Many school security forces are managed by subcontractors who hire personnel to staff security manager positions and similar high priority positions who are not experienced or even trained in security matters. This deficiency becomes apparent when one identifies the plethora of security weaknesses that exist at many of these school campuses. Many security managers have decided to ignore the basic principle of "defense in depth." It is very common for security positions to be laid out in a linear fashion. This means that once one security position is breached, the adversaries have penetrated the school campus. Inexperienced security managers believe that soft alarms and locking mechanisms are valid in-depth security measures. Many school systems and security subcontractors are more than happy to rely on electronic alarms to somehow thwart physical attack because soft alarms are actually used to replace security officers.

Additionally, many school administrations have dropped exterior fence patrols, believing they are a waste of manpower. By ignoring the perimeter, school administrators have expanded opportunities for the adversary to gain access to the school campus. Adversary(ies) may now approach campus perimeters without fear of discovery and subsequent security officer intervention.

Some school administrators and security subcontractors have also condoned the use of nonsecurity personnel to operate certain pieces of security equipment, to staff security alarm monitoring stations, and/or to conduct other security tasks. Additionally, some school systems manipulate postulated threat identification to suit security force strength (as security forces are cut, the postulated threat is reformed to reflect a lesser threat).

Of course, some readers may be thinking; how can these security concerns be allowed to flourish? The answer is simple: in many ways, school systems regulate, inspect, and evaluate themselves. Since many school systems show little interest in security issues, school campuses are evaluated and always deemed acceptable as a result of any audit. These positive findings are generated for a number of reasons. Perhaps the biggest reason concerns the fact that if school administrators find a school campus lacking, the school system will have to spend money to fix the shortcomings. Thus, in the interest of cutting security forces and saving money, many school administrations are unlikely to spend any funds on issues such as security. In many cases, the present mission-to-resource imbalance is causing an inability to conduct adequate safeguards and security mission accomplishment. Indeed, as security forces continue to suffer further budget and manpower cuts, the safeguards and security program capabilities continue to fall further behind requirements.

It is the school system's duty to commit to a viable safeguards and security program. Failing to honor security requirements will not only reduce public trust, but more importantly, it will endanger the students and staff it is obliged to maintain. Decisive measures must be taken to stem any reduction of crucial security program resources and capabilities or schools will be protected at an unacceptable level.

Of course, security technologies are not the answer to all school security problems. However, many security products can be excellent tools if applied appropriately. They can provide school administrators or security officials with information that would otherwise be unavailable, release manpower for more appropriate work, or be used to perform mundane tasks. Sometimes they can save a school money (compared to the long-term cost of personnel or the cost impact of not preventing a particular incident). However, security technologies are often not applied correctly in schools, are expected to do more than they are capable of, or are not well maintained after initial installation. In these cases, security technologies are certainly not cost effective.

School administrators cannot simply rely on any existing or projected security/safety systems to completely prevent violence from occurring in the school environment. However, integrated security systems will demonstrate to community organizations and individual citizens that school personnel and law enforcement entities are aware of security concerns and are proactively involved in addressing these issues. A properly designed, updated, practiced, and implemented integrated security system will ultimately increase a school community's success in (saving student lives).

Finally, high-profile security measures must be effectively balanced with after-school programs, outreach programs, and counseling programs for troubled students who may commit crimes at school. School systems that fail in their attempt to address physical security and emotional well-being issues will likely lose students to private schools and/or home-schooling efforts. Or, in some instances, students may feel obliged to drop out of school. The idea is to address physical security and emotional well-being in a concerted effort. Effective integrated security systems using a number of technologies and programs, discussed in this chapter, will serve a proactive role in promoting peace and harmony within the community, and in ensuring the right of students and teachers to attend a safe school environment.

Chapter 4

EFFECTIVE RESPONSE MECHANICS

Response Plan Purpose

The response effort the author has developed is quite different from what many school organizations call response plans. The author's response plan focuses on the preparation and compiling of elements of essential information which should be used by police response forces when a school violence crisis occurs. This information is designed to enable police responders to quickly and efficiently develop an entry plan which will streamline response time frames and save lives. The focal point of a rapid effective response is to shift the actions of an active shooter from offensive activities to defensive activities.

The author believes traditional response plans generated by educational entities actually focuses on intervention efforts, not true response. The author's concept is part of a trilogy–identification, intervention, and response. There is no doubt school administrators are adept at identification and intervention processes; however, the author believes many school organizations are deficient in the area of true response. The author's response plan focuses on proactive information gathering and response mechanics intended to be employed when identification and intervention efforts have failed and a school crisis is in progress.

Further, the author believes that a response document must be site specific and adjusted accordingly. The end product should contain observed structural and procedural weaknesses and strengths. Applicable recommendations for the enhancement of existing or additional internal defense systems, physical protection devices (hard and soft), and protective forces should be included in applicable attachments. Indeed, a response document can be used as a significant part of a security survey as vulnerabilities or root causes are identified and earmarked for correction. A response document is developed by compiling elements of essential information concerning a target school and the surrounding area into a workable format. An effective response document will neutralize or, at a minimum, decrease security concerns. A condensed oral response briefing should also be prepared and practiced for streamlined presentations.

Further, an effective response plan will enable law enforcement entities to quickly and effectively achieve the following priorities: save the lives of those located in the proximity of the active shooter, protect the lives of citizens located in the area of the event, protect the lives of responding officials, capture and/or neutralize the suspect(s) as soon as possible, obtain area containment, generate communications and multiofficer–multiagency response, and achieve after-event investigation and the return to normalcy of the affected area.

Finally, these events are not usually resolved by SWAT teams. Indeed, the first officers on the scene will have to make a rapid assessment of the situation and move to the area where the active shooter is operating, using speed, aggressive tactics, and knowledge gained through the development and use of a response plan.

Response Planning

Response planning is a very tedious process. School administrators may hear comments from school personnel stating that planning is non-essential or useless because no plan ever works as envisioned. These views are voiced by individuals who are inadequately trained in response planning, misunderstand the value of planning, or have never seen or experienced a "wing it" style response go sour. It is guaranteed that even an incomplete weak response plan is better than no plan at all.

Response planning is not just a leadership task; it requires subordinate participation as well. One person should not plan an entire response document alone; if he or she tries, the chances of failure are high due to time constraints, information overload, and limited thinking. One person considering an operation will be limited to his or her personal mind set and experience, but when a whole team of personnel participates, the options are increased manyfold. Through team involvement, the plan takes on the identity of a team plan instead of "the plan."

Response Planning Mechanics

To begin planning, the school facility must be analyzed; therefore, all elements of essential information available must be collected and collated into a workable format. To accomplish this task, a primary question must be answered: *What is the*

response documents purpose? response documents purpose is to serve as a centrally located document containing elements of significant information designed to be used in support of an overall mission intended to counter a school violence situation. A response document is designed to address many complex contingencies by capturing, fusing, and disseminating information to operational entities. Finally, the response planning effort will represent a significant value in school/law enforcement partnerships; help decide upon and develop action steps for anti-school violence policies, procedures, and programs; and help develop strategies for involving law enforcement, school officials, teachers, staff, students, parents, and community leaders in efforts to prevent school violence.

Another question frequently asked concerns the storage of the response document: *Where should the response document be located?* The response document should be removed from the direct area of concern or what would be called during a real-world event (the target site). The response document should be stored in a central location such as the leading law enforcement entity's headquarters. Of course, if desired, copies may be stored in a variety of places such as the school itself, EOCs, rally points, etc. However, these documents should be considered as very sensitive and protected by applying operations security (OPSEC) techniques.

OPSEC Techniques

Operations security (OPSEC) is a countermeasures program designed to disrupt or defeat the ability of people to gain the inadvertent release of school violence crisis response plans outside established control procedures. The central focus of OPSEC is to decrease transmission, sensitivity, and visibility; establish accountability; and increase protection of school violence crisis response plans. OPSEC may be achieved by reducing the accessibility, volume, and dispersion of school violence crisis response plans. OPSEC efforts can be enhanced by requiring access authorization, limiting distribution or restricting further distribution, controlling copies, consolidating activities, and the systematic destruction of data no longer needed.

To implement an OPSEC program, the following principles should be implemented: restrict the distribution of school violence crisis response plans to only those people who have a "need to know"; start the OPSEC program in conjunction with the beginning of the school violence crisis response plan process; keep a low profile when developing, completing, and practicing the actual school violence crisis response plan processes; and finally, identify and utilize designated personnel to handle sensitive aspects of the school violence crisis response plan.

In conclusion, a balance must be struck between the release of non-sensitive and sensitive school violence crisis response plan information. For example, the media (broadcast TV, print, radio, and electronic–internet sources), community (community population, families of students, school system employees), special interest groups (PTA, teachers union), and the general population will be interested in and require some information concerning developing or existing school violence response plans. Other personnel or agencies interested in this information include school boards, local governments, state government officials and organizations, and federal government entities. However, only a general overview or concept should be released to these entities in lieu of exactly stating what response actions will implemented in any

situation. Only actual responders and planning entities have the "need to know" projected tactical solutions and response mechanics. If this type of sensitive information is "compromised," offenders may develop plans designed to thwart response efforts thereby heightening the likelihood of mission failure and endangering the lives of everyone involved in a school violence crisis incident.

The media spokesperson (discussed in detail later in this section) will need to work "hand-in-glove" with the OPSEC officer (usually the chief planning officer–also discussed in detail later in this section) to identify what information may be released and not released. Information not to be released should be a short list. Examples include: do not release information that could jeopardize anyone's safety or information that could jeopardize the management of an incident or investigation. Additionally, do not reveal key investigative techniques or sources, critical matters of evidence, and/or names of juveniles.

The Response Mission

Our criminal justice system is fundamentally reactive. Indeed, little happens until a crime has occurred; by then, it is too late for identification, intervention, and effective response strategies. The school violence response planning system discussed in this book is designed to be proactive in lieu of reactive, thereby reducing the death, injury, and destruction generated by a school violence crisis event. Furthermore, this system is an effective tool for assisting police officers and other types of first responders to heighten their effectiveness and performance during these types of crisis. In short, the school violence response planning mission is to "save lives." Once this goal is reached, the very important role of the criminal justice system can move forward (apprehending and punishing perpetrators).

The Response Planning Committee

There is a critical need to form a relationship between school administrations and police personnel before any planning or training can be performed. This relationship needs to result in the development of a school violence crisis response team. This team not only plans what to do when violence strikes, but it also ensures that staff and students know how to react during a crisis. This team may also be the personnel chosen to set up and operate an Emergency Operations Center (EOC). This school violence crisis response team should work with police crisis response planners in order to shape and tailor a plan specifically designed to fit the needs of each individual school (each school district, police department, and community is unique). Of course, many aspects of a generic planning process will be applicable to all school systems. The idea is not to "reinvent the wheel" but to use applicable planning aspects, "tweak" some aspects, and develop unique aspects when required.

Each team needs to trust and share what their needs are with each other in order to develop an effective response plan. The following planning positions are only suggestions and may or may not be staffed. Additionally, one position may be staffed by more than one person. Further, one person may conduct the activities of one or more other positions as required. Each position should have a job description which includes a job title, reporting line, job function, specific duties and responsibilities, and the qualifications required to staff the position.

A school administrator may have a staff or the administrator may represent the entire school violence response planning committee. The size of the staff needed to carry out school violence response planning will depend upon the size of the school facility; the financial resources available; the school's past history, present threat level, and projected threats of potentially violent situations. How well the school administrator manages the school violence crisis response planning committee depends in part on whether minimum staffing needs are met. Part of the job of a school administrator is to estimate what the staffing needs are or will be, and then plan to obtain that level of staffing. In some instances, especially when school systems lack financial resources, a volunteer school violence response planning committee may be developed.

School violence response planning committee positions include the following titles: chief planning officer, administrative support, chief of school security (law enforcement or school resource officer), logistics officer, facility architects and engineers, school medical representative, school legal representative, school media/liaison spokesperson, environmental safety and health officer, and other elements unique to the school system, as required.

Chief Planning Officer

The chief planning officer (CPO) has the overall authority and responsibility for the conduct of all activities pursuant to the planning process. The CPO develops and clarifies the concept of the operation to those involved in the planning process, approves the crisis response document, ensures that adequate personnel and resources are available and tasked for completion of the planning process. Additionally, the CPO provides oversight of all aspects of the planning process, keeps higher entities (local, state, and federal agencies, etc.) informed of the status of the planning process as required, and coordinates actions with outside agencies (local law enforcement, fire department, medical support, etc.) as required. Further, the CPO develops a command and control structure (chain of command), develops roles and responsibilities for each position, authorizes policies and procedures, and briefs participating individuals/agencies prior to beginning the planning operation (briefings should continue as needed throughout the operation).

The CPO also authorizes media relations and other policies, for example, OPSEC programs. The CPO is also responsible for training personnel on policies and procedures to include rehearsing the crisis response plan, determines what procedures are needed to meet crisis response plan requirements, coordinates all major activities of the planning process, and establishes and maintains liaisons/points of contact with all appropriate individuals/agencies. Further, the CPO provides an overall view of the planning document by describing school buildings and the activity conducted in each building, prioritizing each building, establishing the sensitivity of each building, identifying any physical or environmental conditions for each building, and addresses any operational considerations.

Additionally, the CPO must decide what types of threats exist and address them in a priority fashion. Examples include gang rivalries, fights behind the gym, drugs hidden in lockers, guns brought to school, outsiders on campus, drinking at lunchtime, vehicle break-ins, graffiti, vandalism, or accidents in the parking lot. Finally, the CPO accounts for all expenses related to the planning operation and is responsible for the development of proactive measures and recording their results, attaching any past security/safety surveys, and compiling

concluding comments and instructions.

Administrative Support Staff

This position is responsible for all administrative support pertaining to personnel involved in the school violence crisis response planning process. This person(s) handles routine office work. If at all possible, the CPO should not try to run a school violence response planning committee without some type of administrative assistance. The administrative staff is expected to handle paper work effectively and efficiently. For example, this position provides input to the logistics officer concerning equipment, supplies and forms needed, and reproduces documents as required. Administrative support also publishes and updates phone numbers, contact list, and locator methods concerning crisis response team personnel; personnel assignment rosters; rosters delineating school personnel responsible for school buildings; and school employee and student information. Finally, administrative support copies all relevant security, safety, and fire regulations for inclusion in the crisis response plan (these regulations may be attached to the master plan through the use of annexes).

Chief of School Security or School Resource Officer (SRO)

This position is responsible for gathering and disseminating intelligence data concerning individuals and groups identified as possible threats; gathers intelligence on expected activities during the planning operation; assesses tactics or actions threat student(s) may utilize during a violent incident; and assesses counter actions previously used by law enforcement agencies in response to violent incidents. The SRO also provides the CPO with an assessment of the crisis response planning document, conducts intelligence briefings as directed by the CPO; and is responsible for retrieving visual representation of effected structures (video and still photographs). Finally, the SRO evaluates internal and external security systems; compiles current and potential threat data; and is responsible for establishing a crime scene etiquette program for the school community.

Logistics Officer

The logistics officer determines and acquires all resources required to support the crisis response planning process. The logistics officer also tracks all operational expenses associated with the crisis response planning process and provides the equipment/supplies needed for the project. Finally, the logistics officer provides required resource support concerning all activities focusing on the crisis response planning operation.

Some logistics officers will be assigned the responsibility of financial planning or at the very least, a person working for the logistics section will be assigned budgeting financial planning duties. Financial planning can be divided into three categories: budgeting, accounting, and reporting. Every school violence response planning committee, no matter how small, must have a budget. A budget is an itemized summary of probable expenditures for a given period of time and is usually prepared on a yearly basis. A school violence response planning committee budget should be developed to maintain an acceptable level of readiness. The size of the budget will depend upon the size of the school system; the size of the school campus; the size of the school violence response planning committee; the past performance of CPO, if any existed; the size of the community; the availability of government

grants; other appropriations; and the responsiveness of the local government/community. A look at past budgets will give a general picture of what to expect in the future.

Accounting is another financial term which refers to the keeping of financial records. Accounting is the procedure by which actual expenditures are recorded. Accounting procedures are likely to be well established within any particular school system. The office of financial management will usually be able to assist the logistics officer with proper accounting forms and procedures.

Reporting consists of making a periodic presentation of the budget and accounts to supervisors or other authorities who have oversight responsibilities over the school violence response planning committee. Actual reporting procedures are likely to be standardized and particular to the school system. These reports may be assigned in an annual fashion or more frequently. The logistics officer should try to turn reporting activities into an opportunity to promote the school violence response planning committee.

This position is important due to the fact that without resources (staffing, funds, and equipment) school violence crisis response planning would be impossible. The point is, in order to carry out any school violence crisis response plan, the CPO must know what personnel and assets are available. Resources may be grouped into four areas: those available from the government, those of the school system, those of a neighboring jurisdiction, and those that can be obtained from the private sector. Resource types include emergency services, medical services, assembly areas, transportation, supplies, media sources, individuals, equipment, service agencies, and community groups.

In order to make use of emergency resources, the logistics officer must know, what resources are available, where resources are located, and the proper steps in the procurement process including proper return procedures as required. Thus, a resource inventory should be developed that will enable the best use of resources during a school violence crisis. The resource inventory should contain exactly who controls the resources and how to contact that person. The resource inventory should contain the position, name, phone number (home, office, and cell phone), pager or answering system, complete home and business, and the service or equipment to be provided. The same information should be collected and recorded concerning the primary source's designated alternate in case the primary contact cannot be reached. Additionally, the resource inventory should be listed in a systematic way to ensure efficient use. Resources should also be sorted into a useful index by title and page number.

Finally, the resource inventory should be updated as often as necessary but at a minimum once a year. A resource inventory is worthless if it is not up-to-date. An out-of-date inventory presents its own hazard. For example, if a school violence crisis occurs and the logistics officer is calling disconnected numbers and promising resources that cannot be delivered, lives may be lost. The fastest way to update a resources inventory is to send a standard form letter to everyone listed in the inventory document. The logistics officer can reproduce previously filed information and send a copy to the contact person asking them to confirm the facts and continued availability of the resource. When the letter is returned, the logistics officer can change information on the inventory record and make note of the last date of confirmation. This process enables anyone using the inventory sheet to identify whether the information is accurate and up-to-date.

Facility Architects and Engineers

Personnel staffing these positions read and interpret blueprints concerning all of the structures located on the school campus. Facility architects and engineers are responsible for compiling a list depicting the location of supporting utilities, e.g., communication lines, electric lines, water lines, heating and air conditioning, etc. Finally, facility architects and engineers serve as a point of contact for building drawings, blueprints, and other structural information.

School Medical Personnel

School medical personnel are responsible for interfacing with local medical support entities; identifying and storing medical supplies designed to meet the needs of mass casualties; assisting in the planning and conducting of mass casualty drills; and answering all questions dealing with medical support operations and programs. School medical personnel should also establish what levels of injury or trauma hospitals can address and their existing capabilities. School medical personnel should also become familiar with stress and the resulting trauma (acute stress caused by a sudden, arbitrary, often random event and chronic stress which occurs over and over again such as child abuse). Further, school medical personnel should become familiar with crisis reactions which may appear in the aftermath of a school violence crisis. Crisis reactions include physical responses, cognitive responses, emotional reactions, feelings of loss, regression, behavioral reactions, short-term recovery, long-term crisis reactions, and long-term stress recovery. Finally, school medical personnel should brief all concerned parties on the aspects of crisis reactions, for example,

A. The physical response to trauma is based on animal instincts such as frozen fright, fight-or-flight, or exhaustion. Frozen fright includes physical shock, disorientation, and numbness. Fight-or-flight includes adrenaline being pumped through the body, nausea, or the body relieving itself of excess materials like ingested food, one or more of the physical senses becoming more acute while others shut down, an increase in heart rate, muscle tremors or twitches, chest pain, difficulty breathing or hyperventilation, sweating, elevated blood pressure, thirst, headaches, visual difficulties, grinding of teeth, dizziness, chills, shock symptoms, etc. Weakness, fainting, fatigue, and/or exhaustion often occurs after prolonged fight-or-flight responses.

B. Cognitive responses to stress reaction include blaming someone, confusion, poor attention, poor decisions, heightened or lowered alertness, poor concentration, memory problems, hypervigilance, difficulty identifying familiar objects or people,increased or decreased awareness of surroundings, poor problem solving, poor abstract thinking, loss of time, place or person orientation, disturbed thinking, nightmares, intrusive images, etc.

C. Emotional reactions can be broken down into three stages. Stage one includes shock, disbelief, uncertainty, and denial. Stage two includes a cataclysm of emotions such as anger/rage, irritability, agitation, fear/terror, sorrow/grief, confusion/frustration, anxiety, apprehension, severe panic, loss of or inappropriate emotional control/response, depres-

sion, feeling overwhelmed, and self-blame/guilt. Stage three includes the reconstruction of a normal/familiar state of equilibrium or balance putting a stop to the emotional roller-coaster.

D. Feelings of loss include loss of control over one's life; loss of faith in one's God or other people; loss of a sense of fairness or justice; loss of personally significant property, self, or loved ones; loss of a sense of immortality and invulnerability; and a loss of future.

E. Feelings of regression include singing nursery rhymes, assuming a fetal position, crawling instead of walking, calling authority figures mommy or daddy, feeling little, wanting mommy or daddy to take care of them, and feeling weak.

F. Behavioral reactions include change in activity, change in speech patterns, withdrawal, emotional outbursts, suspiciousness, change in usual communications, loss or increase of appetite, alcohol consumption, inability to rest, antisocial acts, nonspecific body complaints, hyperalert to environment, startle reflex intensified, pacing; erratic movements, change in sexual functioning, etc.

G. Short-term recovery includes getting control of an event in the victim's/survivor's mind, working out an understanding of the event, redefining values; reestablishing a new equilibrium/life, reestablishing trust, reestablishing a future, and reestablishing meaning. While many students/teachers may live through a trauma and be able to reconstruct their lives without outside help, most people find some type of outside intervention useful in dealing with trauma. Recovery length depends upon the severity of the crisis reaction, the ability to understand what happened, the stability of the victim's/survivor's equilibrium after the event, the supportive environment, and the validation of the experience.

H. Long-term recovery includes experiencing crisis reactions for years. Crisis reactions often occur in response to trigger events that remind the victim of the trauma. They can bring back the intense emotion that occurred with the original trauma. Trigger events will vary with different victims/survivors but often include identification of the assailant; sensing (seeing, hearing, touching, smelling, tasting) something similar to something that one was acutely aware of during the trauma event; anniversaries of the event; the proximity of holidays or significant life events; hearings, trials, appeals or other critical phases of the criminal justice process; and news reports about a similar event.

Long-term crisis reactions may be made better or worse by the actions of others. These negative actions are often called the second assault, and the accompanying feelings are known as a second injury. This second injury constitutes the victim's perceived rejection by and lack of expected support from the community. Sources of the second assault may include the criminal justice system; the media; family; friends or acquaintances; hospital and emergency room personnel; health and mental-health professionals; social service workers; victim service workers; schools, teachers, and educators; victim compensation systems; and the clergy.

Long-term traumatic stress reactions may involve what is called Post-Traumatic Stress Disorder. The following is the description of that disorder referred to in the *Diagnostic and Statistical Manual–Third Edition–Revised,*

"309.89 Post-Traumatic Stress Disorder."

1. The individual has experienced an event that is outside the range of usual human experience and that would be markedly distressing to almost anyone, e.g., serious threat to one's life or physical integrity; serious threat or harm to s children, spouse, or other close relatives and friends; seriously injured or killed as a result of an accident or physical violence.

2. The distressing event is persistently reexperienced in at least one of the following ways: (a) recurrent and intrusive distressing recollections of the event (which may be associated with guilty thoughts about behavior before and during the event); (b) recurrent distressing dreams of the event; (c) sudden acting or feeling as if the event were recurring (includes a sense of reliving the experience, illusions, hallucinations, and dissociative or flashback episodes, even those that occur upon awakening or when intoxicated) (in young children, repetitive play in which themes or aspects of the distressing event are expressed); (d) intense psychological distress at exposure to events that symbolize or resemble an aspect of the event, including anniversaries of the event.

3. Persistent *avoidance* of stimuli associated with the distressing event or numbing of general responsiveness (not present before the event), as indicated by at least three of the following: (a) deliberate efforts to avoid thoughts or feelings associated with the event; (b) deliberate efforts to avoid activities or situations that arouse recollections of the event; (c) inability to recall an important aspect of the event (psychogenic amnesia); (d) markedly diminished interest in

significant activities (in young children, loss of recently acquired developmental skills such as toilet training or language skills); (e) feeling of detachment or estrangement from others; (f) restricted range of affect, e.g., unable to have loving feelings; (g) sense of foreshorted future, e.g., child does not expect to have a career, marriage or children, or long life.

4. Persistent symptoms of increased arousal (not present before the event) as indicated by at least two of the following: (a) difficulty falling or staying asleep; (b) irritability or outburst of anger; (c) difficulty concentrating; (d) hypervigilance; (e) physiologic reactivity at exposure to events that symbolize or resemble an aspect of the event (e.g., a woman who was raped in an elevator breaks out in a sweat when entering any elevator).

5. Duration of the disturbance of at least one month. "Specify delayed onset if the onset of symptoms was at least six months after the distressing event."

Note: Not all long-term stress reactions can be described as post-traumatic stress disorder. Furthermore, the intensity of long-term stress reactions usually decreases over time as does the frequency of the re-experienced crisis. However, the effects of a catastrophic trauma cannot be cured. Even survivors of trauma who reconstruct new lives and who have achieved a degree of normality and happiness in their lives will find that new life events will trigger the memories and reactions to the trauma in the future. **Additional note**: Much of the information concerning stress, trauma, and reactions was gathered from National Organization For Victim Assistance (NOVA)–1757 Park Road, N.W., Washington, D.C. 20010.

Some organizations develop Critical Incident Stress Management (CISM) teams to provide peer support (this includes students, school officials, parents, and emergency response personnel) after a trauma/critical incident to minimize the unwanted effects connected with the critical incident. Some examples of critical incidents include serious injury or death of school personnel, large number of casualties, suicide of a school member, death/serious injury/violence involving a child, expenditure of a large amount of physical/emotional energy without success, incident involving excessive media coverage, bizarre/highly emotional incidents, and an incident involving a friend or relative.

A critical incident, often causes some debilitation to the personnel involved. Debilitation makes one unable to function normally. The reactions to the incident are normal under the circumstances for normal people. However, if the reactions are not dealt with, there is a possibility they will appear again at a later date and perhaps cause permanent mental health damage.

An effective way to address debilitating reactions is to employ a debriefing. In these cases, a trained CISM team may create an environment in which an individual can share his or her feelings and reactions to the incident. Confidentiality is stressed and the session should not be confused with group counseling or any other type of counseling. Rather, debriefing represents an opportunity for the individuals involved in an incident to share their reactions with their peers. The session is conducted by reiterating that the reactions and feelings are normal for normal people under the circumstances.

In conclusion, sometimes one or more of the stress reaction signs described above may predate the incident. These should be considered as signs of critical incident stress only if there is a significant change in their intensity following the incident. Different people react differently to any situation. Indeed, it would be unusual for an individual to experience all of the above mentioned reactions. A person may not experience any of the reactions or may experience one or more. The length and intensity of the reactions will also often vary from individual to individual. Symptoms become of concern if they reflect a significant change in functioning from before the incident to after the incident. Symptoms that predate the critical incident are of concern if they significantly increase in frequency of occupance and/or in intensity after the event.

School medical personnel should develop a coordinated community response including professionals working within the school district and the greater community. These professionals should be called upon to assist individuals who are displaying severe stress reactions. Effective programs should help parents understand children's reaction to violence; teachers and other staff members deal with their reactions to the crisis; students and faculty adjust after the crisis; victims and family members of victims reenter the school environment, and students and teachers address the return of a previously removed student to the school community. Finally, school medical personnel should be fully involved in meeting the needs (validation and healing) of victims of school violence.

School Legal Representative

The school legal representative is responsible for advising the CPO about any concerns which may generate as a result of information gathering, compilation, and/or other use. The school legal representative is also responsible for researching the following areas: federal, state, and local laws concerning emergency plans; response

group interface; and dealing with the press. Further, the school legal representative should also answer any legal issue or concern as required. Finally, the school legal representative is responsible for researching school policies and procedures dealing with referral, corrective actions, and expulsion. **Note**: Attorneys, judges, and probation officers are good candidates to serve in this position.

School Media Spokesman or Public Information Officer (PIO)

During any school violence situation, the statement, "no comment" won't be sufficient. The press will want answers and if the wrong message is given, the resulting damage a school administration and/or system sustains may be irreversible. The school media spokesperson is responsible for acting as media liaison (broadcast TV, print media, radio, and electronic media–Internet sources); community liaison (community population, victims families, families of other students, school system employees); group liaison (PTA, teachers' union); perpetrator('s) family liaison; and general population liaison. The school media spokesperson is also responsible for governmental liaison; for example, addressing school boards, local governments, state government officials and organizations, and federal government entities.

The following information will help the media spokesperson perform his or her duties. The media spokesperson working in conjunction with the CPO, legal representative, and school administrators should develop a public information standard operating procedure (SOP). The SOP should outline the framework within which the media spokesperson will work with the media. Essential elements of an effective SOP include a statement of policy, a policy overview, definitions, designate officials, detail media interface, outline desired media behavior, identify what information may be released and not released, set information formats, and clarify access to school facilities.

A statement of policy should acknowledge that the agency is committed to the free flow of information to the media, subject only to the narrow limitations imposed by the law and the legitimate needs of the school system (the federal Freedom Of Information Act (FOIA) as well as state FOIA require the free-flow of information). A policy overview simply states the basic principle that will guide the school media spokesperson. For example, the school organization will keep the news media fully, fairly, and accurately informed in a timely manner concerning all matters falling within the administration's area of responsibility, within the limits of law and consistent with the needs of the school community.

Terms used in the public information SOP should be clearly defined. Additionally, officials such as school superintendents or other top school officials should always make decisions involving formal news conferences and communicate these decisions or needs to the school information officer. Media interface actions should clarify the stance that all school personnel will treat reporters with courtesy and respect at all times. However, the media representative does not have sweeping privileges; he or she also have responsibilities he or she must meet when involved in a school violence situation. For example, media representatives should be properly accredited and display an appropriate photo ID in plain view. Furthermore, by committing the school organization to keeping the media fully informed, school administrations should expect media accuracy, fairness, and impartiality in their handling of information.

It would be impossible to list every item of information that might be made available to the media; however, the public information SOP should outline, in a general fashion, the information which may be disseminated. Basic information will certainly include "Who, What, Why, When, Where, and How." Once a warrant has been issued for a suspect, additional information can also be released such as name, age, sex, address, nature of charges, further details of the crime, and circumstances of the arrest. For further guidance on what is appropriate to release to the media, refer to the federal FOIA, especially Title 5 U.S.C., subsection b (7), parts A-F; specific state FOIA; the U.S. Code of Federal Regulations (28 CFR 50.2) and the U.S. Department of Justice Rules 7.3, 7.4, and 7.17 governing media policy; and rule 3.6 of the American Bar Association's Model Rules of Professional Conduct.

Information not to be released, in reference to OPSEC principles (discussed in detail at the beginning of this section), should be a short list. Examples include not releasing information that could jeopardize anyone's safety or information that could jeopardize the management of an incident or investigation. Additionally, do not reveal key investigative techniques or sources, critical matters of evidence, and/or names of juveniles. Refer to the resources listed above for additional guidance.

Information formats should outline the different types of contact with the media and who is authorized to make such contact. Information formats include interviews (personal contact or telephone), printed news releases, formal news briefings and news conferences, electronic bulletin boards, and e-mail. Access to school facilities should be extended to accredited reporters on legitimate assignment (entertainment type news entities may be handled in a different manner). In conclusion, an SOP will eliminate confusion for the crisis response planning team concerning who can or should say what to whom. It will also have the added benefit of reducing friction and increasing cooperation between the crisis response planning team and the media.

When addressing the media, brief families first; designate one spokesperson; develop a consistent message; schedule news conferences only when news is available; avoid individual interviews; deny requests for exclusive interviews; speak only on issues the media position is responsible for; speak only about known details–do not respond to questions that require more details than are available; don't package human interest stories; be as factual as possible; do not give out any information that has not been confirmed; and make no predictions. Finally, the school media spokesman should not engage in speculation on what could happen or what is going to happen.

The school media spokesperson is very important because school administrators cannot ignore the media. Indeed, school administrators are responsible for presenting information to the public. When a violent event occurs in a school facility, individuals and the community as a whole may experience a heightened sense of fear that additional events will occur or that there may be a larger problem looming in an educational facility. Thus, the community has the right to know what the motivation of the crime was, whether the police believe it was an isolated incident or an incident related to others that have occurred in the facility in the past.

School violence is complicated and not easy to speak about in sound bites. Thus, reporters should be educated on what steps school administrations and police entities have taken to identify, intervene, and react in school violence situations. Most news organizations, especially at local levels, have minimal experience in reporting school violence incidents because it is an area that has received little exposure until relatively recently.

A school media spokesperson must be prepared; a journalist is expected to ask questions and these questions don't stop with who, what, when, where, and how. They also include internal questions about how an issue is covered. Furthermore, not only reporters will be seeking information, but parents, grandparents, guardians, and other loved ones will be passing along rumors that tend to grow if there is a long delay for an official statement. Some official statement or comment is better than none and can help ensure that an accurate depiction is presented. A lack of comment and information unnecessarily fosters suspicion and mistrust.

The key to a better relationship between school administrators, police agencies, community organizations, concerned citizens, and the news media, when a school violence incident occurs, is being aware of the constraints facing each group. Due to public interest, a high-profile school violence incident will be reported regardless of whether a school administrator or law enforcement entity believes it has compiled all the needed facts or is ready to issue a statement. To contain misstatements and avoid inaccuracies by others, school administrators and law enforcement entities should develop a method to distribute information quickly, offering whatever information has been confirmed and explain why more information isn't available. Some information is better than none and any communication, no matter how limited, presents an opportunity to get the school administrator/law enforcement entity's message across to viewers or readers.

Furthermore, a school violence incident

will develop into a time-sensitive environment. Thus, it is a good idea to develop media packets before an incident occurs, so it can be followed in the rush of events that will follow an incident. A consistent process should be developed for answering questions quickly. The media packet should contain a protocol on answering media questions. Alternate media contacts should be established if the initial contact person cannot be reached.

Getting a message out in a hectic newsroom setting can also be difficult. Generally, the more contact an administrator has with a news organization the better. Administrators should fax information or press releases to an assigned desk or assigned editor. Furthermore, if contact has been made with a specific reporter, also fax the information directly to the reporter.

Because many school violence incidents are considered relatively minor offenses (i.e., a fistfight), they rarely make the news. Indeed, the public hears about school violence only when they reach a level the media considers "newsworthy." These incidents are usually presented as isolated incidents and generate a degree of surprise from the community. In order for the public to deal with school violence, it needs to be informed about ways they can help in the fight against school violence. A school and/or community is not protected by a lack of information and cannot deal with problems existing within or against it if it lacks the information necessary to address the problem at the community level. To address this issue, a media packet may be developed. A media packet should contain the following information: school violence statistics, the responsibilities of the school administration and law enforcement, what steps have been adopted and implemented concerning school violence, a list of school violence definitions and programs, school policy and procedures concerning school violence, a list of local resources concerned with school violence, and sources of further information. This information may be posted on the Web so that both the public and media can freely access desired information.

School media representatives must also be trained in writing and speaking more sensitively about Asian Americans, blacks, Hispanics, Native Americans, people with disabilities, women, and other groups. Stereotypes (all Asians are alike), loaded words (Oriental or Negro), loaded images (buck teeth, heavy accents), ethnic slurs (Jap, Chink, or Chinaman), insensitivity (failing to include responses from all groups involved in a crisis), and military metaphors (war or invasion) must be avoided at all costs. The idea is to improve the effectiveness of information while eliminating cliches. Help can be ascertained from groups such as the Asian American Journalists Association, National Association of Black Journalists, National Lesbian and Gay Journalists Association, National Association of Hispanic Journalists, and Native American Journalists Association.

A school media spokesperson will also have to address electronic media demands. The following information may make addressing e-mail demands easier and more effective. The school media spokesperson should designate a specific person responsible for e-mail replies. To address e-mail inquiries in a timely manner, fact sheets and standard responses should be outlined prior to a violent incident. Further, an area should be set-up for the specific mission of receiving and responding to e-mail messages.

E-mail interaction is not without benefits; for example, e-mail communications may generate tips and information concerning the crisis (naturally, this information should be immediately passed on to investigators).

Further, e-mail may be used to refer concerned people to updates posted on the schools web site. Finally, e-mail inquiries may be used by the media spokesperson to shape communication objectives.

The school media spokesperson will often be required to present victims' briefings. To effectively conduct these briefings the spokesperson must show respect; designate a specific person to perform as liaison with victims' families; schedule briefings for victims' families and other affected persons before news conferences; send the same message to everybody; manage expectations; provide credible answers and explain limitations; and manage the outrage. The media spokesperson must not exploit these people. The media should be told that the school media spokesperson has already met with the families. Additionally, the school media spokesperson should involve the clergy and deal with issues before they go public.

The school media spokesperson will often be required to present community briefings. To effectively conduct these briefings, the spokesperson must designate a specific person as community liaison; schedule briefings after news conferences; send the same message to everyone; refer to established e-mail and web site for continuous updates; involve clergy; manage expectations of the community; provide credible answers and explain existing limitations; manage the outrage typically generated by school violence; avoid the exploitation of personnel or the situation; tell the community that families were met with first; determine if there are any limitations placed on the media by a court order; establish a media site/press area and staff as required; ensure media representatives have media identification; and finally, read media/policy guidelines to all assigned personnel and media representatives.

In conclusion, when a school violence incident occurs, the community as a whole is likely to experience a heightened sense of fear that further incidents may occur, or that the incident may be part of a larger problem in the school and/or community. Any community affected by a school violence crisis has a right to know the motivation for committing the crime, whether the police believe it was an isolated incident, or an incident related to other acts that have occurred in the same school and/or community. Due to public interest, a school violence crisis will be reported regardless of whether a school administration, police agency, or community organization is ready to issue a statement. To contain misstatements and avoid inaccuracies by others, the school media spokesperson should disseminate information quickly, offer whatever information has been confirmed, and explain why more information isn't available. Some information is better than none because a lack of information will often foster suspicion and mistrust. Indeed, the public must be kept informed during a school violence crisis or the response of citizens may be unpredictable.

Finally, it is in the best interest of school organizations to be as forthcoming with the media and community as possible. Furthermore, school media representatives should work with news personnel throughout the year. A good working relationship may help with useful exchanges of information during a school violence crisis, and as familiarity is achieved between entities, the less likely doubts of credibility will occur. Good media relations translates into good public relations.

Environmental, Safety, and Health (ES&H) Officer

The ES&H officer identifies the existence of HAZMAT materials. HAZMAT information should include the type, amount, and location of HAZMAT materials and the ease of access to HAZMAT materials. Further, the ES&H officer should recommend the security requirements of HAZMAT materials. Additionally, the ES&H officer should identify the hazard level of HAZMAT materials and finally, recommend response procedures for HAZMAT material incidents.

Other Elements

Other elements are addressed due to the unique circumstances that may effect any school system. To address unique circumstances, the CPO designates each position by determining necessity, developing and clarifying a scope of duties, directs adequate staffing, and establishes responsibilities. **Note**: A variety of community leaders and/or parents may be asked to support the response planning project by staffing this position; these personnel may include PTA officers, clergy, law enforcement personnel, violence prevention groups, mental health and child welfare personnel, physicians and nurses, business leaders, school board members, and other local officials.

In conclusion, school crisis incidents require immediate, planned action, and long-term, post-crisis intervention. Indeed, the crisis response planning team not only plans what to do when violence strikes but also ensures that staff and students know how to behave. Students and staff will feel secure when there is a well-conceived plan and everyone understands what to do or whom to ask for instructions. Finally, planning will ultimately reduce chaos and trauma generated by any school violence crisis.

School Violence Response Plan Format and Contents

A fourth question commonly asked concerns the school violence response plan format and contents: *What should the School Violence Response Plan document include and how should the information be organized?* Actually, completing the plan occurs in a variety of steps. While there are no hard and fast rules pertaining to plan development, the basic plan is usually written first. From the basic plan, annexes and appendices may also be developed. The basic plan should be treated as the umbrella document that draws together all other parts of the plan. Its primary audience is the chief executive, planning entities, and police personnel.

A school violence crisis plan should be developed using the following suggested format: introduction to the basic plan, statement of purpose, situations and assumptions; organization and assignment of responsibilities, concept of operations, administration and logistics, plan development and maintenance, authorities and references, and the definition of terms. Annexes to the basic plan, appendices, and standard operating procedures and other procedures should be developed and inserted as needed.

A plan begins with a series of statements that serve as the introduction to the basic plan. These include the promulgation statement, foreword, table of contents, instructions, and change record. The promulgation statement is signed by a chief executive to give the plan authority. Next, a foreword is written that describes the planning process, abstracts the contents in an executive summary, and states the goals of the plan. A table of contents should now be developed which lists the total contents to include any annexes or appendices. Another statement concerns instructions explaining the plan's use, the intended audience, and the purposes of its sections and distribution. Finally, a change of record is developed depicting the dates, locations, and specific verbiage of any revisions.

After the introduction to the basic plan has been completed, it is time to develop a statement of purpose. For example, the purpose of the plan is to provide the school community with an effective and efficient school crisis response operation which, when applied, will provide the levels of protection for life and property and recovery assistance which are acceptable to the school system and citizens of the community.

The next section focuses on situations and assumptions. The types of school violence situations which may occur in the school system are described here. The planner must be realistic and develop valid assumptions. The plan of operation for meeting these situations will be based upon the assumptions made in this section. To complete the picture of the situation and assumptions of the plan, a review focusing on the security survey and other proactive measures should be included.

The next step requires planners to establish an organizational structure and assign responsibilities. This is a key section of the plan and will normally be lengthy. It should specifically define the roles of school officials in the planning structure. The organizational structure should also include individuals staffing local government and community positions who may be called upon to provide resources. Certain officials are given specific assignments and lines of authority are identified between the planning positions and emergency responders.

The organizational structure should be as similar as possible to that which is used for day-to-day operations. For example, a school nurse should be assigned as a school medical representative instead of a logistics officer. However, the organizational structure should allow for the expansion and extension of duties as situations dictate. To the greatest extent possible, personnel should continue to work with the supervisor and associates whom they normally work with on a regular basis. This familiarity will often streamline the start-up process by avoiding the need of getting to know new people, establishing territories, dealing with different work ethics, and so forth.

Another important section of the plan is titled administration and logistics. This section should address management of resources, general support requirements, and availability of services and support for all phases of a school violence crisis situation. The plan should establish policy for obtaining and using facilities, material, services, and any other required resources.

Next, plan development and maintenance should be addressed. This portion is normally addressed after completion of the school violence response plan and includes provisions for review, modification, acceptance, and approval by the head of the effected school system. Of particular importance is the continuous review required to update the plan to reflect improvements needed as a result of experiences in dealing with school violence and changing situations and assumptions.

Any authorities and references which were used in plan development should be stated at the end of the document. Authorities and references may include statutes, executive orders, regulations, formal agreements, general planning guidance, plans of other agencies, plans of other levels of government, and the like.

Another section, that is valuable, concerns the definition of terms. This would include definitions of terms which are not commonly known as well as those used in the plan which could cause confusion if misinterpreted. The terms one chooses to define will depend upon the uniqueness of the school community and the audience addressed.

Annexes may be included in order to describe operations for a particular function. Annexes should define a function and show how activities of various participants in the functional organization are coordinated. Annexes are typically action-oriented and are written for, and preferably by, the person responsible for controlling resources available to accomplish the objectives of the function in a school violence crisis. Annexes may include such functions as direction and control, warning systems, communications, public information, evacuation procedures, law enforcement interaction, fire department interaction, resources management, and the like. Of course, the annexes listed are not meant to be all-inclusive. The selection and definition of functions to be covered in annexes varies from school system to school system depending on such factors as the size, organization, and specific needs of each school. Finally, annexes should be formatted in the same manner as the basic plan. To reiterate, there are nine parts to the basic plan and annexes: (1) introduction, (2) statement of purpose, (3) situations and assumptions, (4) organization and assignment of responsibilities, (5) concept of operations, (6) administration and logistics, (7) development and maintenance, (8) authorities and references, and (9) definition of terms.

Finally, the plan should end with an appendices. An appendix contains details, methods, and technical information that are unique to each specific school violence hazard identified as being likely to pose a threat in a particular school. Appendices may also be attached to functional annexes

and should have sections corresponding to those in the annex for which supplementary hazard specific information is required.

Crisis action planning staffs may also include standard operating procedures and other attachments which are deemed necessary to support and provide directions to school violence response personnel. These documents may be attached to any part of the plans elements where they are most readily accessible and most likely to be needed. These attachments may include checklists, charts, maps, standard operating procedures, available resources, call-up lists, and contact lists, etc. Like the basic plan, attachments are living documents. They are changed and revised as required. Indeed, attachments will probably be the most frequently modified part of the plan. School violence response planner should design the plan in this manner, allowing for the removal and insertion of changes and new pages.

School Violence Response Plan Information

Of course, as has been previously discussed, school violence response plans are specific and unique to each school system. However, each school violence response plan must gather information valuable in defining a specific schools assets; defining a school's threats; defining a school's weaknesses; defining a school's strengths, and characterizing a school's environment. All school violence response plan information should contain, at a minimum, the following generic information:

Description of the Building(s)

A full description of each building on campus should be compiled to include the exact physical location (street address complete with written directions). This will prevent responding officials from going to the wrong locations or getting lost. Getting lost will waste valuable time and responding to the wrong location can be deadly to everyone involved in the area of responsibility. For example, perpetrators may see response personnel set up at the wrong location and decide to kill students or fire upon unsuspecting personnel. Many campuses are large and confusing to responders who have never seen the area in question. Further, sometimes buildings look very similar and may generate confusion. Descriptions provide identification by sight and street addresses/written directions will provide clear physical locations.

Activity Conducted in Each Building

What type of activity is normally conducted in each building? For example: mass assemblies, classrooms–learning activities, physical fitness activities, laboratory experiments, the use of power tools, the use of torches, the use of volatile chemicals or solvents, etc. Buildings used for mass assemblies are usually attractive areas for offenders to employ school violence actions, for example, lunch rooms, gymnasiums, and assembly rooms.

Priority of Each Building

Is one building or facility area more important than another? Are musical instruments, tools, special equipment, potentially dangerous chemicals, valuable assets, expensive fixtures, etc., used or stored in certain buildings? Is a building considered by the campus population as a focal point of importance? Are campus buildings protected by security systems operating at different levels?

Sensitivity of Each Building

Sensitivity is an extension of priority. Sensitivity may be assessed as high due to building contents, importance to the operation of the facility (heat, water, electric power), and the level of protection available.

Physical and Environmental Conditions

When formulating this section, planners should consider the aspects of obstacles, cover and concealment, observation, key terrain, and avenues of approach and/or escape. This is an area that may be beyond many school administrator's knowledge and indeed this verifies the fact that this plan should be developed by the number and type of personnel previously discussed. Police officers should specifically tour each building on campus and note the physical and environmental conditions listed above and discussed below. Further, still photographs and videotapes should be produced from all areas of concern. When this is done, there is no question concerning how effective a perpetrator could be if located in these specific areas.

Obstacles should be noted and described, especially in areas located on routes of travel to and into any structure. For example, do obstacles such as fences, open fields, open parking lots, construction areas, etc. exist that will cause a problem for responding forces. Any area that slows down, stops, or allows perpetrator to observe responding forces should be considered an obstacle. When these areas are identified, responding forces can formulate plans to either circumvent the area or develop ways to counter the obstacle.

Cover and concealment aspects focus on areas the perpetrator may use as cover and concealment as well as areas which may be used by responding forces. The availability of cover and concealment will directly correspond with the tactical elements of control, security and speed responding forces will use to travel to, into, and through an area or building. Strengths and weaknesses should be identified and accompanying methods of counteraction should be recorded.

Observation is also a condition of physical and environmental conditions. For example, does the perpetrator have a good view of an area (through huge windows) or is his or her ability to observe diminished by wooded areas, other buildings, blank walls, etc. Observation is evaluated in two ways: first, responding forces must envision what they believe a perpetrator can see from the tactical area of concern and second, consider how well responding forces can see the tactical arena.

Key terrain is also a condition of physical and environmental conditions. For example, perpetrator control an area by taking up a position in a specific area. For example, could a perpetrator take up a position in a bell tower and shoot people at great distances, or can responding forces take up a position in the bell tower mentioned above and control a large area with effective weapons fire if necessary. If areas are identified as key terrain, responders will have to find ways to circumvent the area, neutralize the area by using various tactics, flush the perpetrator out of the area, or physically occupy the area to prevent perpetrator(s) from getting in the area.

A final condition of physical and environmental conditions includes high-speed avenues of approach and escape. For example, are there areas conducive to perpetrator approach or escape? If so, these areas must be physically controlled by responders. Further, can these areas be used by responders as approach and/or withdrawal routes? All non-traditional ingress and egress routes should be identified, for example, air conditioning ducts, elevators shafts, air vents, maintenance tunnels, and adjoining structures.

Of course, the above explanation is only a sampling of physical and environmental conditions which are important to responders. These principles should also be used when evaluating the inside of any structure, for example, obstacles, cover and concealment, observation, key terrain and avenues of approach and escape to some extent. This is another example of why school violence response plans are site specific and unique to each school system.

School Personnel Responsible for Each Building

Who is actually in charge of each building? These people are sometimes known as building managers. A primary and secondary building manager should be identified to include primary and secondary contact methods. These personnel should know more about their assigned building than anyone else on campus.

Operational Considerations

Will the loss of a particular building affect other parts of the campus? Could operations conducted in a building prove valuable to a perpetrator?

Supporting Utilities

A list depicting the location of supporting utilities; e.g., communication lines, electric lines, water lines, heating and air conditioning, etc. should be compiled for each building. A survey of power supply systems should be conducted to include the type of power supply. For example, on-site power, off-site power generation, power supply capacity, capacity for expansion, and condition of power facilities. Distribution systems, and emergency back-up systems may be identified by number, location, capacity, and condition. The fuel supply for power systems should also be evaluated for type, quantity, security, and location.

Visual Representation of Campus Structures

Visual representation should include the following types and areas of concern. Photographs depicting the interior and exterior of each building should include rooftops. These photographs should include aerial still photographs, ground level still photographs, and still photographs taken from a variety of angles. Videotapes are also required to include aerial video, ground level video, and video taken from various angles. Photographs and videos should also include contents of rooms; location of all emergency lighting systems; location and type of all security alarms and monitoring stations; location and type of fire suppression systems; location and type of telephones to include numbers, and the location of all intercoms.

Blueprints and drawings are important and should include building floor plans depicting hallways length and width, direction of travel and destination, and any branching areas. All rooms should include dimensions, door structure, door swing direction, type of door lock, location of light switches, type of lighting to include emergency lighting, location of closets and other hiding places, room use, and windows location and type (can they be opened and closed, thickness, coating materials, curtains, and blinds or other covering). What can a person see from this position and are there

Figure 33. Helicopter being used for gathering aerial photographs.

alternate points of ingress and egress?

Further points of interest include adjoining rooms, structures or hallways, air conditioning and heating ducts, sewer access, basement access, rooftop access and access to elevators and/or elevator shafts. Wall material and thickness are also important. Stairwells should be described by type (straight or winding), dimensions, direction of travel, number and location of ingress and egress points. Finally, planned structural modifications should be addressed, including proposed blueprints or drawings.

A new technology that combines all of the above visual representation methods into a very effective response planning tool is called "Interactive Virtual Floor Plans For Emergency Response Planning & Tactical Operations." This virtual floor plan, developed by Interactive Tactical Group (ITG), uses advanced 360 degree digital imaging to produce photo-realistic visual maps that are accessible on CD. ITG integrates maps, databases, and high-definition visual images into a package that can be quickly deployed and allows responders to "walk through" a building (unknown physical environment), moving from room to room, without physically entering the facility.

Internal and External Security Systems

These security systems include intrusion detection systems (IDS), structure locking mechanisms, building access control, campus access restrictions, etc. Generally, security systems are designed to discourage unauthorized access, provide a warning that an intrusion is occurring, to notify staff members that a security problem exists, and to delay or scare away a perpetrator. However, security systems can work against responding forces and tip off offenders that a response mission is in progress. Thus, the type, number, location, and capabilities of all security systems must be recorded.

Evaluation of Lighting Systems

The evaluation of lighting should focus on types and effectiveness. For example, lights can be identified as timed, manually-operated, motion-activated, sound-activated, or photo-electric. The type of lights used by a school may be of great importance to police officers. Lights can compromise a mission so officers need to know the type of lighting is used in order to formulate effective plans to defeat their operation.

Lights should be evaluated for effectiveness by observing their functioning at night, noting times of operation, brightness, area covered, and ease of access to wires and bulbs. Lights beams may be designed to overlap one-another in a continuous arc or designed to highlight specific areas. All dark areas should be noted and evaluated for attractiveness as an ingress/egress point. Any malfunctioning lights should be noted and replaced as soon as possible (perpetrators hate lights and may telegraph intentions by breaking or removing light bulbs a few days prior to an attack). Finally, lights should be evaluated for any interference caused by foliage such as weeds, shrubs, bushes, and trees. Foliage must be trimmed or removed if it is causing shadows or completely blocking light beams.

There are also some non-traditional lighting systems that may be encountered; they include infrared (IR) or near infrared lighting. These lights may be conducive to responding units that plan to use active and/or passive night vision devices.

Fence Lines

Fence lines should be evaluated for the following points of information:
1. Age and condition
2. Fabric tension
3. Fence material
4. Existing holes to include their size and location
5. Interface of the fence fabric to the ground, anchors, and bottom railing
6. Wire design
7. Properties of the ground
8. Washouts or other erosion
9. Concrete support
10. Gravel base
11. Asphalt base
12. Strength and physical appearance
13. Fence attachment to support poles
14. Condition and location of gates
15. Top guard type and condition
16. Overall fence stability
17. Lighting type and effectiveness
18. Existing intrusion defense systems
19. Foliage type and density

All of this information will assist responders in deciding if, how, and/or where a fence can best be breached.

Survey of Parking Facilities

All parking facilities should be noted and the following information should be included: exact physical location, distance from school buildings, observation points located in the school building, amount and types of vehicles parked (during hours of operation and off-shift hours), access requirements, ingress and egress points, lighting requirements, existing defense systems, and the ability to support response force vehicles and associated operations (field command post, tactical operations center, medical aid station, etc.).

Evaluation of Site Security Forces

Security forces should be examined and the following information should be gathered: size of the available force, training level, intended mission, duty locations and functions, equipment available, and security vehicles number and type.

Survey of Communication Systems

Communication systems should be noted and the information gathered should include types (telephones, cell phones, cordless phones, intercom systems, two-way radios, etc.); capacity; installation (above or below ground); potential for exploitation, current assignments—exact locations, condition, and identified dead spots (areas where radios will not transmit or receive).

Survey of Existing Vulnerability Countermeasures

Vulnerability countermeasures may include the following topics: Barriers—natural or manmade, active or passive, command activated or intruder activated, safe havens—indoors and outdoors; evacuation procedures and routes; and existing explosive mitigation devices.

Survey of Perimeter Terrain

The following aspects of perimeter terrain should be noted: grade—flat and level, rolling and hilly or mountainous; proximity of the perimeter to bodies of water; high volume vehicle traffic, pedestrian traffic, aircraft landing strips, and railways; ground cover—defoliated, rock/gravel, paved/asphalt surfaces, grassy/weedy, heavily foliated, or forested areas; soil composition—type, compaction, stability, drainage, surface coloration, and surface reflection.

Employee Information

The following employee information should be captured: turnover rate, overtime worked, absenteeism, morale, biographic information, current full-face photograph, physical characteristics—height, weight, build, hair color, eye color, race, scars, marks, tattoos, preferred clothing, preferred jewelry, spectacles, medical concerns, marital status, point of contact and method, military experience, and any special skills.

Student Information

The following student information should be captured: discipline record—arrest history, absenteeism, biographic information, current full face photograph, physical characteristics—height, weight, build, hair color, eye color, race, scars, marks, tattoos, preferred clothing, preferred jewelry, spectacles, medical concerns, marital status, points of contact, and method.

Current and Potential Threat Data

Current and potential threat data should focus on the following: past threat activities, past actions and outcomes, firearms used or otherwise available, explosives used or otherwise available, other violent methods, effected areas, and any past demands and deadlines.

Copies of All Relevant Security, Safety, and Fire Regulations

These regulations should include natural emergency plans and standard operating procedures, evacuation routes–primary and alternates, rally points, accountability procedures, security procedures, and containment positions to include police, fire equipment, and ambulance set-up.

Environmental, Safety and Health Considerations

Environmental, safety and health considerations will normally be categorized as hazardous materials (HAZMAT). Hazardous materials include substances or materials which, because of their chemical, physical, or biological nature, pose a potential risk to life, health, or property if they are released. A release may occur by spilling, leaking, emitting toxic vapors, or any other process that enables the material to escape its container, enter the environment, and create a potential hazard. Hazardous materials may be categorized into explosives, flammable and/or combustible substances, poisons, or radioactive materials.

Explosives are substances that release pressure, gas and heat suddenly when they are subjected to shock, heat, or high pressure. Flammable and/or combustible substances are easy to ignite. Related hazards are posed by oxidizers which will lend oxygen readily to support a fire, and reactive materials which are unstable and may react violently if mishandled.

Poisons (or toxic materials) can cause injury or death when they enter the bodies of living things. Such substances can be classified by chemical nature; for example, heavy metals and cyanides or by toxic action such as irritants that inflame living tissue, and corrosives that destroy or irreversibly change tissue. One special group of poisons includes etiological (biological) agents. These are live microorganisms, or toxins produced by the microorganisms, that are capable of producing a disease. Finally, radioactive materials are a category of hazardous materials that release harmful radiation. In conclusion, it must be understood that the above listed HAZMAT categories are not mutually exclusive. For example, acids and bases are listed as corrosive materials but can also act as poisons.

The risk associated with any particular hazardous material depends on the source, the availability of pathways for the HAZMAT to reach the receptor, and the characteristics of the receptors. No single piece of information alone is sufficient, and incomplete information can be highly misleading. To assess a HAZMAT risk the following questions must be answered:

1. What are the hazards properties of the substance and what kind of effects can it have on living things or on the environment?
2. How much of the substance exists at the source, and in what concentration?
3. In what form is the substance?
4. What are the chemical and physical characteristics of the substance?
5. How is the substance contained?
6. What pathways of exposure exist?

7. Where is the population located in relation to the source?
8. What are the characteristics of people who are at risk? The susceptibility of any individual to a toxic substance varies depending on age, weight, sex, and individual characteristics, for example, young students are more susceptible to the effects of HAZMAT than older students or adults.
9. How long does the exposure to the chemical last?

Many of these question can be answered by referring to a substance's Material Safety Data Sheet (MSDS). Any HAZMAT material located on a school campus should include this information. The MSDS is usually prepared by the manufacturer or distributor of a hazardous substance. An MSDS form will include the following information: the identity of the substance, physical and chemical characteristics, physical hazards, health hazards, routes of entry, permissible exposure limits, existence of carcinogens, safe handling methods, control measures, first aid procedures, date of preparation, and manufacturer information.

Another information source includes the National Fire Protection Association (NFPA) 704M system. The NFPA 704M label is diamond shaped, and is divided into four parts, or quadrants. The left quadrant is blue, and contains a numerical rating of the substance's health hazard. Ratings are made on a scale of 0 to 4, with a rating of 4 indicating a danger level so severe that a very short exposure could cause serious injury or death. A zero, or no code at all in any quarter, means that no unusual hazard would result from the exposure.

The top quadrant of the NFPA symbol is red, and contains a numerical rating for a fire hazard. Again, the numerical codes range from 0 to 4, with a 4 representing the most serious hazard. The right quadrant of

the NFPA symbol is yellow and contains a numerical rating for explosive or other reaction. Once again, the numerical codes range from 0 to 4, with a 4 representing the most serious hazard.

The bottom quadrant of the NFPA symbol is white, and contains a numerical rating for any special hazards that may apply. There are three possible codes for the bottom quarter which are OXY meaning the material is an oxidizer; W/ indicating the material reacts with water to release a gas that is either flammable or hazardous to health, and the tri-blade symbol designating a radioactive material that will emit radio-activity. It is important to note that this system is chemical-specific. No chemical identification system can accurately assess the synergistic effects of one chemical combining with another, or the possible effects of combining unknown amounts of several chemicals.

Evaluation of School System Interface with Local Governments and Population to Include Communication Methods and Points of Contact

To begin an evaluation, key personnel and resources must have been identified beforehand. This includes the identification of key agencies, businesses, social institutions, etc. Leadership must also be identified early to include formal and informal leaders (individuals in the community who are important and have clout as perceived by the community). Potential leaders are also identified as those who have status, power, and/or wealth. Of course, all of these key personnel should be listed by address and communication methods (telephone–home and office, pagers, cell phones, radios, etc.). Some of the important key contact agencies, resources, and personnel may be broken down into the following headings: emergency services, medical services, assembly areas, transportation, supplies, media, individuals, equipment, service agencies, and community groups.

Emergency agencies typically include fire, police public works, and public utilities. Medical agencies typically include hospitals, clinics, doctors, dentists, nursing homes, and medical associations. Assembly areas may include parks, shopping centers, schools, churches, government buildings, warehouses, and community centers. Transportation resources may include buses, trucks, vans, four-wheel drive vehicles, tractor trailers, taxicabs, power boats, air assets, snowmobiles, and swamp buggies. Supplies typically include food and medical items. Media resources include newspapers, radio stations, television stations, and news services. Individuals include local government officials, military entities (military assistance to back up response forces or provide equipment), clergy, doctors, dentists, nurses, pilots, amateur radio operators, and building contractors. Equipment may include farm tractors, construction equipment, excavation equipment, chain saws, portable power plants, etc. Service agencies may include the Red Cross and/or Salvation Army. Finally, community groups may include the PTA, chamber of commerce, Boy Scouts, Girl Scouts, Kiwanis, Lions Club, Cub Scouts, Moose, churches, American Legion, VFW, women's clubs, and even senior citizens groups.

Once key organizations and individuals have been identified, memorandums of understandings (MOUs) should be signed by each agency delineating who will provide what resources and services. MOUs, at a minimum, will require an on-going liaison between the police, school, and community officials. At the least, MOUs should address the chain of command—who is in charge, crime scene processing, interviewing procedures and processes, media interface, victim services, and other agency support.

Attachment of Proactive Measures and Their Results

Proactive measures may include, but are not limited to, counseling services; scholastic crime stopper programs; the hiring of school resource officers; gang, drug, cult, and violence training for educational personnel; performing background checks on all school facility employees; and supporting policies. The importance of proactive measures cannot be stressed enough. In many of the school violence incidents listed at the beginning of this book, shooters "leaked" their intentions to other kids. However, this information was not transferred to police officials for a number of possible reasons: people may have felt that the content of the information was not important enough to report; some people may have felt that there was a lack a real proof; others may have been embarrassed to report the information; some may have decided to try to settle dangerous issues by excluding the criminal justice system; and finally, some people may have feared retaliation.

The key ingredient for effective proactive programs concerns the development of a good working relationship between police officials and school authorities in order for essential information to be passed on and acted upon in a timely manner. It is imperative that all school districts implement as many proactive measures as possible in the minimum amount of time. A number of these proactive programs are listed below.

Counseling Services

Intervention counseling for personnel,

students, and their families should be established in advance of any violent event. Information concerning program development and implementation can be gathered from the National Organization for Victim Assistance's Crisis Response Team. Employee assistance programs and other counseling services can be developed and implemented by contacting local services or by researching existing programs. Of course, the entire community must be informed as to where victim services are located. Finally, this service should be isolated from the media.

Scholastic Crime Stopper Programs

The heart of any crime stopper program must include the identification of anti-social behaviors which carry established consequences which will be enforced to the letter. Scholastic crime stopper programs may consist of a number of options; they include telephone tip lines; anonymous tip line box(s); zero tolerance programs; reward programs; gang, drug, cult, and violence training for educational personnel; training teachers and other educational professionals to recognize students at risk of engaging in violent behavior; and finally, background checks on all personnel working in any educational facility. Of course, for any of these programs to work, most students will need to perceive their actions as not "snitching" but doing something constructive to establish a safer and more secure learning environment for all involved.

Telephone Tip Lines

This program may consist of a telephone tip line staffed by trained personnel 24 hours a day. All personnel should be trained in information gathering processes and effec-

tive recording formats. Of course, a clear line of contact personnel must be established in order to pass on time critical information in a coordinated and timely manner. Students should be briefed on the purpose of the telephone tip line and how to contact the service. The idea is to provide students with a safe process for reporting threats, intimidation, weapon possession, drug selling, gang activity, graffiti, and vandalism. This briefing should include the consequences and seriousness of making hoax threats.

Anonymous Tips Line Box(s)

This proactive measure is a viable option for school systems that cannot afford a fully staffed telephone tip line. This box should be readily accessible from both inside and outside of a facility's structure. Of course, the box should be constructed so that unauthorized personnel cannot readily access the contents. Anonymous tip line box(s) must be emptied and the contents evaluated before each school day begins. Like the telephone tip line, a clear line of contact personnel must be established in order to pass on time critical information in a coordinated and timely manner. Of course, it is imperative that information be passed on to the police in a timely manner. Naturally, students should be briefed on the location and purpose of anonymous tip line box(s). Like the tip line, the idea is to provide students with a safe process for reporting threats, intimidation, weapon possession, drug selling, gang activity, graffiti, and vandalism. This briefing should include the consequences of tampering with the tip line box and the seriousness of making hoax threats.

Zero Tolerance Programs

It is important to establish a zero tolerance program targeting weapons, alcohol, drugs, and/or threats made by students. For example, when a student makes threats to kill or assault others, immediate expulsion or suspension procedures should be exercised. Furthermore, if appropriate, psychological evaluation and intervention should be provided in a timely manner. When adults take threats seriously, students will come to realize that violence is not a condoned resolution to conflict. **Note**: The author believes a common sense-based Zero Tolerance Program represents the foundation for countering school violence. Each educational institution must set clear limits on anti-social behavior and determine consequences for offenders. A zero tolerance program must identify exactly which behaviors will not be tolerated, be fairly and consistently applied, and, above all else, be unbiased.

It is important for students to understand the importance of avoiding confrontation if possible. The point should be made that every person should always protect him or herself and not suffer at the hands of an aggressor if it is possible. It should be noted that a passive option may be the best way to survive. The idea is to let the students know that they can defend themselves as required instead of just standing there and absorbing an attack. The main issue is to teach de-escalation techniques in order to diffuse the violence of a situation.

Reward Programs

These programs may be designed to monetarily reward a student who comes forward with information concerning a pending or actual school violence incident. Of course, the reporting student's identity will have to be protected as much as possible. The reward offered will also have to be considered attractive by the student population. Any cost associated with this

program will often be offset by intervention, the speed of investigation process, and a heightened level of perpetrator identification. The reader must understand that many schools cannot afford real-time detection and real-time response to security incidents. Information concerning a pending incident or after-the-fact investigation is extremely important to these schools. Reward programs may enable investigators to quickly identify, catch, and deal with perpetrators. As a result, students may have second thoughts about engaging in anti-social behaviors at school.

Students Traveling and Arriving Safely (STARS) Program

The STARS program described in this section of the book was developed by the Fresno Police Department, the Fresno County Juvenile Probation Department, and the Fresno Unified School District. The heart of the STARS program involves as many people as possible looking out for children as they walk to and from school. This program encompasses seven core components and actively involves police, probation, school personnel, parents, students, neighborhood residents, city employees, and other volunteers. The seven core components are as follows: (1) parent patrols, (2) student awareness, (3) safe houses, (4) city employees, (5) citizens on patrol, (6) school district personnel, and (7) police officers.

Parent patrols involve parents wearing distinctive vests while walking or driving their vehicles (clearly marked with STARS magnetic placards). These parents patrol the streets near schools looking for suspicious individuals or vehicles. Parents do not take enforcement action or place themselves in danger; instead, they use their personal cellular telephone to contact police or use school-issued radios to contact school staff when necessary.

Student awareness includes being aware of the dangers students may encounter when traveling to and from school. Students are taught to walk with other students, when possible, remain alert for suspicious vehicles and/or individuals, take safe routes instead of shortcuts, and report suspicious activity to school officials or police. The training also encourages students to pay attention to the well-being of fellow students. Finally, students provide a great portion of the needed feedback concerning the STARS program to school officials and the police.

Safe houses involve residents who offer their homes as a place of safety for children who are in distress or danger until the police arrive. A distinctive decal placed in the front window of the home identifies the residence as a safe haven. Fire stations and commercial operations also act as safe havens. The police department screens all volunteers and members of their households or businesses before the home or business is designated a safe haven.

City employees who routinely drive in neighborhoods around schools, for example, bus drivers, postal workers, and sanitation workers, are trained to act as the "eyes and ears" for police. These employees are instructed to report any suspicious activity to the police or school officials.

Citizens on patrol include trained uniformed volunteers who drive marked patrol cars (older, out-of-service police vehicles equipped with amber instead of red and blue overhead lights) through school neighborhoods during peak student travel times. These volunteers take no enforcement action but report suspicious activity via their police radios.

School district personnel include staff, teachers, student safety assistants, and parent volunteers who position themselves around the perimeter of the school grounds as students arrive and leave school. They not only observe events occurring on school property but also watch nearby streets for possible problems. These volunteers wear distinctive vests and take no enforcement action but are instructed to report suspicious activity via their personal cellular telephones or school-issued radios. Police officers assist by giving special attention to the streets near schools, as well as to school and city bus stops, at the beginning and end of the school day. Officers may also distribute informative handouts or make safety presentations to parents, students, city departments, and civic groups to encourage STARS program participation.

In conclusion, the STARS program using minimal start-up costs and virtually no on-going expenditures can cause a synergistic effect heightening the safety of any community's school children.

Gun-Safety Programs

Some schools such as Carroll County, Maryland are experimenting with gun-safety programs which are taught as part of health programs to students from kindergarten through high school. This program is a mixture of the National Rifle Association's Eddie Eagle program and the STAR program, Straight Talk About Risks, run by the Center to Prevent Handgun Violence. In elementary grades, children are visited by police officers and shown videos. They also discuss what to do if they find a gun and how to ask whether guns are in their playmates' homes. Middle school children act out situations involving guns. High school students view more graphic videos and listen to a 911 tape containing the conversation of two youths reporting the accidental shooting death of a friend. Gun-safety programs should be viewed as a proactive program in the same manner as drugs, alcohol, and tobacco; AIDS; and sexual awareness courses.

School Resource Officer Assignment

School personnel and law enforcement officials must work together in order to secure the unique environment of schools. School resource officers (officers permanently assigned to the school by the police department) must be trained to identify "positive" information quickly and be able to efficiently weed out rumors. This process is obtained by establishing and integrating liaison, trust, training, and intelligence into an effective mixture designed to prevent a violent act. These officer should develop intelligence systems targeting potential or planned acts of violence; however, intelligence must drive investigations—investigations should not drive intelligence.

The importance of the school resource officer (SRO) should preclude any temptation a police department may harbor in the assignment of sub-standard officer to staff this position. It will do little good and may generate a negative response if school resource officers have been chosen to staff these positions due to poor performance, negative attitude, or a lengthy disciplinary history. This is not the place to "hide" a problem performer. This position should be chosen through a selection process designed to balance sound police skills with strong interpersonal communication skills. Extra training focusing on the American juvenile justice system may also be required. Indeed, laws concerning juveniles, especially at school, are more complex in some areas.

Further, school administrations may choose to hire full-time security personnel in lieu of police officers. If this is the preferred action, school administrators must check the security contractor's business practices, focusing on background checks and training issues. Many states require neither background checks nor formal training. Little effective proactive results will be realized by organizations that insist on cutting cost when hiring personnel. When a budget concern is weighed against the cost of providing a safe learning environment, the choice should be clear.

Of course, school resource officers should not make up the only police presence in schools. Patrol officers should include schools in their daily patrol responsibilities and, whenever possible (at least once a week), have lunch at school. This gives students an opportunity to talk to a police officer about nearly anything once a trust has been established. Periodic visits by patrol officers become extremely important in school districts located in areas where police administrators cannot afford to assign a dedicated school resource officer. In these cases, uniformed officers should visit schools as often as possible in order to establish student rapport and trust. Officers encapsulated in their patrol car will soon find themselves isolated from the community and their role will primarily center around reactive activities.

Regardless of the law enforcement position, the official must demonstrate to the students that he or she can be trusted, really cares, and is ready to take the time to listen to students. Students will then begin to see the officer as a person instead of just another official representing the establishment. One way to achieve this status is to be proactive with students. For example, the officer may ask for time in classes to conduct discussions concerning current problems such as peer pressure, gang activity, drug and alcohol use, violence, or whatever seems to be of concern to the students.

Gang, Drug, Cult and Counterviolence Training for Educational Personnel

This type of training should be designed to enable teachers and other educational professionals to recognize students at risk of violent behavior. While these concerns are not the only symptoms of possible violent behavior, there is a proven connection between gangs, alcohol, drugs, and violence. Thus, it is necessary for police personnel to educate teachers and school officials about these risk factors. It is especially important that teachers and school officials recognize the meaning of graffiti, literature, music, and other art forms that reflect any association with gangs, cults, or drugs. Background checks should be initiated on students who exhibit any involvement in these areas. Of course, positive background checks will probably require the notification of appropriate personnel to include professional intervention.

Background Checks on All Personnel Working in the Educational Facility

Background checks to include a simple criminal record check should be listed as a condition of employment. Criminal record checks are inexpensive (approximately $20.00 per individual criminal record search) and are often valuable in revealing a perpetrator's criminal history and/or some psychiatric problems. Indeed, routine background checks should be performed on all personnel seeking work at any educational facility and the results of these checks should be obtained prior to the hiring of any individual. Parents have the right to expect, and demand, that the people working on a school campus meet the highest standards of reliability.

Pre-employment background checks may also include resume and employment application verification as well as data research from other sources. In some states, falsification of a job application is a criminal offense. Most information comes from public records, except for credit reports, which require a signed release. Some other good sources of information include driving record, education verification, civil litigation, and social security number verification. Employers are normally on firm legal ground as long as the inquiries comply with applicable laws; for example, the Fair Credit Reporting Act, Americans With Disabilities Act, Equal Employment Opportunity Act, Title 7 of the Civil Rights Act of 1964, and the Age Discrimination in Employment Act.

Background checks may be assimilated into a personal assurance program made up of four components: supervisory review, medical assessment, management evaluation, and security determination. Supervision review may include properly executed documents, drug testing, and a pre-employment check. Medical assessment may include physical, mental, emotional, behavioral, substance, and alcohol abuse. Management evaluation may include review of the supervisory review and medical assessment, evaluation based on unannounced drug testing, and rehabilitation or reformation results. Security determination may include initial access authorization, annual or other periodic security access authorization, and termination of access authorization. Of course, a school administration does not have to implement the full complement of the above listed components. The administration may pick and choose applicable components that fit their school system's particular needs.

Finally, employees designated to participate in personnel assurance program should be required to report arrests, other legal issues, mental conditions requiring medication or treatment, any observed unusual actions or mannerisms conducted by other employees, criminal matters, and fraud, waste, and abuse. Of course, some of these issues may be protected by state or federal law; thus care must be taken to avoid gathering information deemed as legally protected. Legal council should be contacted during the development and implementation of any personal assurance program.

Supporting Policies

This section is titled in a rather generic manner due to the number of proactive measures to be discussed; for example, school uniforms, banned, mesh, or transparent book-bags, transparent plastic lockers, and searches of school property. School uniforms may be adopted in order to lessen conflicts that may arise over a wide variety of clothing choices (inflammatory clothing–slogans, sayings, racial/ethnic/religious/political or gang-related symbolism or clothing that may generate teasing). School uniforms may also generate a sense of everyone belonging to a common purpose, goal, or institution. However, students may still carry concealed weapons in or under any type of clothing.

Bookbags may be banned from the classroom or from an institution as a whole, or bookbags may be relegated to see-through types such as clear plastic or mesh construction. However, the items contained in the bookbag are not see-through so weapons can still be easily concealed in these products. Clear plastic lockers suffer from the same deficiencies as see-through book bags. Additionally, students may strategically place items in the locker in order to prevent the viewing of certain areas from the outside. This is not to say that these items and ideas are worthless; they are valuable,

but they must not be considered as a catch-all or the only solution.

Searches

Searches of school property are valuable in bolstering the effects of school security, especially if they are random and conducted without warning. However, inconsistent rulings by court systems can create legal dilemmas. Generally, the standard of "probable cause" still applies to police searches on school property. Thus, this may cause a legal problem for School Resource Officers (SROs) who conduct searches under the "reasonable suspicion" (described below) standard. Courts have ruled in many cases that police searches conducted on school grounds are no different than other searches, and the same basic search principles apply. However, it is generally acceptable for school officials to give police officers consent to search lockers and desks. Further, some states view School Resource Officers as school officials while other states have ruled differently on this issue. Of course, police officers and SROs can seize contraband items which are in plain view.

Search and seizure issues are different for school officials; for example, in *New Jersey v. T.L.O.* (1985), the United States Supreme Court held that school officials can conduct searches based upon "reasonable suspicion." (**Note:** T.L.O. stands for the identity of a juvenile.(However, the Court did not define "reasonable suspicion," and other courts have broadly interpreted the term. Reasonable suspicion, in this instance, is generally recognized as a standard not as demanding as "probable cause." However, reasonable suspicion must still be articulable, explainable, understandable by the "average" person and have some attachment to what is known as common sense. Indeed, while reasonable suspicion is far from being certain in scope and thus is not as demanding as probable cause guidelines, reasonable suspicion must consist of more than just a hunch, feeling, or thought. For example, a student may overhear others or observe others being involved with contraband; the student, acting as a concerned citizen, may report this information to a school official, who having no reason to think the student is lying, searches a suspect student's locker for contraband.

According to the courts, students have lesser protection under the Fourth Amendment (search and seizure provisions) of the United States Constitution while on school property, since school officials acting in the interest of societal interest need to maintain order, discipline, and safety. Further, students do not have the exclusive right to the use of lockers or desks, so no reasonable expectation of privacy exists. Additionally, lockers and desks are school property, and students have little Fourth Amendment protection from search and seizure of items stored there.

Under T.L.O., school officials may search students, as well as their lockers, clothing, possessions, and vehicles. Generally, searches must be based upon the "reasonable suspicion" standard set forth by the U.S. Supreme Court. However, if the school has a policy permitting random and unannounced searches, officials may conduct such searches if the policy is made available to students and their parents. This policy may be distributed to students and their parents through documents such as a "Code of Student Conduct" which frequently detail a school's policy on searches. Official school documents, such as student parking permit applications or locker assignment forms may include a waiver statement that the student must sign to receive these privilege. By signing these forms, the student acknowledges the search

policy and grants permission to school officials to conduct searches.

The results of many searches will be challenged and may lead to evidence suppression and/or possible civil suits. Thus, it is imperative that legal council be sought while developing and before implementing policies concerning the of searching students, personal belongings, lockers, desks, and vehicles parked on school grounds. SROs and school officials must have a clear understanding of search and seizure law as it pertains to searches on school property. For example, school administrators may conduct a search by applying reasonable suspicion; however, if this search is requested by law enforcement officials, the search may then revert to the higher probable cause standard. Finally, it must be understood that state law may be more restrictive than federal law; if so, officials must adhere to the more limiting state law requirements. Of course, the same concept applies to federal law; if federal law is more limiting than state law, federal law will supersede state law.

Further, school administrators must reach a clear understanding with the school district concerning the goal of searches. For example, is the purpose of the search to locate and remove dangerous weapons and contraband from school property or to make criminal cases? Typically, criminal cases will require more effort, resources, processes, legal council, and expense. In conclusion, the results of searches are often effective and all school safety/security programs should be supported by well designed and supported search and seizure programs. Of course, body searches should be performed only with strong, focused probable cause. It is imperative that personal dignity and privacy are maintained.

Without going into to much depth, there are some exceptions concerning the search warrant rule. Remember, search warrant rules apply to school resource officers who are not identified as school officials by the state. Exceptions include plain view, search incident to a lawful arrest, stop and frisk, vehicle inventory, consent to search, automobile searches, and miscellaneous circumstances. Plain view includes but may not be limited to the following: the officer must be at a location where he or she has a legal right to be; the discovery of the seized items must have been inadvertent; and the items seized must appear to be incriminating.

Search incident to a lawful arrest includes but may not be limited to the following: the arrest must be lawful and the search must concentrate on the suspect's person or be within the suspect's area of immediate control–also known as the lunge area. Stop and frisk includes but may not be limited to the following: when a police officer has reasonable suspicion that the person has been, is, or is about to become engaged in criminal activity; the peace officer must have a reasonable belief that the person is armed and dangerous; and the stop and frisk is focused on outer garments only in order to discover weapons which may injure the officer.

Vehicle inventory includes but may not be limited to the following: a matter of standard practice by a peace officer's department performed each and every time to maintain consistency; performed as a care taking policy indicating that the search is performed for the protection of the owner's personal property; as protection against false claims of theft lodged against officers; protection for the officer from unrecognized danger; and the procedure must not be used by the officer solely to discover evidence.

Consent to search includes but may not be limited to the following: must be freely and voluntarily given; based on the totality of the circumstances; the most critical

analyzation process will occur after the arrest has been made, and third party consent focusing on whether the third party has control over the premises or items to be searched. Automobile searches includes but may not be limited to the following: exigent circumstances such as probable cause to believe that the vehicle or containers located within the vehicle contain seizable items. Proactive search of the vehicle includes but may not be limited to the following: lawful stop of the vehicle; reasonable suspicion that the vehicle contains weapons, the search may extend to the passenger compartment.

Miscellaneous searches include but may not be limited to the following: fire scene searches with certain specifications; crime scene searches with exigent circumstances; inventory searches at jail which are custodial in nature; abandonment of property that has been voluntarily relinquished and has no expectation of privacy; canine search establishing probable cause. In conclusion, these rules are subject to constant interpretation and may vary from state to state so annual updates should be given to SROs by qualified instructors.

Interview and Interrogation

There is a difference between interviewing and interrogation. An interview concerns the process by which an official seeks, obtains, and evaluates information given to him by persons who have personal knowledge of an event or circumstances of a crime, accident, or other matters of official interest. An interrogation involves a process by which an official endeavors to obtain information about an event, crime, or accident from an individual who is suspect in that event, crime, or accident and is unwilling to provide that information. Miranda warning is required if an interrogation is custodial in nature. Thus, special care must be observed in order to keep the interrogation non-custodial. Every state has its own laws governing the interrogation of juveniles.

The purpose of an interview is to obtain facts, information and background in order to determine the truthfulness of a matter under investigation. Facts are items known and without question, for example, names, dates and locations. Information includes all other information gained from victims, witnesses and others possibly interested in the matter and background concerns finding out all pertinent information about an individual prior to the presentation of facts and related information.

There are four elements of consideration for conducting an interview: timing, setting, physical barriers, and preparation. Timing includes conducting the interview as soon as possible after the any incident. However, an official may delay questioning, if the juvenile is cold, sleepy, hungry, or otherwise physically uncomfortable. Emotional states may make a person an unsatisfactory subject to interview until a later date. The setting should include a private interview area. Familiarity of an area may be conducive in gaining cooperation and calm an emotional person.

Physical barriers include minimizing physical distance between the official and juvenile; however, personal space should not be violated. Officials should be aware of the arrangement of chairs if the interview is being conducted sitting down. Chairs may be inadvertently positioned in such a manner that open conversation will be uncomfortable. For example, when an official is positioned at one end of a table or on the other side of a desk and the juvenile is at the other end of the table or on the other side of a desk, the perception is one of domination which may negatively impact the free flow of information.

Finally, officials must be prepared to conduct the interview. As a general rule of thumb the following techniques may prove effective when interviewing juveniles. When contracted security guards, school resource officers, or school officials contact juveniles, it must be understood that they are not dealing with an adult. Thus, there are a number of techniques that must be employed in order to realize the most effective interpersonal communication efforts. These techniques will be broken down into positive actions and negative actions.

Positive actions include the following:
1. Treat the juvenile with consideration.
2. Be friendly, but firm.
3. Try to discover the student's problems.
4. Try to gain the student's confidence and respect.
5. Remember, the child of today is the adult of tomorrow.
6. Develop a positive attitude.
7. Encourage the student to do most of the talking.
8. Discuss a common interest.
9. Be a good listener.
10. Identify yourself properly.
11. Encourage the student to tell all of the facts.
12. Word questions to encourage more than a yes or no answer.
13. Give the student a chance to "save face."
14. Talk the student's language.
15. Compliment the student, be patient, and respect the student's personality.
16. Use humor occasionally.
17. Explain why information is necessary.
18. Encourage the student to participate in planning a future.
19. Be aware of what the student does not tell.
20. Encourage the student to clear up all offenses.
21. Let the student know of the contact's

long-term interest.

22. Express appreciation for settlement of an issue, and help the student to tell the truth in cases of neglect.

Treating a juvenile with consideration reflects what the juvenile thinks of the adult contact and the adult's subsequent conduct may influence the student's future attitude in favor of, or in opposition to, social and legal requirements. Be friendly; many juveniles feel that the world is against them. Further, many juveniles are discouraged and believe they are failures. Adult contacts cannot afford to let their own conduct further the development of an anti-social attitude in the student.

Be firm, appeal to the student's intelligence, reason, and sense of fairness. Discover the student's problems, if possible; the student's problems are very important and once they are identified, solutions may be found. Try to gain the student's confidence and respect when attempting to determine a student's role in any overt act. A student who hates the police officer or other authority figure because of the contact's abusive attitude will often, as an adult, have little respect for these positions in the future. Develop a positive attitude, displaying the benefits that come from an attitude of conformity with lawful and social requirements rather than dwelling on the harmful effects of anti-social behavior.

Encourage the student to do most of the talking. Discuss a common interest such as a sport or other activity in which the contact and student share interests. The discussion of a common interest may set the student at ease and generate an open dialog. Be a good listener; concentrate on the interview so that the student feels the contact is truly concerned. The contact should avoid turning his or her attention to any other person or detail while the interview is in progress.

The contact should properly identify his or herself, providing his or her name and rank so that the student knows exactly who the contact represents. This action often helps to put the interview on a person-to-person basis. Encourage the student to report all of the facts, the contact can help by letting the student know that nothing is shocking and that it is understood that there are many reasons why people get into difficult situations. Questions should be worded in such a manner that more than a yes or no answer is required. The more a contact can encourage the student to talk the more the contact can learn about the student and his or her accompanying problems.

Give the student a chance to save face, rather than point out that the student is lying. Give the student a chance to restate the facts. A review of the facts, as the contact knows them, can help the student admit their participation in the offense. Pointing out discrepancies can also help. Talk the student's language using simple expressions which can be easily understood. Avoid the use of technical terms or police jargon. Compliment the student; try to find something constructive to say about his or her conduct, appearance, or attitude. Everyone likes a sincere compliment and this should help the progress of the interview.

Be patient; don't expect to settle every matter in record time. Anticipate a certain amount of resistance and avoid pressing for the facts. It may give satisfaction to the student to frustrate the contact's efforts. Respect the students personality, treat them as a person with real worth, and avoid asking questions which the contact person his or herself would not want to answer. Use humor occasionally; humorous illustrations often ease pressure, especially if the contact person can say something funny about him or herself. Humor may overcome resistance the student is showing in the interview.

Leaving the room may also help as long as the contact person is certain of security measures.

Explain why the information is necessary; make it clear that there is a constructive purpose behind the questions and that the aim is to help plan the student's future better. Encourage the student's participation in planning his or her future. Get the student to think through possible plans for him or herself so that the student learns to be responsible for his or her own future. Students will tend to adjust well if they have a share in future plans. Be aware of what the student does not tell, the contact might learn of certain sensitive areas which the student avoids talking about but which are important in understanding the students problems. For example, the student not mentioning a certain member of the family may reveal hostility toward that person.

Encourage the student to clear up all offenses; once the student has admitted a present offense, it is often easy to get the student to talk about former offenses. If the student balks on this, it would be advisable not to press for the information since often-times the details will be revealed in later contacts with authority figures. Let the student know of the contact person's long-term interest; suggest that the contact person will be available for help in future years if required. Let the student know that the contact officer would like to see the student become a respected citizen.

Express appreciation for settlement of the problem, let the student know the contact officer is pleased with the student's cooperation in helping him or herself and the school administration in clearing up the complaint or problem. Help the student tell the truth in neglect cases. Many times in neglect cases, children have been advised what to say by their parents in order to protect the parents. A contact officer should be aware of the conflict a student faces when he or she is asked to tell the truth about negligent behavior in the home. The student's confidence must be won and the contact person must stress the fact that only by telling the truth can the parents be helped by agencies in the community. Finally, remember the student is a juvenile; don't expect an under-developed child to function as an adult.

Negative actions include the following: don't resort to vulgarity, profanity, or obscenity; don't brand the student; don't lose your temper; don't use physical force; don't lie to gain a point; and don't take notes immediately. Don't resort to vulgarity, profanity, or obscenity because, the use of such language by a contact person is especially reprehensible and should not be tolerated under any circumstances. Don't brand the student; epithets should never be used in reference to students in their presence or in the presence of their parents or relatives, or any of any other person. Nothing is to be gained by epithets, and there is a definite indication that it is very injurious to the student. Epithets often give rise to justified complaints and they are rightfully resented by the parents and other people. The use of epithets towards students is a reflection upon the character and intelligence of the contact person using them.

Contact personnel must not lose their temper–to do so is an admission of inferiority to the student being interviewed. Contact personnel must not use physical force; rough treatment does not gain respect but tends to develop greater hostility. If the contact person cannot settle the problem through accepted methods, he or she must be content to solve the problem at some later date or pass the situation on to another entity. Contact personnel must not lie to gain a point; sooner or later the lie may be discovered and the contact person will lose all of the students respect.

Finally, the contact person should not take notes immediately; instead, wait until the student feels comfortable and ready for the note-taking process. Students may freeze up when they see the contact person writing down statements from the very beginning. Note taking can be enhanced by having ample paper and writing materials available; not writing continually–this may detract from the communication process; writing down information easily forgotten–names, dates, addresses; and, if possible, allow the juvenile being interviewed to write his or her own statement.

There are six qualities necessary in a good interviewer. First, the interviewer should have a good personality, one which reflects confidence, sincerity, and alertness. Second, the interviewer should possess a breadth of interests, in other words, be able to discuss many different topics with a variety of people. Third, the interviewer should be an actor or be able to act a part. Fourth, the interviewer must be a salesman having the ability to sell him or herself to another person to gain his or her trust and confidence. Fifth, the interviewer must have the ability to remain in control of the interview and keep the discussion focused on the topic at hand. Finally, the interviewer must be pleasant.

Upon completion of an interview, the official should close the conversation in a courteous and friendly manner. The official may also wish to summarize the conversation. Finally, the official should let the juvenile know that his or her cooperation is appreciated. Of course, the information gathered must be evaluated. Evaluation may be conducted according to five criteria. First, is the information relevant to the issue at hand? Second, is the information related to all other known facts? Third, is the information source trustworthy and competent? Fourth, is the information accurate and verifiable? Finally, is the information potentially powerful enough to establish proof?

Defense-in-Depth

Of course, each measure described above should be designed and implemented in an effort to make the introduction of weapons and/or dangerous contraband onto school grounds as difficult as possible. These measures are called supporting policies because, if they are initiated as a stand alone policy, their effectiveness will be limited if not totally insignificant. For example, if a school administration focuses only on the adoption and construction of see-through lockers, weapons may be easily hidden in book-bags negating the see-through effect.

Referring to the defense-in-depth security concept addressed in the physical security portion of this book, an effective measure would be developed in the following manner. School officials may stagger reporting times to lessen foot traffic and accompanying mass interaction, activity would be physically monitored by school officials as students enter the school facility, closed circuit television (CCTVs) systems would monitor and record activity, personnel would monitor the CCTVs, school resource officers would be prepared to immediately respond to any incidents, students would be processed through metal detectors and all hand carried items would be inspected or see-through book-bags would be required, student property would be stored in see-through lockers, and random searches of school property would be conducted. The idea of a defense-in-depth process requires students to defeat a number of security measures in order to introduce a weapon into the school facility. Thus, the ultimate ideas is to make the introduction of weapons and/or dangerous contraband into any school facility so difficult that students will not even consider, much less attempt such a practice.

In conclusion, many of these proactive programs discussed above reportedly work best in school communities that:

1. Focus on academic achievement.
2. Involve families in meaningful ways.
3. Develop links to the community.
4. Emphasize positive relationships among students and staff and discuss safety issues openly.
5. Treat students with equal respect.
6. Create ways for students to share their concerns and help children feel safe expressing their feelings.
7. Develop and maintain in place systems for referring children who are suspected of being abused or neglected.
8. Offer extended day programs for children.
9. Promote good citizenship and character.
10. Identify problems and assess progress toward solutions.
11. Support students in making the transition to adult life and the workplace.
12. Finally, actively share information coupled with a quick, effective response designed to ensure that a school is safer and children are less troubled.

Attachment of Any Past Security/Safety Surveys

Please refer to chapter three of this book for a full explanation of the information contained in a security survey. If a school facility has not performed a security survey, the author recommends that one be completed, by a security professional, as soon as possible.

Attachment of Any Crisis Procedure Checklists

These checklists may include subjects such as "lock-down procedures," evacuation procedures, emergency notification lists, emergency operations center (EOC) or incident command system (ICS) involvement, and crisis aftermath procedures), etc. A school administrator may attach natural or technological emergency procedures to this portion of the response plan; however, these type plans are inadequate for school violence response situations. Granted, parts of these plans are valuable and should be used, but there are portions of a school violence response plan which will require different response actions.

For example, a school experiencing a violent attack such as an active shooter will require a police response that will require tactical actions such as cordon operations, scouting operations, tactical operations center (TOC) operation (this is totally different from an incident command center or emergency operations center), overwatch evacuation routes and accompanying rally points in order for innocent students to be screened for perpetrators, search and clear operations, neutralization of perpetrator(s), and subsequent criminal investigation.

Response Plan Exercise 1. Officer practicing containment operations.

Response Plan Exercise 2. Officers preparing to enter a school during an exercise.

Response Plan Exercise 3. Officers entering a school during an exercise.

Response Plan Exercise 4. Officers practicing negotiating a school hallway.

Response Plan Exercise 5. Officers moving in a quad formation during an exercise.

Response Plan Exercise 6. Student posing as an active shooter during an exercise.

Response Plan Exercise 7. Student posing as an active shooter, engaging police personnel during an exercise.

Response Plan Exercise 8. Teacher practicing a room evacuation during an exercise.

Response Plan Exercise 9. Students practicing a lockdown procedure during an exercise.

Response Plan Exercise 10. Officer entering a room during an exercise.

Response Plan Exercise 11. Officers challenging an active shooter during an exercise.

Response Plan Exercise 12. Officers completing an active shooter arrest during an exercise.

Lock-Downs

Lock-down, safe haven, or evacuation procedures are not as clear-cut as they seem. Indeed, these procedures are frequently emotional and dangerous events. School administrators are unlikely to understand that the situation they face during any school violence crisis is tactical. This is an important point because once a situation has turned tactical, solutions also become tactical. Tactical situations are often very fluid and tactical principles are also subject to change. Tactics must be flexible in nature and are always subject to change in a moment's notice. Tactics are chosen to fit the situation; the situation does not fit the tactics.

For example, if a violent action is occurring outside a school facility, it is probably wise to employ lock-down procedures in order to provide a barrier between the students, situation, and perpetrator. However, if a situation is occurring inside the school building itself, it may not be a good idea to lock-down students. A lock-down will fix students in place and provide numerous defenseless targets of opportunity for the perpetrator, plus there will be many more personnel for responding officers to assess while performing dangerous search and clear operations. Would it not be a better choice to evacuate students and personnel from the crisis area? The answer is dependent upon the tactical situation.

A freely moving perpetrator will endanger everyone in the school, while a fixed-in-place perpetrator will only endanger people in the immediate area. In the former situation, evacuation would probably be a good choice while the latter situation would probably require a lock-down. Of course, any tactical situation can be argued in many different ways which only verifies the concept that tactics and tactical responses must remain flexible in relation to rapidly changing tactical developments. Therefore, neither a lock-down or evacuation procedure should represent the sole decision of the responsible administrator. Furthermore, one procedure may come into play or both procedures may be applicable; for example, only part of the school may be locked down while the remainder of the school is evacuated.

Furthermore, evacuation and/or lock-down procedures must be carefully chosen in order to fully protect students and staff from harm. Indeed, it is critical that school administrators identify safe areas "safe havens—a form of lock-down" where students and faculty can go in a crisis situation. A safe haven is actually part lock-down and part evacuation. When implementing a safe haven procedure, students would actually leave the immediate area and proceed to an identified safe area. Many of these areas may actually be located inside the school in lieu of evacuating to outdoor areas. Several areas must be chosen as safe havens because a school violence situation may take place anywhere on the school campus. For example, according to the situation, an area normally considered safe may be subject to perpetrator access or weapons fire and therefore become unsafe.

Safe Havens

The best safe havens are solely dedicated to this purpose and are clearly identified and discussed with students and faculty. Safe havens should not be locked due to problems associated with key control. Safe havens can be protected from tampering through the use of plastic or paper seals (tamper indicating devices) and frequent status checks. If a seal is broken, a complete inventory of the safe haven should be performed. Of course, safe havens can be monitored through the use of security systems or frequently patrolled by the SRO. Some safe havens may be dual use and serve other purposes than just security needs.

At a minimum, any area designated a safe haven should have a telephone, emergency telephone numbers, a flashlight, and a lockable door. Safe havens should have a means of escape (ground floor doors, outdoor stairs, secondary ingress/egress doors, etc.). Safe havens should be located in areas that have natural choke points (stairs, hallways, channeled entrances, etc.). Choke points restrict free movement so these areas may be avoided by perpetrators. The idea is to choose a safe haven that provides students and faculty with the ability to move while outside choke points restrict the perpetrator's ability to maneuver.

If possible, safe havens should be stocked with emergency supplies and a disaster supply kit. These supplies should sustain faculty members and students for at least one day. If emergency supplies cannot be stored in a safe haven(s), these supplies should be stored in a sturdy, easy-to-carry container such as a backpack, duffel bag, or covered trash container. Disaster supply kits should include seven basic kinds of supplies, for example, water, food, first aid items, sanitation items, tools and accompanying supplies, bedding, and special items. Disaster supply kits can be protected from scavengers and/or pilferers through the use of plastic or paper seals (tamper indicating devices) and frequent status checks in the same manner as safe havens.

Water should be stored in plastic containers. Containers that will decompose or break should be avoided. Most people need to drink two quarts of water a day; of course, hot environments and/or intense physical activity can double that amount. As a general rule, store one gallon of water per-person-per-day. At least a one-day supply of non-perishable food should be stored. These foods should require no refrigeration, cooking, or other preparation, and little or no water. Food items should also be compact and lightweight.

A first aid kit should also be developed and stored in the classroom and/or safe haven. This kit should contain the following items:

Sterile assorted bandages in assorted sizes
Two-inch sterile gauze pads (8 or 12)
Three-inch sterile roller bandages (3 rolls)
Hypoallergenic adhesive tape
Scissors
Moistened towelettes (8-10 individual packages)
Tube of petroleum jelly or other lubricant
Bar of soap
Tongue blades and wooden applicator sticks
Latex gloves
Aspirin or non-aspirin pain reliever
Antiseptic or hydrogen peroxide
Three-inch sterile gauze pads (8 or 12)
Triangular bandages (3)
Two-inch sterile roller bandages (3 rolls)
Tweezers
Needle
Thermometer
Cleansing agent/soap
Antiseptic spray
Assorted sizes of safety pins
Basic first aid book
Eye wash
Rubbing alcohol

Sanitation items should include:
Toilet paper, towelettes
Plastic garbage bags and ties
Soap, liquid detergent
Feminine supplies
Plastic bucket with a tight lid
Household chlorine bleach

Tools and supplies should include:

Mess kits or paper cups, plates, and
plastic utensils
Flashlight and extra batteries
Fire extinguisher, small canister, ABC
type
Tape
Matches in a waterproof container
Plastic storage container
Paper, pencil
Medicine dropper
Plastic sheeting
Battery-operated radio and extra batteries
Non-electric can opener, utility knife
Pliers
Compass
Aluminum foil
Signal flare
Needles, thread
Whistle

Bedding should consist of one blanket or
sleeping bag per person.

Note: The first aid kit should be sealed
and periodically checked in the manner
discussed in the disaster supply kit section of
this book.

Students and faculty members must know
where safe havens are located and what
routes are safe to follow in order to reach
them. At least one staff member should
travel the route to the safe haven and quickly
check the safe haven to ensure the area is
clear of perpetrators and explosive devices.
Faculty members and students should then
travel to the safe haven. Next, staff members
should immediately account for their
students upon reaching the safe haven.
Faculty members should also check students
for injuries and render treatment as required.
This procedure will help responding
personnel avoid needless and dangerous
searches for missing persons. Trying to find
out where and how other students or faculty

members are can be the most stressful part
of a school violence crisis.

Faculty members should control the
students while occupying the safe haven.
The door to the safe haven should be locked
once all students are accounted for and
heavy objects should be used to reinforce the
door. Students should not be allowed to
wander around the room; they should be
instructed to remain on the floor, near a wall,
in a far corner away from the door. Faculty
members should place themselves between
the students and the safe haven's door. The
door should be under faculty observation at
all times. Faculty members should call 911 as
soon as possible and give a complete
location of the emergency (address, floor
and room number, city or town, nearest
cross street, and any helpful landmarks), give
your name and telephones number, describe
what happened, pass on how many people
need help and what is being done to assist
them, and finally, let the person on the other
end of the line hang up first.

Faculty members should also call the
police and tell them what is happening and
where, if anyone is injured, where the safe
haven is located, and give a complete
description of the perpetrator(s) (height,
weight, build, age, race, hair color, eye color,
clothing worn, weapon(s) number and type,
equipment carried, and a name(s) if known).
A checklist should be developed listing these
and other topics and this checklist should be
posted near the telephone. A procedure
should also be planned for getting school
facility keys into the hands of the police if
required (a complete set of keys should be
stored with the emergency crisis response
plan). However, if police officers request
keys, they may be thrown from a window to
responding units. To plan for this option,
keys should be placed on an oversize device
to avoid the possibility of losing them in the
dark or in high foliage. Faculty members or

students should not leave the safe haven to assist police with search and clear operations. **Faculty members or students should never pick up a weapon and approach the police!!!**

Faculty members and students should remain in the safe haven until physically contacted by police officers. Additionally, faculty members must remain calm, alert, aware of their surroundings, and avoid the mental state of denying that a school crisis event is occurring. The mental mind-set must be one of survival and winning a confrontation, not panic and defeat. Finally, all instructions issued by the police should be followed to the letter. Complying with these instructions will heighten the chances of a safe and successful conclusion to a very dangerous situation.

Indeed, personnel released from a safe haven by police officers who have entered the crisis site may be in shock or become hysterical. This is understandable and should be expected, especially if responding police officers are dressed in tactical gear including protective masks. Shock and hysteria may be more pronounced if officers have been shooting weapons and/or using distraction devices. Thus, released personnel may panic and perform reactions such as running for exits, trying to hide, or even physically attacking police officers themselves.

Officers will likely be prepared for such actions and perform the following actions: maintain visual and physical control of all suspects and personnel discovered in the crisis site, keep personnel in place, hands in sight, and call for support personnel backup (usually designated as snatch teams). These team members, as soon as possible, begin instituting a non-hostile authority by using calming techniques; being firm, showing anger or disrespect; showing understanding, but not being overly sympathetic; modeling calm behavior; reassuring personnel that everything is under control; repeating instructions as needed; ignoring nondisruptive emotional behavior, and using distractions such as focusing group attention on something or someone else.

When giving members of this group directions, police officers will likely order only one action at a time; use the shortest sentences possible; repeat directions frequently; give acknowledgment and encouragement when needed; and only a team leader will give directions while team members observe personnel to make sure all instructions are understood and followed. If personnel are to be moved under exigent circumstances (a chance of additional firing or the crisis site is not fully cleared), officers will likely take the following actions: keep in place all hand-held items until inspected by bomb squad and/or investigating officials; require each person to place his/her hand on the shoulder of the person to the front, for control purposes, and move in a single file until absolutely clear of any danger; maintain a calm but firm in-charge manner; ensure personnel take proper actions; give clear and concise instructions; use physical guidance, if necessary, especially for hysterical individuals or if subsequent gunfire erupts; and keep personnel reassured until the crisis site is cleared.

There will be a tendency for rescued personnel to rush to families or friends; however, people moved from the crisis site will often be directed to a prepared, secured, holding area. Support personnel (including female officers) should be preselected and standing by to perform the following actions: a professional body search looking for hidden weapons, masquerading active shooters, and body bombs; using prearranged code words or hand signals to alert other officers of any active shooters discovered among rescued personnel;

maintaining close observation; being alert for suspicious behavior; reassuring personnel that normal procedures are being followed; and being constantly prepared to deal with fear reactions or emotional hysterical behavior.

To prepare students and other school personnel for the possibility that a school violence situation could occur and that the above actions may be taken, information should be passed in a manner that will not frighten students. Steps that will enhance lock-down, safe haven, or evacuation procedures should be thoroughly discussed. The idea is to instill in each student and faculty member that the possibility of a school violence crisis is real while raising confidence in the chances of survival. Confidence in survival will be heightened as each student and faculty member learns the appropriate actions to take before, during, and after any school violence crisis.

In the aftermath of high-profile school violence incidents, there have been many scares. Students should understand what rumors are and their seriousness in terms of spreading fear and associated cost in terms of school discipline and legal consequences. Students should know that the school and law enforcement authorities have made plans to respond in the event of an emergency at the school. Students should also know that it is acceptable to tell on someone who has a weapon on school grounds in order to save lives. Indeed, it is vital to stress the importance of reporting the presence of a weapon to a responsible adult. Students should be instructed to report the following information concerning a student carrying a weapon: what the student was wearing; his or her name–if known; where the student was last seen; if he or she had the weapon out, threatening others; where the weapon was located; the type of weapon (knife, firearm, etc.); and what the person said.

Children are capable of relaying a great deal of detail when they are upset or mad at someone.

All faculty members should learn how to render basic first aid to include cardio-pulmonary resuscitation (CPR). Emergency telephone numbers should be posted near all telephones and all students should be taught how to effectively summon help in an emergency. For example, call 911, give a complete location of the emergency (address, floor and room number, city or town, nearest cross street, and any helpful landmarks), give your name and telephones number, describe what happened, pass on how many people need help and what is being done to assist them, and finally, let the person on the other end of the line hang up first.

Evacuation

The next task is to discuss with students and faculty members what steps to take in the event of an evacuation. Evacuation can be a frightening experience, knowing what to do can make the process safer and more efficient as well as reduce the fears and uncertainty of leaving. It is a good idea to develop an evacuation checklist in order to remember what to do during an evacuation. This checklist should include the steps to be taken and who is in charge of performing each step. The following items should be included, but this list should by no means be considered all-inclusive.

1. Answer how the children will be evacuated from the school in a safe and orderly manner.
2. Plan for transportation in case a full school evacuation requires completely leaving the school grounds. When transportation is assembled to transport students and school personnel away from school grounds, it should be

inspected for immediate security concerns law enforcement personnel should be assigned as security escorts. Transportation should be positioned in a manner designed to expedite a safe and rapid traffic flow. Drivers should have in their possession copies of evacuation routes and be familiar with them to include the destination. Students may be held inside the transportation conveyance unless other plans to safely secure them have been made. No vehicle should leave the school grounds unless a roll is performed and everyone is accounted for.

3. Each teacher should have a "grab and run" emergency kit that is designed to be as light as possible. The kit should include a class roster, emergency contact information, emergency medical information, small first aid kit, flashlight, and other items deemed necessary by the individual school.
4. A buddy system should be used by the students. If for any reason the students becomes separated from the main group, they will have someone looking out for them. The buddy system will often lessen or even prevent panic.
5. It is a good idea to designate at least two ways out of each room and/or building.
6. An area should be designated for assigned personnel to meet parents and explain the situation and if practical set up a procedure allowing parents to check students out.
7. All students and faculty members should listen to and follow all instructions issued by emergency officials.
8. Police officers will normally treat all evacuated personnel as suspects. This precaution is taken because active shooters may try to escape or even

attack people after they have mixed into the evacuating population. Thus, everyone who exits the scene will be directed to a safe area, frisked, separated, and perhaps handcuffed until a debriefing is performed (normally in a secure area).

In conclusion, the best way to develop evacuation or lock-down procedures is for school administrators to work with faculty members, students, police administers, and other emergency responders by participating in a number of mock school violence scenarios. Mock scenarios will often revel the best options to choose in a number of circumstances. The more mock scenarios that can be practiced, the higher the likelihood that an effective decision can be made in a real-world crisis. Furthermore, practice will help students and faculty to evacuate an area in safe and orderly manner. Students and faculty with knowledge and who are assigned responsibilities often feel less vulnerable or panicky during emergency situations. The central focus should be on the sharing of responsibilities and working together as a team.

Emergency Notification List

An emergency notification list is more stable and clear-cut than lock-down or evacuation decisions. Indeed, this is one area which can be directly pulled from a well-planned ICS procedure. Emergency notification lists should be in place so that in the event of an emergency, the assigned person(s) can go down a list notifying the needed agencies and personnel as designated. The emergency notification list should be structured in a hierarchal fashion. Of course, emergency responders should be listed and contacted first. Finally, the time of notification should be recorded next to the contact's name or agency instead of using a check mark or other symbol.

Incident Command System (ICS)

An Incident Command System (ICS) is the model for command, control, and coordination of a response and provides a means to coordinate the efforts of individual agencies as they work toward the common goal of stabilizing an incident and protecting life, property, and the environment. ICS is a sound program and federal law requires the use of ICS for response to HAZMAT incidents. Indeed, many states have adopted ICS principles for responding to all types of incidents. However, many administrators, both school and police, are overly dependent on incident command systems. This is a dangerous mistake in relation to a "real-time" school violence crisis. Consider the fact that incident command systems are time and information dependent, meaning, by the time a full blown ICS is operational, the perpetrators inside the school facility will be or have been free to commit any acts they originally planned.

Granted, ICS is valuable in the long term if situations continue over a period of time and when performing aftermath operations. However, an ICS will do nothing to stop perpetrators from continuing to kill students and school personnel. A well-planned school violence response plan implemented immediately upon notification that a school violence crisis is occurring will enable police officers to stop the violence.

Of course, parts of any existing ICS should be used when developing rapid response operating procedures for educational systems. The reader will find many of the elements of the ICS to be valuable. Some of the more important areas include the emergency operations center, incident command post, and staging areas.

Aftermath Checklist

Aftermath check lists should include such things as media releases, notification of parents, injury assessments, damage assessments, assisting with criminal investigations, debriefing students and school personnel, and getting the school back into operation.

Acquiring Response Planning Information

A final question often asked concerns information gathering processes: *Where do school administrators acquire response planning information?* Information gathering methods are diverse and unique to each location, but generally the methods consist of the following:

1. Reconnaissance and surveillance—administrators should observe the area of concern from as many angles and heights as possible. One view may reveal what another cannot. Air assets are valuable, if available. Administrators should make maximum use of photography, video, and sketches. Furthermore, the area should be observed at different periods of the day and night in order to record any significant changes such as vehicle traffic, pedestrian traffic, lighting conditions, etc.

2. Conversation—enter into general conversation with students; these personnel may see, hear, or know elements of essential information. Hotlines may also be established to gather this type of information. Also, converse with building managers, workers, custodians, etc... to verify and identify any school building weaknesses or unusual circumstances. It is

interesting to note that in most of the recent school tragedies, the shooters actually talked about their intentions to other schoolmates or associates.

3. Records–Personnel, medical, and school performance information should be developed into an information bank complete with updated photographs. A hot file may be developed concerning high risk students.

4. Documents–Analyze all notes and messages obtained during day-to-day school operations.

5. Maps, photographs, terrain models, and touring similar buildings. Procure maps of the immediate and surrounding area. Procure photographs, videos, and all other means of visual representation including photographs of the immediate and surrounding area. Procure floor plans of the school building and adjacent buildings. Question building managers, workers, custodians, etc... to verify floor plan accuracy. If possible, develop a three-dimensional model of the school site.

6. A professionally developed school site security survey will contain a great deal of essential information which can be easily assimilated into a school violence response plan.

Response Procedure Completion

The elements of essential information gathered by the different team members should be evaluated, compared, and ultimately compiled into one master response document. When complete, the leading school administrator should review the response document in order to ascertain effectiveness. An effective response document should be evaluated for workable format, completeness, and feasibility. **Note:**

The response document should then be filed in a known central location complete with facility keys. The response document may be useless when only one person knows the location or has sole access to the document.

The leading school administrator is also responsible for critiquing the end product, rendering assistance during information gathering efforts, and answering questions concerning the end product. The goal is to keep the information flow focused, efficient, and effective. Ultimately, the crisis response planning procedure should serve as a process for securing immediate external support from law enforcement officials and other relevant community agencies. All provisions and procedures will also require monitoring and review by the core developers and the lead administrator.

Characteristics of a Good Plan

A plan must be based on facts or, at the least, valid assumptions. If assumptions must be made, they should be checked out to make sure they are as close as possible to the actual situation. The plan must also provide an organizational structure and should clearly define the relationship between the various functions and fix the responsibility of who is to do what. To strengthen organizational structure, people should be assigned functions which are close to their day-to-day operations and existing work groups should be kept intact as much as possible.

Cumbersome words and long sentences should be avoided so the plan will not be misunderstood. Additionally, the various elements of the plan must be coordinated and fit together. Finally, a completed plan must be reviewed and revised as necessary. Indeed, there may not be agreement from everyone on every point. Thus, the CPO may have to serve as a negotiator between departments. If no agreement can be reached, the CPO will have to recommend a final course of action and present the plan to managing entities as required. The final page of any plan should contain signature blocks for all affected administrators and heads of entities to sign signifying they are all in agreement.

In conclusion, a plan is considered good if it provides for an organizational structure and offers a definite course of action to meet a school violence crisis. Finally, for any school violence crisis response plan to be effective, it must be evaluated for validity. Validity may be measured by testing methods designed to see if the plan will actually work. The most effective way to test a plan is by simulating a real school violence crisis in order to exercise responsible personnel and applicable procedures.

Response Plan Exercises

The most effective way to evaluate a plan and accompanying programs is to perform a dry run or exercise. An exercise will often identify strengths and weaknesses in any plan which can then be addressed, revamped, and/or corrected. Further, procedures can be modified or deleted as necessary. Finally, exercises provide personnel with specific emergency response assignments to understand and practice the exact duties they are expected to accomplish. The goal is to eliminate any confusion in the accomplishment of an assignment.

There are five different types of exercises that may be used to test a school violence crisis response plan. Each exercise is progressively more realistic, more stressful, more complex, and more difficult to conduct. Therefore, school systems should plan on exercising in successive steps—each building on the experience of the past exercise. These five exercises are designed to provide both individual training and

improve the response system as a whole.

The five types of exercises include orientation, drill, table-top, functional, and full-scale exercises. The orientation exercise is a preparatory training exercise that uses simulation materials to set the stage. This exercise is very low-key and is used as a building block to other, more difficult exercises. The second type of exercise, called a drill, is typically a single emergency response function targeting single agency involvement. This exercise is often used to evaluate a field component during a full-scale exercise. **Note:** For more information concerning a drill, see the description of a drill and full-scale exercise listed below.

The third type of exercise is called the table-top exercise. The characteristics of this exercise include low stress, little attention to time, lower level of preparation effort, and only rough attempts to simulate reality. The focus in these exercises is on training and familiarization with roles, procedures, responsibilities, and personalities working in the school violence crisis response system. The table-top exercise introduces participants to messages which simulate a realistic school violence event. It is to these messages that individuals respond with decisions. Thus, the table-top exercise serves the purpose of emphasizing the many problems associated with coordination among responding agencies.

The more advanced exercises include functional exercises and full-scale exercises. The functional exercise normally takes place inside a classroom or actual emergency operations center (EOC). This exercise involves complex simulation supported by various forms of message traffic (written, telephone, radio) and exhaustive attempts to recreate a realistic environment through simulation. Training is realized through the practice and testing of personnel and procedures under complex conditions which generate high stress levels that in turn evoke responses approximating a real school violence crisis, even though actual equipment and personnel are not physically operating. The functional exercise typically brings key personnel into the EOC to run through their decisions and responsibilities. This exercise tests the organization of the plan, its task assignments, and the liaison necessary among responding agencies. Conflicts in authority or responsibility often emerge in a functional exercise as do gaps in task assignments in the plan. These authority and responsibility conflicts plus gaps in task assignments can be identified and neutralized during the training exercise in lieu of an actual situation (authority and responsibility conflicts plus gaps in task assignments can easily result in additional death and destruction in a "real world" school violence crisis). In conclusion, the conducting of regular and periodic functional exercises should be a major goal for every school violence crisis response program.

A full-scale exercise typically combines a functional exercise with a drill in which field personnel, representing one or more responding emergency services, actually operate. The actual movement of equipment and personnel is important for emergency service organizations, but a drill alone does not suffice to test the school violence crisis response plan. Too often, agencies feel confident that they have tested their plan after running a drill. However, unless the EOC is activated and full interagency coordination has been exercised, there is no complete system test. Therefore, the goal of exercising should be to conduct a full-scale exercise to include EOC activation. Drills alone cannot substitute for simulation of emergency coordination—the most important task of the school violence crisis response manager.

Drills do serve a valuable purpose in support of a full-scale exercise. For example, before the conduct of a major exercise, the school violence crisis response manager or designated person should make certain that the plan calls for the alert of all the required personnel by conducting a notification drill. This drill consists of pretending that a school violence crisis has occurred and observing whether the correct people and agencies were notified at the proper time. This drill achieves the purpose of making certain the plan contains the proper information concerning roles and responsibilities. Of course, any of the annexes can also be tested in this manner by observing annex initiation, response, and effectiveness. Drills also enable the testing of specialized activities such as the EOC and communications equipment, to verify it is in working order.

Conducting Drills and Full-Scale Exercises

In order to conduct a drill and a full-scale exercise, a great deal of preparation activity will have to be made. Safety is paramount in the conduct of exercises involving firearms, explosives, chemical agents, pyrotechnics, vehicles, unarmed self-defense techniques, tactical individual movements, and tactical team movements. Collectively this material provides the essential ingredients for effectively planning and carrying out exercises designed to support training and evaluation efforts in a safe manner. Of course, the magnitude and scope of a particular scenario will determine the applicability of the following observations.

These observations will be broken down into the following headings: general safety, participant responsibilities, weapon safety, blank ammunition, pyrotechnics, vehicle safety, rules of engagement, explosives, pre-exercise briefing, command and control functions, controller/evaluator training, and concluding remarks.

General Safety

Safety rules must be followed to minimize the potential for accidents/incidents during exercises. Maximum effort should be made by management, controllers, and participants to anticipate and react to unsafe situations. As a matter of exercise policy, realism must be achieved and safety must be considered in the actions of all participating personnel. By integrating realistic safety requirements into exercise scenarios, safety application by participants is enhanced under both operational and exercise conditions.

All exercises must be governed by plans that specifically address safety issues while remaining consistent with realistic training. Safety plans should include procedures for any materials, equipment and/or operations which are identified as potential hazards during the conduct of a specific scenario. Preparations should also be made to react with appropriate levels of medical assistance to situations that could occur.

Exercises and related activities should be regulated by controllers who have final authority regarding safety matters. During an exercise, controllers are responsible for ensuring that operations are conducted safely. Controllers may stop exercise activity for safety or administrative reasons. Any individual may stop exercise activity for safety reasons.

Participant Responsibilities

Personnel acting as aggressors and response force operators must be briefed on their individual responsibilities, they include:

A. Avoid identified hazardous areas.
B. Monitor personal physical condition for signs of overexertion.
C. Render first aid and notify a controller if injuries or assistance is required.
D. Report injuries, no matter how slight, to the nearest controller or safety officer.
E. Handle and use all weapons in a safe manner.
F. Inspect weapons, equipment, and personnel to ensure that no live ammunition is present in the exercise area.
G. Limit physical contact during an arrest or physical control maneuver to searching and hand-cuffing, refraining from violent physical contact.
H. Refrain from attempts to disarm any individual by grabbing their weapon or person.
I. Ascending or descending from elevated positions by a ladder, stairway, or other safe method, jumping from elevated positions should be avoided.
J. Avoid hot propellant gasses vented from weapons.
K. No person acting in the role of a hostage may be physically abused.
L. All personnel occupying a target facility must be provided with appropriate safety equipment during assault phases.
M. Any damage to vehicles, equipment, or facilities must be reported to a controller by the end of the day's exercise.
N. Eliminated participants must immediately cease fire, movement, communication, and other actions, and remain in place until the exercise is terminated or the eliminated participant is released by a controller.

Weapons Safety

A. All weapons should be equipped with approved blank fire adapters or blast deflectors.

B. Exercise firearms should be inventoried by serial number and stored separately from live ammunition.

C. All exercise weapons, if possible, should be fitted with live round inhibiting devices to prevent the accidental introduction of live rounds.

D. All exercise weapons must be inspected at the beginning of each scenario, clearly marked as an exercise weapon, closely controlled, and kept separate from any weapon not associated with the exercise.

E. Exercise weapons should not be loaded until authorized by an exercise controller.

F. Blank firing weapons are to be fired only at participants who are at least 10 feet away from the weapons muzzle.

Blank Ammunition and Blank Fire Adapters

A. Only blank ammunition magazines, clips, and belts that have been distinctively color-coded and modified to inhibit live rounds may be used.

B. Blank ammunition must be stored separately from live ammunition and inspected prior to issue by an exercise controller.

C. Prior to each exercise and each scenario, participants must inspect their weapons and person to ensure that only blank ammunition and marked exercise weapons are in use.

D. Prior to each exercise and each scenario, designated controllers must inspect exercise weapons and all ammunition to ensure that only blank ammunition and marked exercise weapons are in use.

Hand Thrown Pyrotechnics, Distraction Devices, and Chemical Agents

A. Participants should never pick up thrown pyrotechnics, distraction devices, or chemical agents. Duds should be reported as soon as possible to the controller.

B. Duds must be handled by following the manufacturer's disposal recommendations or site-approved procedures implemented by properly trained personnel.

C. Pyrotechnic devices may be used only in areas identified as safe in the exercise plan.

D. When pyrotechnic devices are authorized for use in an exercise, appropriate fire fighting equipment must be readily available.

E. Participants who will be using pyrotechnics, distraction devices, chemical agents, or other hazardous materials must have appropriate training.

F. A chemical agent decontamination area and method (natural, passive, or active) should be set up and organized to facilitate the decontamination of personnel suffering from chemical agent exposure.

Vehicle Safety

A. Only specifically designated vehicles may be used by the participants during an exercise.

B. Vehicles may only be mounted or dismounted after they have come to a complete stop.

C. All personnel in moving vehicles

equipped with seat belts must wear seat belts at all times. Personnel in the open back of moving vehicles must remain seated within the body of the vehicle.

D. Vehicles may only be driven within posted speed limits and in accordance with safe driving rules.

E. Vehicles may not be used to crash, block, or endanger another vehicle in any way.

F. Vehicles may not be used to chase down personnel.

G. Vehicle must be turned off, placed in park, and the emergency brake set, prior to the driver departing the vehicle.

H. All non-exercise vehicles will be conspicuously identified, and the identification methods will be included in participant briefings.

Rules of Engagement

Specific rules of engagement should be developed and documented for each exercise. Typical rules of engagement focus on halting the exercise. An exercise may be halted at any time for safety, emergency, or administrative reasons.

A. **Exercise Freeze**: An Exercise Freeze is a command that is used to halt an exercise when it is necessary to correct safety-related problems or respond to a "real world" emergency. Any person observing a life-threatening safety problem should announce "Exercise Freeze." Controllers should relay the "Exercise Freeze" announcement throughout the exercise area and on the radio net. Every participant must immediately freeze in place (i.e., stop at their locations and cease fire, movement, communication, and other related actions) until the command "Resume Exercise" is given by the controller. A code word may be designated to serve as the order to freeze the exercise.

B. **Administrative Hold**: An Administrative Hold is a command used to halt an exercise when it is necessary to correct exercise problems of an administrative or procedural nature. The effect of an "Administrative Hold" will normally be limited to specific locations rather than the entire exercise. The command "Administrative Hold" will not be used to correct safety problems or respond to emergencies. Only a controller can administratively halt exercise activities. The controller will announce the hold in the affected area and all participant activity in that area will immediately halt until the controller give the command "Resume Exercise."

Explosives

A. Organizations handling explosives must provide safe operating procedures to the Safety Staff. These procedures will identify the hazards, assess the risks, and establish the necessary safeguards for the particular operation.

B. Explosives will only be authorized for use by tactical units who are thoroughly trained in the use of such devices, and in applicable safety requirements.

C. The quantities of explosives used will require review and preapproval by the Senior Controller and Senior Safety Officer.

Pre-exercise Briefing

The following example is not meant to be all-inclusive for every scenario. Briefings should be tailored to specific exercises and to the participants. Specialized briefings may be necessary to ensure selected participants are aware of detailed information and/or requirements pertaining to a specific event or role. Responsible personnel must ensure that participants are provided these briefings.

A. Scenario
B. Assignments and Responsibilities
C. Communications Requirements, Procedures, and Methods
D. Safety
   1. Controllers
   2. Safety Officers
   3. Participants
   4. Equipment, Weapons, Ammunition, etc.
   5. Vehicles
   6. Risk Assessment Reports, Hazards, and Mitigating Controls
   7. Actions to Be Taken in the Event of Emergency
E. Questions and Answers
F. Identify the Number of Scenarios to Be Conducted
G. Establish Pass/Fail Criteria
H. Exercise Control Measures
   1. Exercise Control Chain of Command
   2. Describe Controller Responsibilities Specific to the Scenario
   3. Describe Non-Participant Control
   4. Describe Exercise and Emergency Communications Systems
   5. Describe Accountability and Control of Weapons and Ammunition
I. Identify Required Supplies
J. Safety/Health Issues
K. Training Requirements
L. Exercise Coordination Requirements
   1. Emergency Medical Personnel
   2. Fire Department
M. Compensatory Measures
   1. Safe Exercise Halt Procedures
   2. Emergency Response into an Exercise Area
   3. Weather
   4. End of Exercise Accountability (personnel, weapons, ammunition, and equipment)
N. Coordination and Approval
   1. Site Specific Control Authority
   2. Facility Authority
   3. Environment, Safety and Health

Command and Control

A system of command and control is necessary to maintain an environment free of the recognized hazards associated with major drills/full-scale exercises and performance tests. The command and control system helps to ensure that rules of engagement are followed, specific hazards and safety concerns are appropriately addressed, and exercise continuity is maintained. The chain of command is as follows:

A. Exercise Director: Responsible for assuring that all appropriate safety measures are in place prior to the start of the exercise and during scenarios, plus has the final authority for exercise halts due to potential safety problems.
B. Senior Controller: Reports directly to the exercise director and is responsible for coordinating, establishing, and supervising the exercise controller staff; identifying the number of personnel required to control the exercise; ensuring that appropriate controller training is conducted and developing and implementing the concept of operation for

the exercise director.

C. Controller: The controller staff must be organized in a manner that facilitates the control of all affected locations and the control and coordination of all events to be initiated during the exercise. Individual controllers may have several duties assigned depending on where they are and what activities are occurring in their areas of responsibility. Their first and foremost responsibility is ensuring safety during exercise activity. This includes ensuring that all participants adhere to the safety procedures and rules of engagement. In most cases, the event controllers at a particular exercise location will be the only personnel watching for potentially hazardous situations during the exercise and they must be prepared to take prompt action to prevent accidents or unsafe conditions. In the event these situations develop, controllers take action in accordance with established safety procedures. Personnel assigned as controllers are responsible for enforcing or implementing the following general requirements during exercise:

1. Conducting safety checks and inspection of all personnel under their control for live rounds, prohibited articles, and general safety, and reporting the results to the senior controller prior to the beginning of the exercise.

2. Ensuring no live firearms or ammunition of any type are allowed within the exercise area.

3. Ensuring exercise participants wear appropriate safety equipment.

4. Ensuring that personnel under their control comply with the exercise plan to include the rules of engagement and the safety regulations.

5. Stopping a specific activity or the entire exercise if unsafe conditions or acts are observed.

6. Ensuring the accountability of personnel and equipment at the termination of the exercise, and reporting the results to the senior controller.

D. Safety Controller: The safety controller is responsible for assessing the exercise plan, conducting walk-downs of the exercise area, and conducting safety briefings which specify the rules of engagement, medical response, munitions and weapons safety, and vehicle and personnel safety. The safety controller reports to the senior controller and should remain in contact with the senior controller at all times during the exercise. In addition, the safety controller:

1. Assists the senior controller in the development and conduct of pre-exercise controller training.

2. Ensures that adequate safety walk-downs are conducted to determine site suitability prior to the exercise.

3. Conducts a safety walk-down with the exercise director, senior director, event controllers, and other selected controllers prior to the exercise.

4. Ensures emergency medical and fire protection services will be present or on call for the duration of the exercise.

5. Establishes high speed avenues of ingress and egress to facilitate the movement of medical personnel.

E. Event Controllers: Event controllers report to the senior controller and are responsible for executing control over specific categories of exercise activity including one or more exercise events. Event controllers are responsible for ensuring that non-participating facility personnel in the exercise area are aware that an exercise is to be conducted and that they are not to interfere with the flow of the exercise. Event Controllers must ensure that all exercise participants under their control:

1. Are aware of procedures for halting an exercise for safety reasons or an actual emergency.
2. Are not in possession of any live weapons or ammunition.
3. Are fully trained and qualified if programmed to deploy hand-thrown pyrotechnics, distraction devices, explosives, and/or chemical agents.
4. Are instructed that if distraction devices are used, that they are not to be thrown within 50 feet of personnel in open areas or into occupied areas or rooms.

F. Special Controllers: In those exercises involving special weapons, explosives, pyrotechnics, rappelling, etc., the exercise plan should specially designate controllers for the special activity. Special controllers are responsible for ensuring that the following safety requirements are implemented, as applicable to their assigned area of involvement:

1. All exercise participants are fully trained and provided with specific instructions on the hazards of special weapons, explosives, and other similar devices prior to the exercise.
2. Distraction devices are not to be thrown within 50 feet of personnel in open areas or into occupied areas or rooms.
3. All explosive simulators are

returned to their point of issue at the conclusion of the exercise activity.

Controller/Evaluator Training

The command and control system is dependent on a contingent of personnel selected and specifically trained to control drills and full-scale exercises. In addition to being trained to oversee exercises, controllers must receive training commensurate with the scope, complexity, and special nature of the activity. Based on the nature and complexity of the exercise, specific controllers may be required for special or high-risk activities. Training should focus on formal and scenario specific aspects. Formal training should include the following topics:

1. Controllers/Evaluator
   a. Purpose
   b. Responsibilities
   c. Duties
2. General Knowledge
   a. Equipment/Pyrotechnics
   b. Safety
      1. Firearms
      2. Vehicle Use
      3. Participants
      4. Environment, Safety and Health
      5. Medical
3. Exercise Plans
   a. Schedule
   b. Scenarios and Variables
   c. Participant Actions
   d. Controller/Evaluator Actions
   e. Role Player Actions
   f. Suspension/Resumption/Termination
   g. Rules of Engagement
   h. Communications
   i. Administration

Scenario Specific Training should include the following:

1. Briefing on tasks and responsibilities.

Brief on the specific tasks and responsibilities prior to exercise initiation.

2. Rules of engagement. Brief each controller on the procedure for the following: exercise freeze, administrative hold, rules of engagement for participants, vehicle safety, explosives, weapons and ammunition, distraction devices, pyrotechnics, general safety, and actual emergencies.

3. Documentation. Describe and demonstrate the desired method for recording information concerning the events that transpire during the exercise. Describe required reports.

4. Simulation/Artificialities. Describe planned simulations/artificialities; how they will affect the exercise; when they will be injected; and the procedures for formulating and introducing other simulations/artificialities, as needed, after exercise initiation.

5. Transportation arrangements. Describe how controllers, exercise participants, data collectors, and visitors are transported to the exercise location.

6. After-action meeting. Describe the purpose of the after-action meeting; the information that should be brought to the meeting; and the location of the meeting.

7. Equipment. Describe the location of the issue and turn-in of equipment, accountability measures, and detailed instructions on the equipment required for each controller during the exercise.

8. Radio usage and call signs. Provide a detailed description and demonstration of the radios the controllers operate during the exercise. Explain the importance of operating only on the channel and frequency specified in the communications plan.

9. Route familiarization and exercise site. Provide each controller with a map depicting the route of the exercise site and walk-down the exercise site with all controllers as necessary.

10. Emergency procedures. Review and provide all controllers with a copy of exercise emergency procedures.

11. Information protection. Review the guidelines for information control and established policies and procedures for the protection of exercise related information.

12. Controller identification. Describe how controllers will be identified and demonstrate the proper method of donning and wearing any apparel to be used for identification purposes.

13. Non-player/observer identification. Describe how non-players or observers will be identified and demonstrate the proper method of donning and wearing any apparel to be used for identification purposes.

14. Controller meetings. Provide directions to and scheduled time for any controller meetings.

15. Scenarios scripts. Participants must stay faithful to scenario scripts or be ejected from the exercise by the controller.

In conclusion, full-scale exercises must be conducted with the highest regard for the safety and health of personnel, protection of the environment, and the protection of property. Safety issues must be considered from the inception of any exercise to the completion of a scenario. Furthermore, planners should conduct a test of all or part of the school violence crisis response plan. Planners should take notes as the test is in progress and pay particular attention to what went as expected and what went wrong. A review should be held after the test to discuss the outcome, and the plan should be modified as necessary. Additionally, exercises should not be "one-shot" efforts; rather, exercises should be an integral part of improving each school violence crisis response plan. Finally, advanced exercises, especially full-scale exercise, should not be attempted until all participants and agencies have participated in the more basic exercises and drills. The surest way to fail the test of any plan is to attempt to launch a full-scale exercise with insufficient practice of basic exercises and drills.

Concluding Remarks

In conclusion, once the school violence crisis response plan has been completed and tested, everyone in the community should be informed. This is an excellent time to begin a full public information push concerning school violence and accompanying programs. It is also an excellent time to do a little promotion within the school system. School administrators should use the completion of the plan as an opportunity to renew contacts with other agency officials, volunteer groups, parents, and the public. The information shared with different groups will depend upon the type of group, their role in the plan, and their stated interest in the plan. There are several ways to inform people about the plan. Examples include the local news media (radio, television, and newspapers), speaking to local community groups such as the PTA, and the dissemination of brochures (the boy scouts, girl scouts, or adult civic groups could distribute these brochures). The idea is to have a well-informed and active community involved in the identification, intervention, and response efforts designed to counter school violence.

Chapter 5

TACTICAL CONSIDERATIONS

The purpose of this chapter is to focus on some information and tactics which have been used or will likely be used when responding to school violence crisis situations. Reading this information will help school officials to understand some of the reasons why law enforcement entities perform certain actions. This information will also assist law enforcement officials to develop new skills or perhaps refine dated skills.

Concealed or Disguised Weapons

Illegal prohibited articles may be difficult to identify. Indeed, since the 1950s, the marketing of concealed and/or disguised weapons has blossomed, and designs have been copied at an enormous rate. These weapons are turning up on many American street corners and will increasingly find their way into school campus areas. Concealed weapons are manufactured in all sizes and shapes, thus the following list of descriptions is not intended to be all-inclusive. Some of these deadly devices are fabricated (there are numerous publications available to the public which provide detailed descriptions of how to construct concealed/disguised weapons) for sale on the black market; fabricated in home workshops for personal use; and/or sold through specialty magazines and at flea markets. Many of these devices are advertised as self-defense tools and are shipped directly to the buyer's residence with few or no restrictions on the purchase. Numerous novelty shops are also currently selling these items. Finally, some of these devices are of high-quality and expensive; others are of poor quality and inexpensive.

The following list is compiled to serve as a guide to familiarize security officers, SROs, and school officials with the types of concealed/disguised weapons typically encountered on the street. The first device, the executive ink pen, looks and works like an ordinary pen. However, this pen pulls apart to reveal a blade approximately 2 $\frac{1}{2}$ inches long. These pens are normally painted black or silver. Another device disguised as an ink pen is called the "Executive Protection." This device is a 360-degree pivot, one handle Balisong type knife. The Executive Protection is .50 inches in diameter, has a 2.85-inch long blade, is 5.50 inches long when closed, and 8.50 inches long when opened. This knife comes in the following colors: black, blue, burgundy, silver, or gold. Finally, some pens do not conceal edged implements, but are actually disguised tear gas dispensers, for example, the tear gas pen. This device is a 5 $\frac{1}{2}$-inch long pen and contains a 10 percent formula of Oleoresin Capsicum (OC). The effective range is approximately 12 feet.

There are a number of knives disguised as harmless devices. For example, the bracelet knife is pulled apart to reveal a thin 1-inch blade. Another device, the sword umbrella, is made from a telescoping umbrella that has been modified to conceal a 10-inch blade complete with a sturdy fiberglass handle. The blade is housed in an undetachable sheath located inside the base of the umbrella. The belt buckle knife is a clever device which houses a 3-inch double edged knife in what appears to be an ordinary belt buckle. The blade can be quickly detached without loosening the belt. Some models contain a knife hidden in a built-in sheath. Another device, the comb knife, is an 8 $1/4$-inch, fully functional comb that snaps apart to reveal a 3-inch blade. These combs are available in a number of colors. The walking cane sword is a clever device used to house are a number of different sized blades. Approximately 36 inches overall, they typically offer either one sword blade or a combination of a long blade and a shorter dagger-type blade fitted in the handle. These devices are available in black lacquer or a mahogany finish.

Another edged weapon, a common necklace type knife, is called the cross knife. The cross knife contains a 1 inch long x $1/2$ inch wide blade. Furthermore, some knives are disguised as the common key. The key knife is approximately 1 $1/2$ inches in length and $1/2$ inch wide. These devices are commonly attached to key chains and may be easily overlooked. There are also credit card knives which are approximately twice the thickness of a normal credit card. These devices house a retractable 2-inch long by 2-inch wide blade and are easily concealed in a wallet or purse.

An additional device, the lipstick knife, is a cleverly disguised 1 $1/2$-inch knife housed inside an aluminum lipstick tube. This device is available in a number of different colors; the blade is extracted by twisting the tube's base. A final device used to conceal edged implements is the hollow wrist watch. This device is not a weapon in itself but can be used to conceal weapons. These units consist of a leather or nylon wristband and a molded plastic watch face that opens to reveal a hollow compartment large enough to conceal two standard razor blades.

There are also a number of plastic weapons readily available on the open market. These devices are actually made from fiberglass-filled nylon or other space-age plastics. These devices include plastic knives, the devils dart, etc. Plastic weapons typically do not have great slashing and cutting power; however, they do have incredible penetrating capabilities. Thus, users adopt plunging type attacks. These devices usually weigh less than one ounce, are very tough, and won't register during metal detection efforts.

Beepers and pagers are known to be used to be a disguised weapon or hide weapons. One device looks like a personal beeper/pager but is actually a pepper spray (Oleoresin Capsicum) device. This pepper spray pager is the same size as a personal beeper/pager and may be attached anywhere a conventional pager would be placed. The pepper spray pager contains a 10 percent formula of Oleoresin Capsicum and has a range of approximately 10 feet. An additional device that uses a pager as a disguise is not a weapon itself; however, this hollow pager shell is capable of concealing a small firearm inside the cavity. When in use, the case pops open and hinges downward at the press of a button allowing instant draw of the weapon. Another variation of this device includes a hollow pager case that houses a small handgun which is fired while contained in the pager case by pressing an externally positioned firing button.

Many devices are disguised firearms; for example, the cigarette lighter gun is made from a traditional Zippo type lighter. This weapon is capable of firing a .22 caliber round by opening the lighter's cover and applying pressure to a firing mechanism located in the base of the lighter. Another disguised firearm, the tire gauge gun, appears to be an ordinary tire gauge. This spring-loaded weapon is capable of firing a .22 or .25 caliber round when a striker is pulled to the rear and released.

Some disguised firearms such as the bolt gun resemble a normal piece of hardware but are capable of firing a .25 caliber round. The bolt gun is fired by pointing the threaded end of the bolt toward the intended target, pulling rearward on the spring-loaded bolt head and releasing the bolt head which moves forward firing the round. Another disguised firearm, the pen gun, is available

in numerous calibers—the two most common being the .22 or .25 caliber. These devices are available in a variety of designs and many display quality machine work. Pen guns are spring-loaded, thus the operator points the device at the intended target, pulls back on a cocking knob which is in turn releases driving the firing mechanism forward, firing the round.

Stun guns may also be discovered at entry control points. These devices are usually easily recognized; however, one device, the stun gun umbrella, is not so obvious. The stun gun umbrella resembles an ordinary collapsible umbrella measuring approximately 18 $\frac{1}{2}$ inches overall. This device is capable of delivering approximately 80,000 volts.

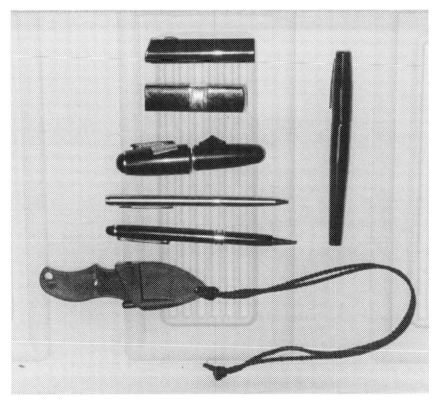

Figure 34. Concealed weapons—closed.

The Knife Wielder

Probably more people are carrying knives or other edged weapons today than at any time in history. Attacks by knife-wielding subjects are becoming more common. Even though firearms and explosives receive the most publicity, the primary weapon in school violence is the edged weapon. Security officers or SROs should not judge knives in relation to their small size. A dedicated wielder using the element of surprise can cause serious injury or death by attacking a victims eyes, face, and throat area. Indeed, it is amazing what damage even a small 2-inch blade can do to human flesh. A small knife can be hidden easily and can be used to penetrate an artery before the victim realizes what has happened. A small knife can be manipulated in the hand with ease and can be used in a wide variety of ways by an attacker. Make no mistake; any edged weapon can be used to kill.

However, many security officers and/or SROs do not respect or realize a knife wielders capabilities, know their tactics, or understand their intent. This section will cover these points so the reader will know to beware of the knife wielder. The knife is one of the most vicious weapons available and is used in a staggering number of homicides and assaults. Once a knife attack begins, it is almost impossible to stop without sustaining injury. Most people attacked by a knife wielder won't even know a knife was involved until after the fact.

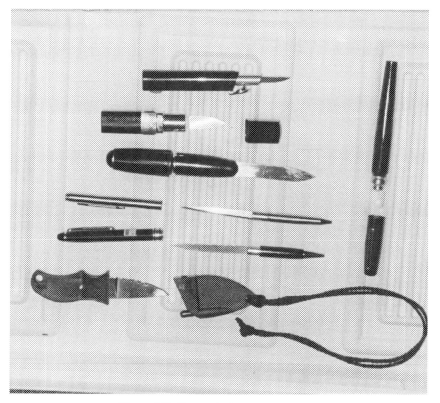

Figure 35. Concealed weapons–open.

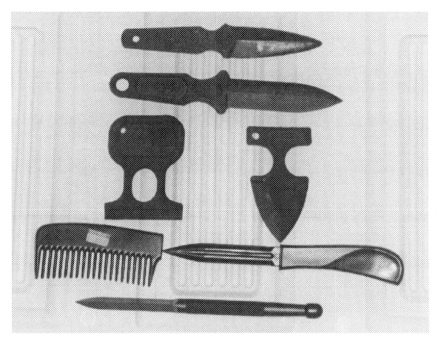

Figure 36. Space-age, plastic-edged weapons.

Figure 37. Concealment containers–closed.

Figure 38. Concealment containers–open.

The knife wielder may possess no training or skill and still inflict serious injury or kill. Normally, all that is required is a series of rapid slashes or thrusting motions. Officers should never evaluate the knife wielder capabilities due to stance, appearance, or grip on the knife. A trained knife wielder will use surprise, stealth, aggressiveness, and ruthlessness to devastating effect. He will usually slash repeatedly with the intent to rupture arteries, sever nerves, and destroy tendons. His goal is to injure or destroy life-sustaining organs and to incapacitate his victim quickly.

Many knife wielders learn knife fighting techniques from street fighting experiences, martial arts schools, and other formal or informal schools. There is an abundant amount of schools that teach knife fighting–some good, some bad. Furthermore, school children may acquire knives with little or no restriction and learn to use these knives by purchasing and watching videotapes extending distance learning instruction on the deadly use of knives and other edged weapons. There are also a variety of ways knife wielders grip knifes; the two most common are the straight grip and the back hand. The straight grip involves grasping the knife by the handle with the blade tip pointing away from the attacker. Slashing may be accomplished from this grip, but plunging is more likely. The back hand grip involves grasping the knife by the handle with the blade pointing toward the attacker and is usually hidden behind the inside of the forearm. Slashing is very comfortable from this position and it lends itself well to speed and power. Stabbing can still be accomplished from this position as well. Whichever grip is used, the knife wielder will often conceal the knife behind his body or an object until it's time to strike. This is why in any type of possible physical confrontation, the adversary's hands must always be watched.

Stabbing or plunging targets include the solar plexus, abdomen, bladder, kidneys, and clavicle artery, all targeted in an effort to destroy vital organs. Stabbing in these areas avoids the body's protective chest and rib bones. Slashing targets include the neck, forehead, inside the arms, inside the thighs, stomach, pelvic area, and chest. The goal is to sever arteries causing the victim to bleed out, to cut tendons and muscles to disable the victim, or in the case of the forehead, strike to blind the victim through profuse bleeding. A quick cut not delivered with full slash momentum is often called a flick. The flick is designed to cut the hands, knuckles, fingers, forearms, etc. of an officer fending off a knife attacker by using his or her hands and arms for protection. The goal is to cause the defending person to drop his or her arms and uncover vital organs.

A trained knife wielder may also be adept at throwing his knife accurately up to sixteen feet or more. The trained knife thrower will usually carry anywhere from three to six knives. This assailant will not normally throw his one and only knife. Also, security officers or SROs should not expect the knife thrower to remain stationary, they practice throwing while moving forward, backward, laterally and diagonally. The knife may be thrown handle first, blade first, overhand, underhand, weak hand, backhand, or sidearm.

A knife thrown with only moderate force can be buried up to the handle in a person's breast bone. Even if the knife only penetrates an inch or two, massive injury and blood loss are likely. The knife doesn't even have to penetrate to cause severe injury. Upon impact, the knife will start to penetrate causing an initial incision and puncture wound. As the knife ricochets off a bone, the knife will often continue to cut in a twisting, turning, or sliding motion. Each knife has its own wound signature due to balance, mass, weight, and blade design. Once the assailant has thrown a knife, he will either disengage, throw another, or close the distance to continue the attack.

Regardless of the type and size of the knife, all are deadly, if used properly. Many people have the misconception that the attacker's knife will be a fixed blade hunting, chopping, carving, fighting, military, switch-blade, or exotic type. Far more prevalent are the folding types due to their ease of carry and concealability. Indeed, extremely large folding knives are easily carried and con-cealed. Further, folding knives are so common place that they normally never attract attention when seen by the public.

When a security officer or SRO encounters a knife wielder, he or she should maintain distance: remember, a person can cover seven feet in approximately two paces or in about one second! A forty yard dash can be completed by a great many people within six seconds. Do not crowd a knife wielder! The tactic for the security officer or SRO involved in a knife attack is to disengage and gain distance, if possible.

If a safe distance or disengagement is impossible, the security officer or SRO must be mentally prepared to sustain a cut(s). This mind set will help the officer deal with the enormous psychological effect that profuse bleeding causes. The officer must try to protect his or her torso with his or her hands and outer arms if no other defensive or offensive device or technique exists. The officer must convince him or herself that he or she will survive. Defending oneself from a knife wielder requires specific training in controlling the knife, stunning the attacker, grounding the attacker, and disarming him if possible. An officer may seek knife defense training taught by police academies, martial artists, or personal defense companies.

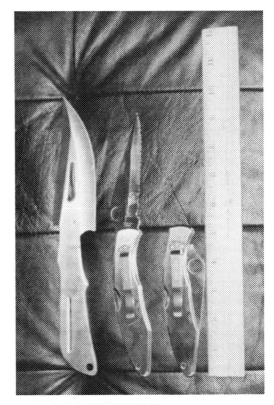

Figure 39. Knives.

Concealed Carry Methods

Concealed weapons can be hidden virtually anywhere; for example, behind/inside the sweatband of hats or the underside of the brim; front and back surface of the neckline; held in place by a holster, cord, or decorative chain to dangle down the back or the center of the chest; in folds of the skin and overhanging masses in obese subjects.

Additional concealment locations include the belt line–inside the waistband, attached to a belt, on the underside of belts or belt loops, and inside, on, or behind belt buckles; wrists–all surfaces can be used with rubber bands, elastic bands, velcro strips, or tape; ankles–again, all surfaces can be used, inside socks, inside shoes, boots, or other types of footwear; jackets–inside internal or external pockets, inside front panels, inside sleeves or down the back; pants–pockets, groin/anal area, along the inside of the leg, items may also be sewn inside belt loops in the middle of the back; and packages–internal and external compartments, between hidden dividers, and inside hidden compartments. Finally, males most commonly attach items to the waistline, hide items in pockets the groin or ankle area, and/or hide items in brief cases or fanny packs. Females commonly hide items in pockets, bras, purses, and other types of handbags.

Thus, when officers employ security scanning devices, physical search techniques, or approach suspicious individuals, great care must be taken to watch for any movements involving the person's hands. Officers must be aware of the inventiveness and deceptiveness of the modern criminal. Thus, caution must be practiced with every item found on a suspicious person. Close examination of seemingly harmless items may appear unorthodox, but may save the lives of school residents.

Free Carry

This is probably the least desirable way to carry a concealed weapon. To use this technique, the person either sticks the handgun in their waist band or a pocket without a holster. While sticking in the waist band, the firearm is not secure and may fall down into the pants or out onto the ground, during the wearer's normal range of movement. While carried in a pocket, the handgun will be slow to draw (the grip may have moved into an inconvenient position; the pocket may be to tight for easy access to the weapon, and the weapon may be prone to printing). People may try to avoid printing by placing a handkerchief between the weapon and the outer material; however, the

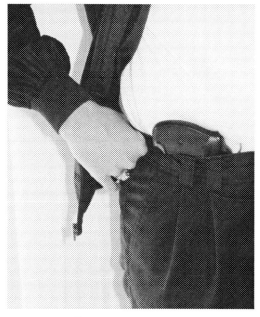

Figure 40. Free carry.

handkerchief may prevent the wearer from easily grasping the weapon. Finally, the pocket will often sag or the weapon's weight will pull the supporting garment to one side telegraphing the possibility that a weapon is being carried.

Elastic Medical Aids

These devices are elastic bands made in a variety of sizes to fit a variety of extremities. Small weapons may be inserted under these bands. Accessibility may be fast, depending upon the location of the band. Concealability is good due to the band's ability to tuck the weapon into the body. Even if the band is seen, it will be considered a medical aid and not a concealed carry device.

Officers may see parts of the weapon, especially the grip, supported under the band. The muzzle may also extend past the band or the front sight may snag the edge of the band, when drawing. An especially popular carry position is inside the weak side

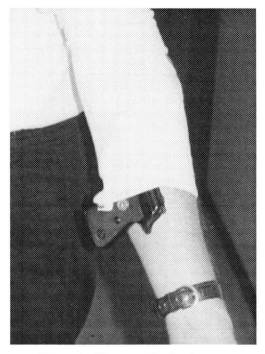

Figure 41. Elastic medical aid carry.

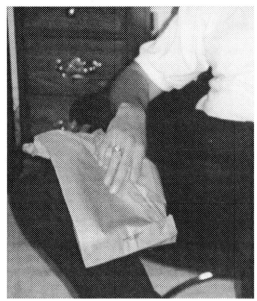

Figure 42. Paper bag carry.

forearm with the grip of the weapon pointed toward the hand. In this position, the weapon is accessible from almost any position. The weapon may be drawn by simply grabbing the grip and pulling straight to the strong side of the wearer's body. Offenders may use the ploy of crossing their arms at the first sign of danger. This action will normally be perceived as non-threatening, but the handgun will be instantly available. However, vigorously moving the weak arm may cause the weapon to flip out on the ground and reloads will often be carried elsewhere on the body.

Naturally, the elastic band may be covered by an outer garment and tight shirts will often be avoided. Shirts having loose cuffs or stretchable cuffs such as those found on sweat shirts are often favored. The shirt may either be shoved back, in order to draw the weapon, or the hand will be slipped

under the cuff. People with larger forearms may be able to carry larger firearms.

Paper Bag

A variety of weapons can be carried in a paper bag–the limitation is the size of the bag. The bigger the bag, the bigger the handgun that can be carried. Naturally, the bag can't be translucent. Further, the weapon may be housed in a holster or free carried inside the bag. The advantage of this technique is the ability to fire the weapon without opening the bag. The offender just stabilizes the handgun, pushes the trigger finger through the bag, and fires. A bag can even be prepared ahead of time, by taping the weapon down and tearing a small hole for finger insertion. Like the other carry methods described, reloads will have to be carried on the body. Normally, the bag will not look threatening and accuracy won't be precise; this is a close range proposition. Another option is to approach areas with the

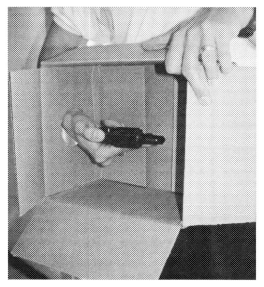

Figure 43. Cardboard box carry.

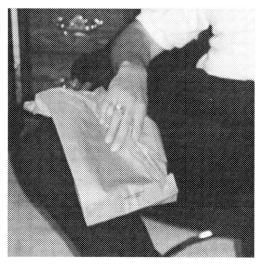

Figure 44. Garment over the hand carry.

weapon already in the hand but still enclosed in the bag.

Cardboard Box Carry

The cardboard box carry is the same as the paper bag carry except it is not quite as flexible. Offenders may or may not open the box to access the weapon. This procedure may be slow and awkward. If firing from the box is chosen, the offender will often prepare the box ahead of time—a hole may be cut for hand access. Further, the weapon is stabilized so that, when the hand is inserted, the weapon is readily available.

Garment Over the Hand Carry

This type of carry uses a weapon already held in a firing grip. Usually, the weapon will be cradled in front of the user's body by one hand, and a garment is draped over the weapon hand for concealment purposes. The weapon may be fired through the garment or the garment may be flung to the ground just prior to firing.

Figure 45. Briefcase carry.

Briefcase Carry

The briefcase carry is a variety of purse, day-timer, portfolio, camera bag, and/or camcorder bag carry methods. Any of these devices are commonly observed on school grounds and often attract little, if any, attention. All of these devices offer good concealment since they house the handgun inside an outer covering that prevents casual observation and printing. These devices also offer the user the option of carrying larger handguns, and more reloads than are usually

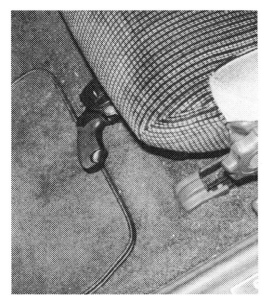

Figure 46. Under the seat carry.

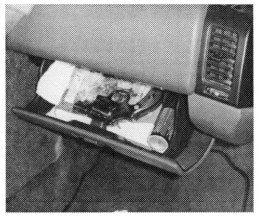

Figure 47. Glove box carry.

carried on the body. Further, these devices are not prone to flagging others that a handgun is concealed due to their prevalence in our society.

Under the Vehicle Seat Carry

This is a style of free carry where the handgun is placed under a vehicle seat. The firearm may be holstered or free of any covering. There are plenty of problems with this carry method. Many people will think this is not carrying, but it is. Many states consider any weapon within "lunging distance" or "arm span," inside a vehicle, as carrying.

Glove Box Carry

A vehicle's glove box is slightly more common and secure than the "under the seat carry." This is due to the user's ability to control the weapon by locking the glove box. Many states consider any weapon within "lunging distance" or "arm span,"

Figure 48. Map pocket carry.

inside a vehicle, as carrying, even if the glove box is locked. However, a weapon carried in a glove box will be stabilized in a smaller area enhancing accessibility. The size of glove box will dictate the size of handgun carried. Further, the weapon may be holstered or free carried in the glove box. A variation of this concealment method is the console carry. However, accessibility may be faster than the glove box due to the close proximity to the driver and the front seat passenger.

Figure 49. Vehicle hook carry–weapons are suspended in the plastic device.

Vehicle Map Pocket Carry

Another possible carry technique consists of placing the weapon in a map pocket. Map pockets are elastic topped pouches or molded indentations found on the lower part of a vehicle's front and back doors. The only security these devices provide is the housing of the weapon in a small area. The size of map pocket will dictate the size of handgun carried.

Vehicle Garment Hook Carry

This type of carry is performed by using a Doskocil Hang 'n' Hide. The Hang 'n' Hide is a plastic box fitted with a lock and a strap that is designed to be slipped over a garment pole or hook. The box is large enough to house two or more handguns plus spare ammunition. A garment is hung over the device concealing the system.

Figure 50. Vehicle trunk carry.

Vehicle Trunk Carry

Even though this is not a true concealed carry method, it is an option for transporting a firearm in the general vicinity of the vehicle operator. Indeed, most states do not recognize this method as carrying. However, a great number of weapons, ammunition, and explosives can be transported by using this method. This is an excellent example of why vehicles should be parked in a controlled area.

Body Cavity Carry

Believe it or not, some people carry weapons in their body cavities. Of course, this is normally a short-time proposition and can be very uncomfortable. The mouth, between the breasts, between the anus cheeks, and inside the anal cavity and vagina cavity are the logical choices for body cavity carry. This type of carry is only effective with very small weapons. Larger weapons may be carried in the vagina by extending part of the weapon into the canal, with the rest supported by the underwear. The weapon

Figure 51. Belt buckle carry–first view.

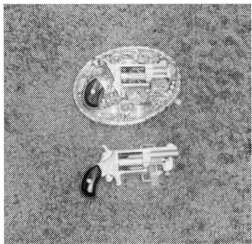

Figure 52. Belt buckle carry–second view.

may be covered with plastic wrap for hygiene purposes. The mouth carry offers the best accessibility of the body cavity methods. Of course, small firearms may be taped under the arm, in the cleavage area of well endowed women, and between the buttocks.

Lanyard Carry

This system is unique to the North American arms revolver. This small handgun is attached to a key ring type device which is then attached to a lanyard. It may be worn around the defender's neck or under an outer garment. When used with athletic apparel, the lanyard may be mistaken for a whistle. For extra control, the weapon may be taped to the chest using medical tape. The weapon may be accessed by simply pulling the lanyard out of the shirt.

Belt Buckle Carry

This system is also unique to the North American arms revolver. This small handgun is attached to an ornamental belt buckle

or a skeleton type belt buckle. The weapon is held in place by metal clamps. This system may be covered by a pullover type outer garment or left in the open in hopes the general population will mistake the weapon for an ornament only.

Self-Contained Firearm/Holster Combination Carry

A final system unique to the North American arms revolver is the attachment of the firearm to a plastic device which serves as a carrying device and handgun grip. This plastic device may be clipped to a pocket or carried as a pocket holster. It is effective in avoiding printing, and the device enhances the handling of such small grips found on this small revolver.

Hollow Book Carry

Many of these "secret compartment" books are made of actual pages which have been glued together, and hollowed out in the center. A plastic insert is often placed in this hollow space intended to store valuables or small handguns. These books are covered

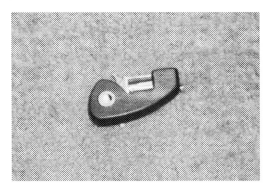

Figure 53. Self-contained carry–first view.

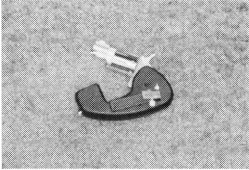

Figure 54. Self-contained carry–second view.

with a variety of titles so no one title is indicative to the carry system. This book is a very effective way to conceal handguns in a car, in brief cases, or when hand carried, etc.

Medical Sling Carry

A handgun can be easily carried in a standard medical sling. The handgun can be inserted between the "injured" forearm and sling material. The handgun's grip will often be facing toward the open end of the sling. The weapon is quick and easy to reach by inserting the opposite hand into the open end of the sling. The "injured" arm may also

be pulled free of the sling to provide a two-hand firing grip. A medical sling is very disarming and may give the defender the edge in a violent encounter.

In conclusion, the above carry methods are by no means all-inclusive. However, they do represent the majority of concealed carry methods likely to be encountered on a school campus. School resource officers, security officers, and school officials should all be briefed on these types of carry methods. Any suspicious actions or items should be inspected in accordance with school policy and procedures.

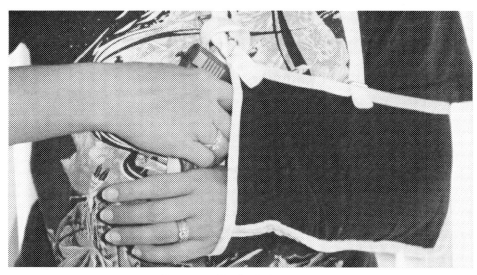

Figure 55. Medical sling carry.

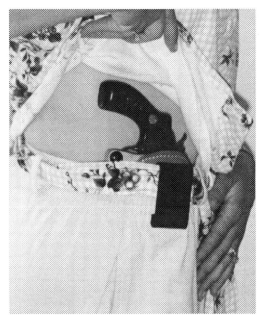

Figure 56. Inside the waistband carry.

Figure 57. Holster attached to pager.

Figure 58. Handgun in fanny pack.

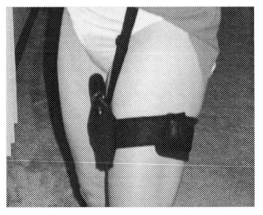

Figure 59. Thigh carry.

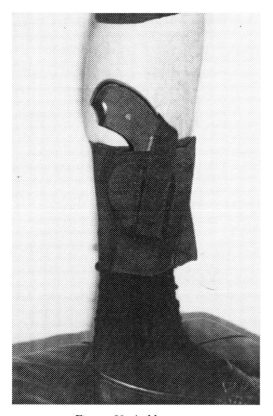

Figure 60. Ankle carry.

Figure 61. Boot carry.

Figure 62. Shoulder holster and multiposition holster.

Emergency Operations Center (EOC) Operations

In the law enforcement arena, tactical operations will often require the manning of an EOC, tactical operations center (TOC), and a field command post (FCP). For the purposes of this book, only the EOC will be discussed due to the fact that during a school violence crisis response, this is the only location where both the school administrators or school violence crisis response planners/committee members and law enforcement operators will intertwine in order to resolve the crisis.

The EOC should be developed to coordinate all available resources required to deal with school emergencies effectively–

to include school violence crisis events, thereby saving lives, avoiding injury, and minimizing economic loss. The EOC is staffed by individuals who are responsible for guiding the direction of emergency operations. Staffing is a departmental/school system management function. Their mission is to manage and support the response to emergency situations, keeping required personnel informed about the status and plans for crisis resolution.

The EOC approves the responders' operations order unless compromise procedures are initiated and the EOC also coordinates the responders' request for support or logistics; for example: explosive ordinance personnel, canine handlers, lightly armored vehicles, etc. Finally, the EOC maintains contact with other officials, the media, and public as required. **Note:** *The EOC is not a command and control element for responders operating in a tactical arena.* To clarify: the EOC approves and orders the mission but does not command and control responder processes or tactics. Support is the key concept.

The EOC may be established anywhere except in the crisis area or mixed in with the TOC. If the EOC is too near the crisis area, its ability to function will be curtailed. Also, if the EOC is setup in conjunction with the Tactical Operations Center (TOC), meddling, confusion, and disruption of operations will result. The ideal place for an EOC is in a local government building which may be already equipped with the necessary communications equipment and other support features. How the EOC is made operational and how the response phase is controlled will often determine the success of plan implementation and subsequent effective results. Staffing the EOC may mean as little as moving people out of their offices and down the hall, or it may be as difficult as moving people all over town.

A sequence of steps is required in order to make the EOC fully operational. Of course, these steps may vary depending on the scope of the school violence crisis. The following operational steps are common: alert EOC personnel; activate communications equipment and support facilities; initiate the message flow system; ready appropriate logs, maps, and status charts for the operations board; prepare a shift schedule; announce briefing schedules; and provide for necessities.

The alerting process should be clearly stated in the school violence crisis response plan as a standard operating procedure (SOP). A common alerting process requires a chain of calls where one person calls another on an alert roster. If one person cannot be reached, alternate names should be provided to ensure the EOC is fully staffed. Activating the communications equipment and support facilities normally requires the activation and testing of communications equipment. Activating the support facilities may include anything from starting an emergency power generator to plugging in the coffee pot.

Initiating the message flow system is simply a method of recording messages as they arrive so that they are documented and appropriate/timely action can be taken. Usually all incoming messages are routed through one person who records the messages and forwards them to an operations officer. The operations officer then assigns the responsibility to act on the messages to someone within the EOC. The operations officer should then be advised of the action taken. Actions taken should always be recorded and posted. To simplify matters, some type of preprinted form should be developed to document and handle incoming and outgoing messages. The form should be an easily recognizable document and contain space for the members of the staff to take notes. A good format contains the following: title of document; status–incoming or outgoing to include time and date, method of information delivery, name, position, and title of person receiving the information; name, position, and title of person acting on the information; name, position, title, and location of person requesting information, message space, action taken space, and notes space.

This information processing is one of the keys to the success of any school violence crisis response effort. How well personnel perform will often depend upon how well they respond to the information received. Thus, information processing includes how information goes into the EOC, how the information is passed along inside the EOC, and how the information flows out of the EOC. Furthermore, written information is important because it documents the actions taken during the response phase. This information may be referred to in the event verification of actions is required.

It is vital that personnel maintain a log of events within the EOC. Of course, other support documents will also be required such as maps, photographs, videos, drawings, blueprints, and the location of utilities, etc. EOC personnel must be prepared; many of these items should be prepared well in advance of any school violence crisis. It is a good idea to create a set of credentials which will allow only certain personnel access to the EOC.

If the EOC is to be in operation for any length of time, a duty roster should be developed and posted within the EOC so that personnel are not on continuous duty. This schedule should include on and off duty times as well as relief breaks. This is done due to the fact that operations can get very intense and accompanying fatigue is likely. Fatigue of key personnel should be avoided

if at all possible.

Briefing schedules should be established and announced as soon as possible. The EOC staff should be briefed when shifts change and at any other times when situation changes or major events and accompanying decisions are required. It may be a good idea to develop and position an update chart or status board just inside the entrance of the EOC. This action informs newly arriving staff of the situation as well as provides a central place for the staff to update themselves. The media will also need a briefing schedule so that they know when to expect a report from the EOC. Finally, providing for the necessitates of operating an EOC includes appropriate food, water, clothing, and housekeeping supplies.

It is essential to control access to the EOC. The EOC is no place for non-essential personnel. The idea is to be able to run the EOC with minimum interference from those who are not part of the emergency management effort. The best way to do this is to have controlled access to the EOC. As soon as the EOC goes into operation, some type of check-in procedure should be established. A guard may be placed at the EOC door to check for EOC credentials and/or an access list. Anyone who does not have credentials and/or is not on the access list should be cleared through the EOC operations officer prior to admittance. Two lists may be required; one list would contain those individuals who have EOC access at any time, while another list may identify individuals who have only limited access to the EOC. It is also a good idea to have some type of sign-in procedure, so that at any time, one can tell who is in the EOC. A separate room should be established outside the EOC for media personnel and other visitors. If logistics do not enable the establishment of a separate area, a restricted area may be established inside the EOC to accommodate these personnel. However, they should not be allowed to loiter; once their task is complete they should be escorted out of the EOC.

In conclusion, once the staff arrives at the EOC, there should be no question as to what they should do. Each staff member should have a personal copy of the EOC standard operating procedures. EOC personnel should be briefed on the situation as soon as possible. This can be done through the use of a quickly prepared handout which is given to them as they sign in or through a general briefing. The initial briefing will normally be brief, while follow-up briefings will be more detailed as additional information arrives over the course of the crisis event. The EOC should be placed into operation as soon as physically possible.

Tactical Containment Operations

School resource officers, being police officers, quite frequently participate in containment operations in response to natural disasters, accident scenes, crowd control functions, and in support of tactical operations, etc. All of these containment operations have many elements in common; however, tactical containment operations require a variety of unique requirements which must be considered. Poor containment operations can endanger the school campus population, contiguous civilian population, law enforcement officers, support personnel (firemen, emergency medical technicians, tactical consultants, command, control, communications and intelligence personnel, etc.) permit adversary attack, reinforcement, or escape. Proper containment operations will diminish or avoid many unnecessary situations, thus heightening mission success and officer survival.

Once an incident has developed into a containment situation (a subject has taken a defensive posture), e.g., hostage situation, barricaded subject, hostile takeover of an area or valuable asset, etc., immediate steps must be taken to gain control of the situation through the implementation of a tactical containment operation. Containment procedures should be initiated to achieve the following goals: contain the problem in the smallest area possible; confine the perpetrator to his current location; isolate the perpetrator from all outside contact; provide 360-degree observation and fields of fire; and slow down the adversary's action so tactical units can plan and prepare to resolve the crisis through applicable negotiations or tactical actions.

The first officer arriving at or otherwise encountering a crisis scene should perform steps designed to contain and, if possible, confine a perpetrator in the smallest area possible by establishing and maintaining an inner perimeter. This concept is of vital importance to response teams who may have to eventually enter a stronghold (the smaller the area these officers have to search and clear, or assault, the safer the operation will be). Smaller areas often enhance logistics, manpower, tactical solutions, team techniques, and time factors, etc., which all directly reflect upon officer survival and may even heighten the chance that hostages may be rescued. Granted, a lone officer will probably be unable to contain a perpetrator completely; however, he or she can help ensure that the adversary will be contained quickly when additional officers arrive by first, taking cover; second, establishing and maintaining communications with the dispatch section, and third, maintaining surveillance of the perpetrator. The most important goal, at this point, is for the officer to stay alive and to act as an intelligence collector until additional officers arrive.

The inner perimeter should isolate the perpetrator from all outside contact. Outside contact must be controlled or the perpetrator may call for reinforcements from family, friends, or criminal associates; coordinate with the media causing detrimental peripheral problems to develop; or gain sympathy from the general public, etc. The inner perimeter should also provide 360-degree observation and fields of fire (blind spots, dead space, or otherwise unobserved areas may allow the perpetrator to escape, enable the adversary to plan a method of attack, or generate feelings that the perpetrator still possesses some control of the situation). As officers arrive, the initial officer should provide safe approach directions and verbally guide officers into containment positions located on diagonally opposing corners or other configurations in order to gain 360-degree observation and containment.

Finally, the inner perimeter should slow down the adversary's actions and gain tactical units time by (preventing perpetrator escape, generating feelings of surrender vs. deadly confrontation, fostering a willingness to negotiate a solution, etc.). A strong inner perimeter will often enable tactical units the opportunity to thoroughly plan and prepare the resolution of a crisis through applicable negotiations or tactical actions.

Naturally, the size and shape of the inner perimeter will be determined by the location of the suspect, the perpetrator's weaponry, manpower constraints, physical constraints of the target area, and by the physical characteristics of the surrounding area. A perpetrator located on a first floor may have access to multiple escape routes but may not be able to view very much of the tactical arena. A perpetrator located on a second floor may be able to see more of the tactical arena but may not have many escape routes. A perpetrator located on a roof top may be

able to observe a huge portion of the tactical arena; however, to do this, the perpetrator will often have to silhouette their body against the horizon offering a clear target for precision riflemen or containment forces. Plus, there may be no escape routes on a rooftop.

The perpetrator's weaponry will impact the size and shape of the inner perimeter example, officers may be able to choose containment positions located closer to the target area if the perpetrator has a two-inch barreled revolver in lieu of a scoped hunting rifle. Manpower constraints also impact the size and shape of the inner perimeter For example, multiple adversaries will require more officers to be deployed in order to cover additional threat areas. Furthermore, if fewer officer are available, different containment configurations will have to be chosen in order to provide effective target area coverage.

Physical constraints of the target area will also impact the size and shape of the inner perimeter. For example, a multifloor industrial building will be much more difficult to contain than a single floor family dwelling. Finally, the physical characteristics of the surrounding area will impact the size and shape of the inner perimeter. For example, heavily wooded areas may allow officers to choose containment positions that are very close to a target area while large open areas (huge mowed lawns, parking lots, etc.) may cause officers to choose containment positions located a great distance from the target area. Of course, armored vehicles or other heavy duty vehicles may be used in these situations to provide closer containment positions while also providing cover and concealment.

Containment positions may be located in a diagonal shape (on two opposing corners), square shape for 360 degree coverage, U-shape to cover three sides of an area, or an

L-shape to cover two sides of an area. Of course, all of these configurations may afford partial views of other areas. To further develop an inner perimeter, officers should take up positions which afford cover and concealment, permit observation of the largest area possible while avoiding cross-fire situations, cover all possible routes of escape or high speed avenues of approach, and deploy weapons which can effectively cover required distances; e.g., a 2-inch barreled revolver will be of little use deployed 100 yards distant from the contained area. **Note**: Inner perimeter officers should not be tasked to perform any duties that would detract from their primary containment duties.

An ingress/egress (control) point should be established in order to control all personnel moving into or out of the containment area. **Note**: Uncontrolled ingress/egress will weaken containment efforts and may be dangerous (unidentified police personnel may be mistaken for escaping perpetrators). Established control points may also be used as safe routes to evacuate citizens or released hostages, coordinate negotiated deliveries, and facilitate the movement of support personnel. Of course, tactical units may use other avenues of approach other than through an established control point; however, all perimeter personnel must be advised that tactical units are moving inside the area especially when an assault is underway.

After the inner perimeter is in place, officers should develop an outer perimeter. Outer perimeters are designed to isolate the area of operations, further contain the perpetrator (if a breakout is attempted and the inner perimeter is breached, the outer perimeter acts as a safety net), and prevent unauthorized personnel from entering the area. Of course, more than one outer

perimeter may be developed depending on the tactical situation. An inner perimeter coupled with outer perimeters provide defense in depth both inside and outside the crisis area (layers of officers will have to be penetrated during any escape attempt or penetration from outside assets) (see diagram five).

Inner and outer perimeters are actually made up of a series of blocking positions. Blocking positions can be established in two ways: observation and fire, or physical blocking. Observation and fire techniques allow officers to block more than one escape route. A containment position conducive to this technique must allow observation of any movement within an established sector, provide proper cover and concealment, provide clear fields of fire, and be within range of the officer's weapon; "there is no need to fire a weapon from a location that is beyond the weapon's effective range or the officer's ability to accurately engage a perpetrator." Indeed, doing so may endanger officers located in the general area due to resulting inaccuracy! There is a "golden rule" officers must adhere to in this situation: containment officers should not fire into a stronghold once a tactical team has entered; likewise, tactical teams should not fire outside of the stronghold once they have entered. Violations of this "golden rule" heighten the chances of friendly fire casualties! Officers must exercise discipline and honor designated areas of responsibility.

Physically blocking a perpetrator involves developing a position that will require the perpetrator to overrun during any escape attempt. These blocking positions should be manned by more than one officer (one officer cannot remain alert at all times especially during operations that become protracted). Indeed, the field commander may have to institute relief systems in order to feed, water, or otherwise take care of officers manning perimeter positions. Physical blocking techniques may require the massing of available materials, utilization of vehicles–especially large trucks, spike sleds, or other tire puncturing devices, utilization of existing terrain features, utilization of existing obstacles; e.g., dumpsters, adjacent buildings, fences, etc. The idea is to completely block the route of travel. Furthermore, physical blocking positions must be under observation and fire techniques at all times. Finally, containment positions are not necessarily static–officers may reposition themselves at night in order to operate more effectively during the hours of darkness then move back to the original position for daylight operations.

In conclusion, proper containment operations protect the school campus population, civilian population, law enforcement officers, support personnel (firemen, emergency medical technicians, tactical consultants, command, control, communications and intelligence personnel, etc.), and thwart adversary attack, reinforcement, or escape attempts. Furthermore, proper containment operations will diminish or avoid many unnecessary situations, e.g., cross-fires. Finally, proper containment operations will heighten mission success and the chances of officer survival.

Responding to Booby Traps and/or Explosive Devices

The intent of this section is not to train police officers on how to construct or use booby traps, but instead, to increase their awareness and ability to identify certain booby traps. Awareness will be heightened through the use of a descriptive narrative and the photographic display of a variety of booby traps now in general use. This new knowledge concerning the booby-trap threat will enable officers to be prepared through preconceived response procedures and safety guidelines to prevent inadvertent booby-trap initiation. This gathering of knowledge is the first step toward becoming familiar and proficient in the avoidance of booby traps–a valuable survival tool. This skill may well mean the difference between life, death, suffering, or serious injury when a booby trap is encountered.

Many school violence crisis response incidents have included the threat or actual use of booby traps. Booby traps are attractive to some offenders because they do not require sophisticated explosives, controlled or hard-to-obtain components or materials. At the basic level rope, string, fishing line, fish-hooks, razor blades, and a shovel are all the materials needed to construct a booby trap. The deadliness of a booby trap is limited only by the builder's imagination.

Further, booby traps generate considerable media attention when discovered or detonated, and provide an easy impersonal means of causing damage, injury, death, or terror without the perpetrator's presence. A single booby trap can receive more publicity than many murders and it may take considerable time, assets, and effort for authorities to catch the booby trapper. Booby traps are particularly vicious because they do not discriminate between intended or unintended targets–they are solely designed to neutralize targets of opportunity. Finally, officers involved in a school violence response operation must be aware of the possibility that booby traps may be deployed in the target area. An officer should always look before acting.

The Definition of a Booby Trap

To help identify a booby trap, a definition should be developed. A booby trap is an explosive or non-explosive device used to target the unwary or unsuspecting, usually concealed, designed to detonate or otherwise cause injury or death when some hidden or harmless appearing device is triggered. Triggering may be sophisticated such as the use of a photoelectric cell or simple such as physical triggering, for example, stepping on the device.

Prerequisites for Booby-Trap Deployment

Before a person deploys a booby trap, he or she must first develop a motive. After a motive has been established, three basic conditions must be satisfied in order to field a device. First, the booby-trap builder must have the know-how to construct and deploy the device. Second, he must have access to explosives or the raw materials from which the booby trap can be made, and third, he must have the opportunity to emplace the device at the desired target area. The threat of booby traps' use is great today because each of these prerequisites can usually be satisfied.

Booby-Trap Information Sources

Information concerning how-to-build many types of booby traps is easily accessed and readily available to the public. A number of specialty publishers produce books devoted to the subject showing how-to-build booby traps using improvised materials, commercial products or surplus military components. Another source of information is military manuals, for example, U.S. Army Manual, FM5-36.

Military manuals can be purchased over the counter at any number of Army surplus stores, found in yard sales, or obtained from the personal libraries of armed forces veterans.

Not only are books or pamphlets available, but the Internet is becoming a major source for this type of information. For example, in 1992, booby-trap plans were posted on a computer bulletin board. This booby-trap information was first gathered by college students, then high school students. As a result, this specific booby trap was popularized, experimented with, and/or actually deployed in a number of incidences. This device, known as a Drano bomb, pool acid bomb, or soda bottle bomb, consisted of a one or two liter plastic or 16-ounce glass soft drink bottle, locally available acid, and metal filler. As the acid and metal interact, they rapidly produce hydrogen gas within the capped bottle. Usually, within 15 to 90 seconds, the bottle will shatter showering the immediate area with acid and fragments from the container. In addition, if an ignition source (open flame) is close to the detonation area, the escaping hydrogen gas will explode into a large fireball. Furthermore, acid residue may burn the skin, destroy clothing, or damage equipment and property. This device became so popular that it was adopted for use by some crack house operators, to function when entry teams kicked in a door. Once initiated, this device cannot be stopped, or if it misfires, cannot be safely approached by police officers due to the danger it may still explode (bomb technicians can render this device safe).

Booby Traps Used as Alarms or Early Warning Systems

Booby traps designed primarily as alarms or early warning devices may be chosen for a variety of reasons. First, offenders may not feel comfortable with handling devices designed to injure or kill. Second, offenders may fear that while operating in a booby-trapped area, they may accidentally trip the device themselves, and third, offenders may feel that the area or operation protected does not warrant the use of deadlier devices.

Alarm type booby traps may be designed as a passive device–designed not to injure, only alarm, or active device–designed to injure/kill plus sound the alarm. Alarms or early warning devices have three purposes, they are as follows:

1. To warn the perpetrator that someone is approaching. This warning enables the offender to choose between the options of fighting, fleeing, or a combination of the two. Remember, the police officer is operating on the offender's home territory, and if the perpetrator has ample advanced warning and the desire, he or she may choose to fight, if for only a brief period of time before fleeing. The idea may be to cause additional injury or death through the use of small arms fire prior to making an escape or committing suicide. If a number of perpetrators are present, they may decide to spring a hasty ambush on the approaching officers. After all, once an early warning device has been tripped, the adversaries will know that response personnel are in the area as well as their direction of approach.

2. To impede access. The first device triggered may cause the response team leader to choose an alternate route, costing the police time and gaining the offender time. Also, the first device triggered will certainly cause officers to initially stop, then proceed slowly, while looking for additional devices. Remember, just because one device is

an alarm doesn't mean the next booby trap won't be designed to injure or kill. Additionally, the device believed to have been an alarm may have been a deadly device which malfunctioned.

3. To slow or stop the police pursuit of a suspect, the perpetrator may plan an escape route which goes directly through an area seeded with booby traps. The booby trapper will know where the devices are, but pursuing officers will not. When pursuing officers trip the first booby trap, all officers will, at a minimum, slow down or even discontinue further pursuit.

Passive Alarms

Some passive devices which can be used as early warning devices include the following:

Artillery simulators–the military artillery simulator will discharge a small volume of smoke and flame and produce a very loud whistling sound and explosive report. This explosive report will easily be heard from a great distance. When tripped (normally by hitting a trip wire), the officer may panic, thinking they have been injured by an explosive device, and run into other more deadly devices. These artillery simulators are a pyrotechnic device, so fire is possible when they are discharged in some types on indoor structures.

Hand grenade simulators–the military hand grenade simulator will discharge a small volume of smoke and flame plus produce a loud explosive report. This explosive report, while not as loud as the aforementioned artillery simulator, will easily be heard from a great distance. When tripped (normally by hitting a trip wire), like the artillery simulator, the loud explosive report may cause the officer to panic and run into other more deadly devices. Again, like

Figure 63. Officer in gas mask.

the artillery simulator, hand grenade simulators are a pyrotechnic device so fire is possible.

Chemical grenades–(Chloracetophenone, CN or Orthochlorobenzalmalonotrile, CS). Once tripped (normally by hitting a trip wire), the military CS grenade (Fig. 63) will discharge a large volume of CS chemical. This chemical may affect the officer's eyes, nose, ability to breath, and irritate the skin. These effects may cause the officer to panic and run into other more deadly devices. At the very least, the acts of searching an area or pursuing a suspect will be delayed or terminated. Even if protective masks "gas masks" are carried by police officers, time will be expended by the officers during the donning procedure. This chemical grenade is also a pyrotechnic device so fire is likely.

Smoke grenades–when tripped, again (usually by hitting a trip wire), will discharge a large volume of smoke easily seen from a great distance. The smoke cloud may appear in a variety of colors such as yellow, red, green, white, purple, etc. The smoke produced may interfere with the officers vision and ability to breathe. **Note**: The perpetrator may intermingle smoke and chemical grenades in order to trick the officers into thinking that only smoke grenades are in the area, thus heightening the chance that officers will not don their protective mask and become affected by the resulting chemical agent exposure. These smoke grenades are also a pyrotechnic device so fire is likely.

Military trip flares–when tripped– (usually by hitting a trip wire), will discharge a fair amount of smoke and a very bright flame (light) easily seen from a long distance. Trip flares are especially effective during darkness or dim light (dawn or dusk) conditions. An officer who looks directly at a trip flare will often suffer temporary vision problems–black spots, fuzzy vision, difficulty focusing, and a loss of night vision. Trip flare-generated vision problems will normally last for approximately 30 minutes. Naturally, an officer should never look directly at a burning flare. These trip flares are a pyrotechnic device so they can cause serious skin burns and fire is likely.

Military perimeter alarm–when tripped (usually by hitting a trip wire), will emit a very shrill whistling type noise. This whistling noise can be heard from a long distance. **Warning**: smoke grenades, chemical grenades, and trip flares burn at extremely hot temperatures. Personnel should not try to pick up one of these devices in an attempt to throw it elsewhere or stomp the device out. Serious skin burns may result from the handling of a hot device and clothing may ignite!

Animals–while not a formal booby trap, may be brought into a school building as live early warning devices. Dogs may attack approaching officers or just bark repeatedly.

Be advised, the heavy skull structure and rounded shape of some K-9 breeds may cause handgun/submachine gun rounds to deflect or otherwise fail to penetrate. Multiple shots may be required to stop this animal's attack.

Active Alarms– Designed to Injure

Active devices are a sort of hybrid alarm which will sound the alarm plus cause injury or death when tripped–noise is considered a secondary by-product. Noise may be a product of the device firing or a by-product of the individual tripping the device, screaming out in pain and/or fear. One example of an active device consists of a few fish-hooks strung on monofilament fishing line suspended at face level. The fish hooks will cause pain, injury, and may permanently disable anyone caught in them.

Another device consists of a board with nails driven through it. This device is typically placed at the bottom of a hole made in the floor–the opening is covered with cardboard and camouflage materials to conceal the hole and device from view. The intruder's foot will collapse the cardboard and the subsequent weight will impale the foot, ankle, and/or calf on the nails. The nails may be cut in a jagged manner to make the removal of impaled body parts more difficult. The nails also be coated with fecal matter, poison, or other toxic substance to promote infection. Computer rooms are areas where these devices may be easily deployed. For example, most computer room floors have panels which may be easily removed to access wiring. The offender may remove one of these panels, insert the booby trap, and cover the opening with a rug or office papers, etc.

Figure 64. Smoke grenade.

Booby Traps Designed to Maim or Kill

Some booby traps are deliberately designed to maim and/or kill–their deadliness is limited only by the builder's imagination. Some examples include a firearm trap; the firearm may be attached to a fixed object and pointed at a likely avenue of approach– a thin wire will be attached to the firearms trigger and strung across a doorway. When the wire is tripped, the weapon will fire in the intruders direction of approach. Shotguns are favored for use in this booby trap due to their ability to send multiple projectiles into a general area. Some exotic ammunition such as flechette's, strung buck, flame-producing propellants, incendiary ammunition, smoke projectiles, chemical agents (blast dispersion loads), and noise makers (bird bombs or screamers) may be loaded into the shotgun.

Another booby-trap example uses spikes instead of the aforementioned nails, driven through a board, and placed point-up in the bottom of an opening which will be covered by a light material used to camouflage the opening. Spikes have the potential to cause more severe injury than nails due to their size. Working the same as the afore-mentioned nail trap, the intruders foot will collapse the cover material and the subsequent weight will impale the foot, ankle, and or calf on the spikes. The extent of injury will depend upon the depth of the hole, velocity of the officers foot, the officer's weight, and the foot's angle of entry. The spikes may be cut in a jagged manner in order to produce multiple barbs which will enhance physical damage and make the removal of impaled body parts more difficult. The spikes may also be coated with fecal matter, poison, or other toxic substance to promote infection.

A variation of the spike booby trap consists of placing "Punji Sticks," wooden stakes, at the bottom of a small hole described above in the nail or spike traps. These wooden stakes are light, easy to carry, and thwart the searcher's use of metal detectors. The wooden stakes can cause severe puncture injuries due to their huge diameter and usually serious infections if coated with excrement or another toxic substance as described above.

A similar example of the above booby trap includes using the hole in the computer floor without "spikes or stakes." The opening will be concealed by a camouflaged material and an officer can break a leg or receive a bad sprain as their foot impacts the bottom of the hole. Once again, the extent of injury will depend upon the depth of the hole, velocity of the officer's foot, the officer's weight, and the foot's angle of entry. A running officer can be seriously injured. These pits may also be used to make the officer fall into other booby traps or to channel officers into booby-trap seeded areas. This narrow pit trap may be favored by some perpetrators due to the ease of deployment, lack of material, and low maintenance.

Another popular example of a booby trap designed to maim or kill consists of a fragmentation device. These booby traps are normally explosive devices. When the explosive is detonated, primary fragments including shattered fragments of the container and deliberately added casualty producing missiles are hurled outward from the point of detonation at great velocity. Secondary fragments (glass, wood splinters, etc.) from the area immediately surrounding the explosion may also occur. Fires may also start as a result of the heat and flame produced by the explosion.

A common fragmentation device consist of a demilled or practice military hand grenade. These devices are readily available through surplus stores and gun shows. A new fuse is either obtained or made, the grenade body sealed, and gunpowder or other explosive is inserted into the body. For booby-trap use, the fuse is often instantaneous, providing a very deadly booby trap. Of course, stolen military hand grenades may be used instead of reconstructed practice grenades.

A final example of a booby trap designed to maim or kill consists of military land mines. Naturally, these stolen land mines are explosive devices. When detonated, primary fragments, including the shattered fragments of the container and the accompanying explosive force, will often cause serious damage, injury, or death. Secondary fragments (glass, wood splinters, etc.) from the area immediately surrounding the explosion may also occur. Ignition is often instantaneous, making these devices very deadly.

Figure 65. Fire bomb detonating.

Figure 66. Fire bomb detonating.   Figure 67. Fire bomb detonating.

Figure 68. Military practice grenade with fuzes.

Figure 69. Spike trap.

Figure 70. Nail trap.

Figure 71. Rat trap device.

Figure 72. Homemade napalm.

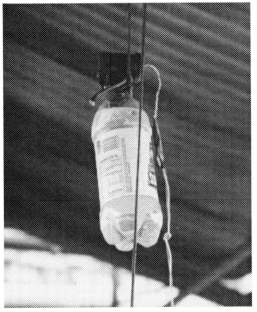

Figure 73. Homemade napalm.

Figure 74. Shotgun shell trap.

Figure 75. Military artillery simulator.

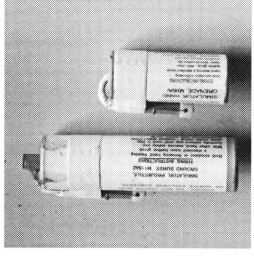

Figure 76. Military hand grenade and artillery simulator.

Booby-Trap Construction

As depicted in the aforementioned examples, a booby trap may consist of a stolen military device, a clever well-constructed device, or may be a crude device, as dangerous to the maker as the intended victim. Booby traps may be constructed from stolen military components, purchased commercial components, or from improvised components.

For example, common household commodities and common chemicals can be also be used for making improvised components and used in booby-traps. Improvised components include cheap commonly available components such as gunpowder, household chemicals, farming chemicals, lumber, batteries, mousetraps, pipes, and common electrical wire.

A piece of plumbing pipe can serve as a one-time use shotgun barrel and a common triggering device may consist of a mouse trap configured with a striker (fabricated firing pin) attached to the yoke. A piece of monofilament line can serve as a trip wire trigger designed to set off explosives, cross bows or a conventional firearms.

Various types of chemical fire-bombs can also serve as booby traps. These devices often consist of bottles containing flammable liquids designed to break or otherwise mix when dropped. One such device consists of a container filled with a chemical and wrapped in paper or cloth soaked with another chemical which will ignite upon contact. This is known as a binary device– both chemicals may be stable by themselves but once mixed, become unstable. The attractiveness of this device is found in the ease and safety of transport to the target area (the reacting chemicals are kept separate until the device is deployed). Another device consists of a light bulb, modified to contain gasoline or explosive compound, once an electric charge is introduced into the improvised filler, an explosion or fire will result.

Battery-powered, electrically fired booby-trap circuits are simple and easy to make for use in the wilds. A few dry cell batteries can provide enough power to heat a piece of resistance wire to red-hot temperatures. If this wire is placed next to gunpowder or gasoline, it serves as an igniter. A photo flash bulb can also work very well as a igniter. A clothes pin with an electrical contact on each jaw works very well as an improvised pull-switch. A piece of plastic, wood, or other nonconductive material with a string or trip-wire attached keeps the electrical contacts apart until someone bumps into them.

Booby-Trap Initiation

Initiation of some kind is necessary to "set-off" all booby traps and runs the gambit from simple to complex. Booby traps may be initiated by mechanical, electrical, chemical, or a combination of these triggering devices. No attempt has been made to cover all existing triggering devices since, like booby-traps, the amount and combinations of triggering devices available is limited only by the builders imagination. Note, mechanical and electrical triggers are by far the most common initiators.

Mechanical Triggers

Mechanical triggers set the booby trap into motion through the physical relation of force and matter. Examples of mechanical triggers include pull types–a fine wire attached to the trigger of a shotgun; pressure types–spring loaded device designed to fire when pressed; and pressure release types–a spring loaded striker armed when pressure is applied and fired when pressure is released. A simple mechanical trigger consist of a trip wire attached to a bell or even a tin can full of pebbles which when disturbed causes a noise designed to alert the booby trapper of

possible intrusion.

Electrical Triggers

Electrical triggers set the booby trap into motion through the use of a power source, usually batteries. One popular type of electrical alarm which is advertised in survivalist magazines consists of a fine electric wire strung around a perimeter. The wire is very thin and breaks easily, interrupting an electrical current which initiates a buzzer. These alarms are light and compact using D-cell batteries for power. The D-cell batteries make this alarm very convenient and popular for use in isolated areas. Electrical triggers are popular due to their capability of firing several devices in a chain reaction–almost simultaneous fashion. The number of devices fired is limited only by the power of the electrical current and the capability of the wire to carry the current.

Chemical Triggers

Chemical triggers set the booby trap into motion through the use of a chemical reaction–corrosives such as acid are often used in chemical triggers. An example consists of a binary device; as the acid eats through a barrier material, two flame producing chemicals interact causing fire. Chemical triggers are rarely used with booby traps due to the problems associated with a consistent time delay. A great deal of expertise is required to obtain consistent short duration time delays. Normally, booby traps need to detonate quickly, in order to be effective, as the target will not be in the area for long periods of time. Also, mechanical and electrical triggers are simpler and easier to work with than chemical triggers.

Combination Triggers

Combination triggers consist of different types of triggers working in conjunction with one another; for example, a pull-type electric trigger, pressure-electric device, or magnetic-electric device. A pull type-electric trigger is initially activated by the mechanics of pulling to allow an electric source to initiate the actual device. A pressure-electric trigger is initially set off by the mechanics of pressure to allow an electric source to initiate the actual device, and a magnetic-electric device is initially set off by the mechanics of pulling the magnet from its position, allowing an electric source to initiate the actual device. Combination triggers are sometimes used by perpetrators as built in safety devices.

Multiple Triggers

Multiple triggers are stand alone triggers attached to a booby trap, acting as a back-up to another trigger or to booby trap a booby trap. When used as a back-up, if one trigger fails, the other trigger may initiate the device. When used as a booby trap, for a booby trap, when one trigger is neutralized by an officer disarming the device, the clandestine trigger is designed to keep the booby trap active. Multiple triggers serve as a very good reason for letting only "bomb technicians" disarm booby traps.

Discovering and Reacting to Booby Traps

Because booby traps may or may not look like dangerous devices and may or may not be concealed. The thoroughness of any search and likelihood of success depends on the skill of the searchers and the ingenuity of the perpetrator. To avoid booby traps, the police officer needs to know where they are likely to be deployed.

Booby traps are point defense devices, most useful for blocking an approach or defending a specific place. Perpetrators may place a few booby traps at the side of a hallway where officers may seek cover during an operation. Hallways and other approach routes such as stairways and roof hatches are logical places to place booby traps. Any gate or doorway is also a logical place to put a booby trap, because the suspect knows exactly where the officer will be upon passing through.

Recognizing a Booby Trap

Even though perpetrators who utilize booby traps have devious minds, and they disguise their work cleverly, there are some telltale signs. First is location; the officer must be very suspicious and alert around any access point leading into a suspected area. Second is physical evidence– naturally if a trip wire is visible, the officer must be cautious. Remember, just because a trip wire has been discovered doesn't mean the booby trap has been located– the trip wire only represents the triggering device. The booby trap may be very close to the discovering officer or a fair distance away; indeed, other officers may actually be closer to the booby trap than the officer discovering the trip wire.

Fishing line is a danger sign, a light piece of cloth, small stick, or a weed may be used by an officer to detect trip wires. The items listed above are held at arms length and moved slowly from the ground to waist high then waist high to over the head in an attempt to brush against and reveal any hidden trip wires. Many times an officer can squat or lay on the floor looking upward in order to silhouette a trip wire against dark colored objects. Flashlights may be valuable for spotting booby traps in darkened areas.

Mirrors are also valuable for looking into small or other hard to observe areas. Mirrors may also be used to reflect sunlight into dark areas–sun reflected light is clearer and brighter than any existing flashlight source.

Third, officers should look for abnormal depression in the floor; these may suggest tampering with the structure. Fourth, be wary of any rearranged objects, a pile of papers observed in a particular spot where no other papers are may hide a booby trap. Fifth, imprints on the floor from recently moved objects such as filing cabinets, desk, office equipment, etc., may represent a warning sign that objects have been moved to other locations. Sixth, the officer must also be wary of any object or area which channels foot traffic into a specific area; for example, a filing cabinet may be placed in a hallway to either conceal a booby trap designed to initiate if the filing cabinet is moved or the filing cabinet obstacle may be designed to force officers to circumvent the object and thus walk into a booby-trap seeded area.

Seventh, look for shiny objects, colors, shapes, and other suspicious items. Finally, the officer must also be suspicious of inconsistent odors, lack of movement, and follow "gut feelings." A booby trap may contain a component that is highly reflective which the criminal may not realize during the set-up process. The reflection may also only occur during certain parts of the day according to the sun's position. An officer should look for colors that are inconsistent with the area. Electrical wires are often brightly colored and other parts of a booby trap may be brightly colored as well. If a color is inconsistent with the immediate area, beware!

The officer should be wary of items not normally found in certain areas such as wires, tape, cans, etc. Also, the officer should take note of discarded empty packages and be especially observant to what they originally contained. These empty packages could mean booby traps are in the area. Officers must be wary of any item apparently left behind, it may be a booby trap. Often, attractive boxes, pornographic magazines, bogus documents, possible evidence, etc. will be left behind to either conceal a booby trap or be a booby trap.

Officers should consider intelligence that reports offender movements leading to an area which then returns in the same direction of origination. Many booby traps require maintenance–this path may indicate visits to the device. Officers should use their sense of smell; petroleum-based products used in incendiary devices may be detected by their odor. Officers should look for unnatural movement or lack of movement. A fan may move objects supporting a booby trap in a different direction than surrounding items or the weight of a booby-trap may hold an item still while the wind moves other items. Finally, officers should follow their "gut feeling"; if something doesn't look or feel right, it probably isn't right. Any object or condition perceived to be out of place should be viewed with suspicion. First look, then move; do not hurry.

Searching for Booby Traps

Officers should not succumb to the movie or television tactics of having the perpetrator search for the device. Remember, the perpetrator may be suicidal and deliberately trip the device or the perpetrator may make a mistake and injure or kill him or herself and the accompanying officer. The act of letting a perpetrator actively search for a booby trap, voluntary or not, will likely be viewed by the public the same as soldiers using prisoners of war to walk through mine fields–a definite war crime. Of course, there is nothing wrong with interviewing the perpetrator to ascertain the presence, type, description, working mechanism, and location of a booby trap.

If booby traps are thought to be in a building or vehicle, the surrounding area should be evacuated, cordoned off, and police supervision notified. Depending on the situation, the area may be destroyed (even a perpetrator with limited skill can turn a building into a labyrinth of death and destruction) or a search by police officers may be required.

Note: except for the most unusual circumstances, bomb technicians do not perform searches. In fact, in some large metropolitan areas, local bomb teams do not even respond to a bomb threat until a suspicious object is discovered. Indeed, even Army explosive ordnance teams (EOD), should they be called upon for assistance, are prohibited by Army regulations from searching any building or area.

It is the duty and responsibility of police supervision to decide whether a booby-trap search will be conducted; if so, the search must be planned, organized, and implemented through the use of trained personnel. A variety of conventional bomb searching methods can be tailored to fit booby-trap searches.

First, the building should be broken down into segments (room by room) and established search patterns should be developed. Search patterns enable searchers to conduct methodical thorough searches designed to avoid the likelihood of missing devices that unorganized random searches often generate. Second, and perhaps the main ingredient for an indoor booby-trap search is "trained search teams." These search teams should contain officers who are trained in search techniques and booby trap recognition. Once the search team is formed, officers will need to make sure the effected area and adjacent areas have been evacuated.

Standard operating procedures should direct the practice of conducting the search from an established exterior perimeter to the building's interior and from bottom levels to top levels. One team may be formed and assigned the task of searching the outside of the target area and another team assigned the indoor search. Outdoor searches should begin at ground level and focus on ledges, ornamental facings, porches, overhangs, trash cans, shrubbery, and parked vehicles. The outdoor search team must be very cautious since the adversary will know that many of the areas listed above will be searched by police officers during the collection of evidence. The outdoor search should be conducted before the indoor team approaches the building. This procedure will clear the way for the indoor search team to approach the building.

The indoor search team should approach the building, when the outdoor search team has given the "all clear." Before entering the building, the indoor search team should peer into windows, and any other points of observation and scan the interior for obvious devices or suspicious areas and items. When entering a building, it may be best for the search team to enter through a non-traditional point such as a window. Officers must be conscious of the difference between non-traditional points of entry and seldom used points of entry. Non-traditional points of entry, such as upper story windows, usually won't be booby-trapped, but seldom used entry points such as alternate doors to the same area are logical areas for booby-trap placement. Multiple doors to the same area enable the perpetrator to choose which door(s) to booby-trap and which one to use as a primary ingress and egress point. **Note**: if a suspect is observed leaving the building through a window instead of a door, it is a safe bet that the building contains one or more booby traps.

Once the building has been successfully entered, rooms will have to be searched. The best technique for room searches is the utilization of two-man teams–one member will be in charge of the area searched. Once again, the search team should look into the room prior to entry. If the room's lights will be used, the officer must first examine the switch for signs of tampering–paint chipped off retaining screws, uneven or crooked cover plate alignment, visible wires, etc. Be advised, the light switch may be used as a triggering device for a booby-trap. Next, the officer should examine the light fixtures for visible wires or devices affixed to light sockets. The light bulb itself should be examined for solid or liquid fillers. One popular light socket booby-trap involves filling a light bulb with explosives or gasoline; when the light switch is turned on the electric current will fire the device. Finally, the light switch should be operated from outside the room, if possible, by reaching into the room in lieu of complete entry. The officers may decide to search the room through the extensive use of flashlights–a difficult procedure.

Upon entry, the room should be divided into two equal parts or as near equal as possible. This equal division should be based on the number and type of objects in the room to be searched and not on the size of the room. An imaginary line is then drawn between two objects in the room, e.g., the edge of the window on the south wall to the desk top on the north wall. Next, the average height of the majority of items resting on the floor should be noted. This procedure establishes the first searching height, usually from the floor to waist height, or to the working level of the room such as desk tops.

Both searchers should begin at one end of the room–the starting point, and start from a "back-to back" position. Searchers must walk softly checking for trip wires, bulges in carpeting or throw rugs, or unevenness in other floor coverings. Next, searchers should check all items on the floor around the wall area, scanning in a horizontal sweep. **Warning**: nothing should be inadvertently moved, tilted, jarred or lifted! "Hands off scanning" is the order of the day. When the searchers meet at the opposite end of the room, the middle of the room is checked upward to the preselected height.

Searchers then return to the original starting point and select a second search height, usually from waist height to the top of the head. The second search is conducted in the same manner as the first and usually covers pictures on the walls, tall table lamps, cabinets, etc. When cabinets, doors, or drawers are manipulated, first, slightly open the area of concern and peer inside with the aid of a flashlight, then inch-by-inch check for signs of a booby trap until the area is cleared. Fiber optics are excellent tools for looking into areas without disturbing contents or surfaces.

Again returning to the starting point, searchers begin a third search height, normally from the top of the searchers head to the ceiling. Areas to be searched include air conditioning/heating ducts, hanging light fixtures, intercom ports, etc. The final search pattern includes returning to the start point and searching the area above false or suspended ceilings, attics, lofts, etc. When the final search pattern is completed, the room should be marked to ensure that no rooms or areas were overlooked. Indeed, some departments require search teams to trade areas and perform a redundant or back-up search.

If while conducting any of the above search patterns, the searching officer discovers a booby trap or suspected booby trap, he should freeze, sound the alarm–don't use the radio, clear the area, mark the area (with tape, paint, felt markers, signs, etc.), isolate the area, and notify police supervision who, in turn, will notify the bomb technicians or explosive ordnance personnel. If absolutely necessary, place sandbags, bomb blankets, mattresses, etc. around the suspicious object, but do not attempt to cover the object. **Do not attempt deactivation–this is a job for specially trained and experienced personnel!** Upon arrival, bomb technicians will take appropriate action with any object determined to be of a suspicious nature.

The above search method represents only one of many methods and may be used to search any enclosed area. If another search method is chosen, it must possess the same methodical and careful steps. As the reader can imagine, indoor searches are dangerous, time and manpower consuming, and best left to specially trained personnel.

Searching for Booby Traps in Vehicles

The number of triggers, types of booby-traps, deployment locations, and complexity of remote entry procedures make vehicle searches more dangerous than searching outdoor locations or the interior of buildings. The only advantage a vehicle search has over the aforementioned locations is the condensed search area. **Note: only personnel specifically trained in bomb disposal and vehicle search procedures should physically search a suspect vehicle**. Police officers should conduct only a "hands off" visual scan of the suspect vehicle and surrounding area.

Visually searching a vehicle should follow the same procedural pattern as searching a building. The officer should start the search at an established perimeter–50-75 yards is often used as a reference distance. Perimeter searches should start and finish at the same point; begin at ground level, and focus on dumpsters, trash cans, shrubbery and other parked vehicles. The vehicle should never be touched or otherwise moved, and officers should avoid using radios near the vehicle.

Next, the exterior of the vehicle should be scanned. The officer should look for mud, dirt or snow knocked loose from the underside of the vehicle. An excess of vehicle fluids located underneath the vehicle should be noted; this may signal vehicle tampering. Ground impressions should be evaluated for the possibility that someone knelt or laid next to or under the vehicle. Handprints, fingerprints, and other smudges on a dusty or muddy exterior may signal tampering. The exterior of the vehicle should also be scanned for fresh signs of forced entry or tampering around the doors, window seals, hood, trunk, hatch latches, gas tank cap, hub caps, or wheel covers. Finally, all loose wires or strands of wires located around the vehicles lighting systems should be treated as suspicious.

Next, the officer should scan the interior of the vehicle through all of the windows and windshield. A flashlight should be used to illuminate the floor boards and other dark areas. Particular attention should be paid to vehicle operating pedals, switches, door panels, and storage areas. Unusual packages or items located inside the vehicle should be noted.

Finally, the officer may check the underside of the vehicle by using a small hand-held mirror or larger inspection mirror. If the mirror image is dark, the officer may shine a flashlight onto the mirror's face and reflect the light into the area of concern. The mirror inspection should be conducted slowly and thoroughly, beginning at the front of the vehicle, moving from one side to the other then rearward. Particular attention should be paid to the engine compartment, exhaust system, fender wells, both sides of tires, under bumpers, top of the drive train, under the gasoline tank, and other crevices. If a suspicious item is observed in the mirror, another officer should look into the mirror and state consensus—some officers are aware of what car parts look like, others are not. If while conducting any of the above search patterns, the searching officer discovers a booby trap or suspected booby trap, the same process should be employed as described in the section above.

Bomb Dogs

Bomb dogs may be a valuable asset when searching for booby traps; however, they may also be a hindrance. Dogs can trip booby traps the same as their human counterpart. If explosive booby traps are expected in an area, dogs may be useful in detecting them by odor. However, remember, a booby trap may not incorporate an explosive compound for the dog to detect.

Perhaps the most effective bomb dog breeds are Labradors, Spaniels, and German Shepherds. Through training, these dogs learn to shut out all odors except the odor they are trained to detect, even when other overpowering odors are in the area. Perpetrators may try to confuse or otherwise disguise an odor by lacing the area with pepper or other irritants. Normally, these actions will only cause the dogs nose to run and actually once the dog has finished sneezing and the mucus has cleared, the dogs sense of smell may be enhanced. **Note**: a dog working alone is useless, but when teamed with a competent dog handler, dogs are often an effective resource.

Reacting to Booby Traps

The first action the officer must perform upon seeing something that appears to be a booby trap is FREEZE. Next announce in a loud voice "device or booby trap." This is accomplished as a warning to alert other officers that a booby trap has been found and that more devices may be in the area. Other officers in the area should also freeze and resist the temptation of rushing over to the discovering officer's position in order to see the booby trap. Not only may the officers rushing over to the discovered booby traps location set off another device, but the discovered device may be command detonated. The perpetrator may be watching and waiting for officers to "bunch up," then detonate the device.

Officers must look carefully around the area before taking another step in any direction. Never assume that the trip-wire, trigger, or device discovered is the only one in the area. The best thing to do is to leave the device alone, mark it, work around it, and send for a bomb technician to disarm it. One way to mark a booby trap is with a spray can of paint to ensure that the discovering officers and others will see it upon return for disarming procedures. Plastic ribbon, string, or crepe paper also make good marking tools. If retreat from the area is the chosen option, the officers must make every attempt to exactly retrace their steps.

If a booby trap has been discovered the hard way, tripped, all officers should FREEZE. Rushing to cover or throwing oneself to the ground may set-off other devices. Next announce in a loud voice where the device was and if there are any casualties. Other officers in the area should also freeze and resist the temptation of rushing over to assist injured officers. Officers rushing over to the wounded officers location may set-off additional devices resulting in more casualties. Assisting officers should be quickly designated (usually the closest officers to the scene) and look carefully around the area before taking another step in any direction.

Never assume that the tripped booby trap is the only device in the area! Assisting officers should plan a route to the injured officer and work slowly and methodically while negotiating the terrain. When retreating from the area, officers must make every attempt to exactly retrace their steps. Naturally, civilian medical personnel should be alerted and stationed at a safe location. Requiring civilian personnel to enter the booby-trapped area is not a good option.

If the urgency of a situation requires that officers immediately do something with the device, they must work carefully, placing personal safety first. Officers should remove any hats, unnecessary equipment, loose equipment, loose clothing, etc., before working around a booby trap. Unnecessary equipment and loose items may snag or hit the booby trap, setting it off.

Next, officers must conduct a "hands-off" scan of the triggering device and booby trap before touching anything. Never try to remotely trip or deactivate a booby trap alone; always work, at a minimum, in a two-man team configuration. A team concept generates both psychological and physical advantages. Two men will conduct a more thorough search and personal security is heightened. An officer can never be sure that, while all of their attention is on the device, a suspect won't attack. The officer needs someone to watch his or her back and perimeter while operating in the tactical arena. Always try to leave disarming a booby trap to the experts!

Booby traps may be tripped in lieu of disablement because trying to disable or dismantle a device is tricky and the officer might set it off during the attempt. Another problem is that the officer may not find all of the triggers leading to the device. If the officer must trip the device, the simplest way is to attach a light rope or wire to it and pull the device from a safe distance, while remaining behind cover. Do not succumb to curiosity and watch the device trip; if the officer can see the device, he certainly isn't behind cover. Remember, even a device that appears to be non-explosive may be a ruse.

Before any device is tripped, all officers in the area should be warned, accounted for, and assume a covered position. Next, the officer must check the entire area for additional trip-wires, and examine each end of any trip-wire found because a chain of devices may be wired together. Other officers may be in the vicinity of these connected devices. Never cut any electric wire found until the officer knows what is at the end of it. If the wire is part of a firing circuit, cutting it will deactivate the device; however, if it is part of an arming circuit, cutting it will activate the device. The officer should never pull a slack wire or cut a taught wire. If possible, leave the tripping or disarming of a booby trap to the experts!

Booby Trap Training Courses

The author strongly recommends all police officers involved in school crisis response operations attend a booby-trap familiarization class. Good booby-trap courses are few and far between. When considering a class, look at the following areas: class focus, length of class, class displays, instructor's background, practice exercise "jungle walk," and an emphasis on teamwork.

Class focus—make sure the class is pinpointing booby traps and not bombs. Bomb recognition and search techniques require a different approach. Length of class—approximately eight hours is required for a good familiarization effort; remember, the intent should not be on disarming, construction, or setting booby traps. Class displays—hands-on mock devices are critical; the bigger the display the better. Mock booby-traps of all types should be available for the students to look at and physically handle. Look at the instructors background–military experience is paramount, especially combat engineers, EOD personnel, special forces, and other select combat arms personnel. Please understand, the author is not "slamming" civilian EOD personnel; they are experts in their area of operations, primarily bombs, and they will certainly be called upon to disarm or otherwise destroy any device police officers discover. To reiterate, the author has the highest respect and admiration for "bomb technicians." However, the military personnel addressed have an abundance of experience setting and disarming booby traps in both urban and rural areas. Many have wartime or other hostile conflict experience.

Perhaps one of the most important aspects of any booby trap class is the requirement for students to physically negotiate a mock booby-trap area. The author can assure the reader that when a trip wire is experienced or a practice booby trap is tripped, the feeling is never forgotten. The mock area should be set up so the student can identify some devices and find other devices the "hard way." Finally, teamwork should be emphasized during the negotiating of the "jungle walk."

In conclusion, the odds are against encountering a booby trap, but if an officer becomes the unlucky one, knowledge is the first line of defense. The information covered in this book should reinforce the officer's survival needs to remain alert in certain situations, and present the know-how to recognize the physical evidence of an alarm or booby trap. Knowledge of personal limitations will also keep an officer safe by accepting the concept that dismantling a booby trap is a job for a specialist. Keep these points in mind and the chances of officer survival are greatly enhanced.

Using Distraction/ Diversionary Devices

Diversions and distractions have proven effective in many tactical situations, often providing tactical teams with a decided edge in surprise and intimidation in order to safely overpower armed or otherwise dangerous subjects. A diversion may be defined as "diverting or turning aside," whereas a distraction may be defined as "anything that distracts or diverts attention." Furthermore, diversions and distractions can be placed into two categories: deceptive or physiological.

Deceptive diversions focus on deceiving as an illusion or the forming of a false conclusion. Deceptive diversions have a greater chance of failure than physiological diversions since this type of diversion depends on a subjects inference. Furthermore, a subject's reasoning ability may be dulled due to drugs, alcohol, emotion, fatigue, or mental deficiency. On the other hand, a subject's reasoning may be enhanced by training, intelligence, alertness, suspicions, or experience. There is always the possibility that the perpetrator may not be fooled. To succeed, deceptive diversions must be misleading. Furthermore, deceptive diversions often last longer than physiological diversions because deceptive diversions generate a course of action causing a subject to act on current information until something happens to generate a decision change. Finally, deceptive diversions require a great deal of planning, preparation and communications (police officers can be fooled just as easily as the perpetrator).

On the other hand, physiological diversions involuntarily affect one or more of the five senses of an organism. For the purposes of this book, distraction or diversionary munitions may include specialty impact munitions, chemical agent munitions, or distraction devices. The author believes any or all of these devices should be made available to security officers and/or school resource officers in order to provide these officers with an alternative to deadly force options. Of course, officers will require training in the effective and safe use of these devices. Furthermore, only a brief discussion concerning each device will be conducted. A complete discussion would require a book length endeavor.

Distraction devices are available in several shapes, sizes, colors, weights, container styles, and configurations. However, they all have a few several things in common; for example, most distraction devices are made of cardboard and/or metal body, use a bouchon or fuse assembly, and contain a derivative of black powder or flash powder. This powder often contains a metallic additive such as nitrocellulose, aluminum percurate, magnesium, or sodium to assist in the burning of the payload.

Typical modern distraction devices produce approximately 2,700 degrees centigrade of heat, 165-185 decibels of sound (similar to a jet aircraft at takeoff), less than 5 pounds per square inch (PSI) of over pressure, and between 2.5 and 7.5 million candlepower of brightness. To understand this brightness level, consider the fact that automobile headlights produce about 100,000 candlepower. Distraction devices initiate in lieu of detonate because the powder in the device is classified as a deflagrating and characterized by progressive reaction rates and buildup of pressure. Indeed, distraction device initiation more closely approximates a propellant than an explosive. A detonating explosive is characterized by rapid chemical reactions causing tremendously high pressures and brisance (shattering action). Thus, distraction devices emit only the byproducts of combustion: light and sound and are not grenades which produce shrapnel, gas, smoke, projectiles, etc. Total distraction device initiation lasts about 50 milliseconds; compare this to the blinking of an eye which takes approximately 200-250 milliseconds.

Due to the temperatures distraction devices generate (approximately 2,700 degrees), there is always a fire hazard. However, fire hazard levels are considered very low because the duration of the heat is measured in milliseconds which is not long enough to raise most materials to their kindling temperature. If fires do start, it is usually the result of flammable materials coming in contact with the distraction device at the instant of ignition. Although most distraction devices are not fragmentation-producing devices, secondary objects cannot be ruled out. Secondary objects may include loose objects such a gravel, fuse parts, or distraction device bodies. Some devices loft themselves into the air upon initiation and some device will launch parts of the initiating fuse, both situations may cause serious injury. Personnel assigned to deploy distraction devices should be trained and wear Nomex gloves, safety goggles (fog resistant), and a Nomex balaclava at a minimum. Non-Nomex gloves/balaclava's such as those constructed of extremely combustible materials should be avoided.

Many distraction devices also generate a great deal of smoke upon ignition. To best exploit the effects a distraction device causes, it is necessary to enter the target area as soon as possible after ignition (no more than 1-2 seconds). During this time period, the bulk of the smoke will usually rise and be suspended near the ceiling, thus vision is usually good at ground level. Within ten to fifteen seconds, the smoke will begin settling toward the floor and frequently vision will become obscured. In addition to obstructed vision, the smoke is noxious, and prolonged exposure at concentrated levels (more than a few minutes) may cause nausea, watery eyes, coughing, and runny noses. These effects are short-lived (less than twenty minutes) but should be avoided whenever possible. When the situation requires operators to remain in the target area for long periods, occasionally evacuate to a clean air source or ventilate the area. Finally, smoke may set off smoke detectors which in turn hinder hearing and communication efforts.

A distraction device is designed to produce a loud bang (most devices produce a sound of approximately 165db to 180db at a distance of five feet from the device which lasts for approximately nine milliseconds). No permanent hearing loss should result from a single exposure to a distraction device (temporary tinnitus–ringing in the ears is all that should occur). However, high-frequency hearing loss can occur from multiple exposures, since the effects of loud noises are cumulative and irreversible. This hazard must be addressed since many officers may be repeatedly exposed to distraction device reports during training and while conducting numerous operations such as narcotics raids. Multiple unprotected exposures should be kept at a minimum and hearing protection should always be worn during training. Some distraction device manufacturers offer training units which produce a lower db level in order to reduce the likelihood of hearing damage during training sessions. Distraction devices also produce a brilliant light (flash–approximately 2.5 million to more than 18 million candela–2,420,000 candela is reportedly 121 times brighter than a typical police flashlight) which causes temporary flash distorted vision for several minutes through rapid pupil constriction and the bleaching of rhodopsin (the pigment in the eye essential to sight in low-light environments).

Additionally, distraction devices generate an atmospheric pressure change of more than 10 percent (1.6 psi) which causes perpetrators near the device to become dazed, confused, and experience a sensory overload which temporarily renders a suspect unable to react to stimuli in a rapid, logical, and organized fashion. These effects are temporary in nature (approximately 6-10 seconds), depending upon the perpetrators position in relation to the distraction device during initiation and other personal factors. For example, drugs and/or alcohol, extreme emotions, fatigue, mental deficiency, previous shock, fear, poor health, poor nourishment, and tension may lessen or heighten the physiological effect of a distraction device. Furthermore, if the device initiates under a chair or behind a couch, a perpetrator may be only slightly affected or wholly unaffected. Remember, a distraction device's ignition force will follow the path of least resistance. Thus, some of the device's designed effects will escape through open doors, windows, or be lessened due to the size of large rooms or areas. However, rooms with closed windows and/or doors and of normal household dimensions will facilitate a distraction device's effects. The ultimate initiating positioning of a distraction device is in the middle of a targeted room, air igniting approximately waist high in order to realize a maximum even distribution throughout an area.

Modern distraction devices neither stun a suspect nor create dangerous concussion. optimum conditions, distraction devices are designed to provide a tactical team a few seconds of perpetrator disorientation in order to exploit the tactical situation and ultimately control the subject before recovery can take place. Ideally, a distraction device will generate a lag time (the normal interval between when an organism is stimulated and when it responds). For example, officers may be able to exploit perpetrator disorientation (lag time) by rapidly entering the tactical arena in order to close the distance between the officer and the perpetrator to neutralize the individual through the use of open-hand, self-defense tactics or to heighten the effectiveness (accuracy) of weapons fire during a hostage rescue or other deadly force situation. Suspects exposed to the effects of a distraction device should be handled by using the same procedures established for suspects under the influence of drugs and/or alcohol.

Of course, distraction devices may also be used for area denial; for example, a distraction device may be used during "break and rake" (windows are broken from the outside of a structure and officers rake any remaining glass shards away while maintaining a covered and concealed position) operations designed to deny a subject access to an area.

Remember, distraction devices are not 100 percent effective. They are not designed to be a solution for all tactical situations and should be viewed as only another tool with which to safely control dangerous suspects. Furthermore, distraction devices are not intended to be a substitute for good tactics, however, they often do offer officers and the suspect a greater chance of survival.

Warning: Not withstanding the obvious benefits of distraction devices, several features of these devices can lead to the death and injury of a suspect should they be improperly used. There is always a slim chance that personnel may be injured by fire or heat (if the device lands on an individual), over pressure (if the device lands between a person and a fixed obstacle), noise (if the object lands next to the ear of a person), secondary projectiles propelled outward from the point of initiation (if the device lands on loose objects such as gravel, broken

Figure 77. Officer holding a distraction device.

glass, spent fuses, etc.), and the temporary increase in the heart rate and blood pressure of surprised individuals may cause medical emergencies. Generally, in many instances, the risks that would result from not using a distraction device far outweighs the risk of using a distraction device.

Remember, each individual perpetrator will react differently due to the following factors: intoxication, extreme emotions, fatigue, mental deficiency, previous shock, fear, poor health, poor nourishment, the will to fight, training, and experience. Prolonged tactical incidents may afford officers the opportunity to exploit or generate fatigue, fear, and tension in adversaries. However, it should be noted that the above psychological/physiological conditions are a "dual edged sword" and may dull the effects of a distraction device. Thus, some agencies always announce the deployment of distraction devices, others never announce deployment, while others weigh the situation and decide on a mission to mission basis (this procedure is probably the best solution).

Specialty Impact Munitions

Specialty Impact Munitions (SIM) are becoming sterling examples of less-lethal systems One definition widely preferred by law enforcement personnel concerning less-lethal systems is stated as follows: "A weapon system or device that, when properly applied, can stop the undesirable action of an individual and induce compliance by means that have a low probability of producing lethal effects." The concept of a SIM is the reduction of the number of fatalities produced in encounters where lethal force was previously acceptable and within the rules of engagement. When a less-lethal munition is used as the first round, knowledgeable courts and investigative boards frequently recognize this action as a legitimate attempt to avoid lethal injury. Indeed, the desired effect should be incapacitation of the intended subject to a point which allows officers to take control of the situation, and make a decision on what follow-up actions are required.

SIM are not new; as early as the 1960s American law enforcement organizations were experimenting with and using SIM with varying degrees of success. For example, wooden baton rounds were used to quell riots and the first "bean bag" rounds appeared. Recent years have seen a great deal of interest placed on SIM resulting in increased research and subsequent new developments. For example, a great interest in SIM has resulted from the rising occurrence rate of "Victim Precipitated Suicide" "Suicide by Police" and other frequent encounters with mentally disturbed individuals. "Victim Precipitated Suicide" is a clinical term for the action of an individual who chooses to be killed by law enforcement personnel as an alternative to a conventional suicide. Keep in mind, these individuals are very dangerous because they may kill a law

enforcement officer in the process of achieving their goal.

SIM addresses the dangerous gap which exists in the range of use of force tools generally available to police officers. Historically, the most common use of force tools, the baton and firearm, were found to be too weak or too strong in many response situations. Thus, officers may have to choose an unnecessarily strong response for lack of an effective alternate weapon. Additionally, SIM are extremely valuable use of force tools designed to provide effective law enforcement while at the same time minimizing the risk to life. Finally, SIM can be viewed as an alternative to deadly force and as an effective tool designed to subdue subjects with little or no harm.

SIM offer a viable choice in controlling target specific situations, and riot control situations. Target specific situations include barricaded subjects and the arrest of some violent subjects. Statistics reveal that the majority of incidents where SIM are used involve suicidal subjects. As stated above, many of these situations include "suicide by police situations." SIM may be utilized to arrest violent subjects armed with knives or other non-firearm type weapons. Finally, SIM may be used to arrest subjects brandishing firearms in a non-threatening manner. In riot control situations, SIM may be used to disperse a crowd, deny access to an area, and discourage looting. SIM may also be used to target a specific individual who is providing motivation or otherwise instigating civil disorder. SIM should be considered an extended range impact weapon serving in the role of the traditional police baton to control the subject's behavior through pain compliance. Indeed, record numbers of police agencies are intending to deploy SIM devices/systems that incapacitate subjects from expended ranges.

Specialty Impact Munitions (SIM) have

many classifications and descriptions which require differentiation. **Note**: A particular SIM may have more than one classification. SIM are generally classified under the following headings: high and low energy, flexible projectiles, non-flexible projectiles, rigid projectiles, single projectile, multiple projectile, direct fire projectile, indirect fire projectile, and method of delivery.

High and low energy refers to the projectiles movement or speed and should not be confused with the degree of force which the projectile delivers to the target. Flexible projectiles are generally composed of powdered lead; lead shot; gelatin-like substances; silica housed inside a heavy cloth, canvass, or nylon bag, or flexible foam rubber. Characteristically, flexible projectiles are designed to be direct fired (see below) and conform to the contour of the surface they strike. Common projectile velocities typically travel in the 200-300 feet-per-second range.

Non-flexible or rigid projectiles are generally composed of rigid or semi-rigid materials such as wood, rubber, plastic, or dense foam material. Rigid projectiles should be relegated to the role of indirect fire (their hardness may cause serious bodily harm to include death). Common velocities for these projectiles typically travel in the 200-1000 feet-per-second range. Non-flexible projectiles may be loaded as a single projectile which are generally intended to be used as a indirect fire munition, (some exceptions may be encountered, always follow the manufacturers warnings and directions), whereas multiple projectiles are often intended to be skip fired or in some circumstances, direct fire deployed.

Direct fire projectiles, sometimes referred to as target specific projectiles, are intended to be fired directly at a subject. Direct fire munitions typically provide superior targeting capabilities. Indirect fire projectiles,

sometimes known as skip fire munitions, are intended to be deployed approximately three to six feet in front of a subject(s). Typically, once these projectiles impact an area in front of a target, they will ricochet into the target at about the same angle of initial impact (**Note**: the greater the angle of deflection, the greater the decrease in velocity). Of course, the impacting surface must be conducive to producing ricochets, e.g., asphalt, concrete, stairwell landings, hallways, or other hard surfaces. Naturally soft dirt, mud, sand, grass, weeds, carpet, etc. will often disperse the projectile's energy or, at the very least, overcome any tendency to ricochet. In some limited instances, indirect fire may consist of a high angle lob delivery method. In riot situations, wooden baton rounds are sometimes fired high into the air above the crowd's heads in order to produce a lob effect. This procedure generates what is termed as wooden rain.

In conclusion, police officers are increasingly encountering unconventional situations such as suicide assistance by police, or armed subjects directly threatening no one but refusing to put down their weapons, etc. These situations often do not call for the use of deadly force and accompanying deadly weapon platforms. Furthermore, many other use of force tools such as batons and chemical aerosol sprays are not practical options when the suspect is armed (leaving cover and closing the distance to the perpetrator often places the officer in range of the subject's weapon). Additionally, closing the distance to the subject increases both officer and subject jeopardy (the officer may be in range of the subject's weapon and the subject may feel forced to act as officers approach). Remember, officers may have the best of intentions but actually play a role in a fatal outcome which will certainly generate public criticism and possible litigation. This is not to say that direct intervention isn't the right thing to do.

Indeed, when properly used, less lethal options such as SIM can assist in these circumstances by avoiding tactics that are unsafe, avoiding actions performed outside accepted police practices and training, avoiding an outcome that is in conflict with the primary objective, and reduce the likelihood of death or serious injury to all involved. Finally, SIM should be considered just another tool, an additional option to consider when seeking the successful resolution of certain critical incidents.

In the author's opinion, SIM will one day be as prominent in the field as an officer's sidearm. Indeed, it is not to farfetched to project that the public will demand the use of SIM in almost all situations. This philosophy may be generated by the judicial system as a whole, special interest groups, and families of perpetrators. The reader should not misinterpret this statement; the need for a variety of force options is necessary and has always been apparent to law enforcement officers. SIM will certainly play a huge role in future use of force continuum and, if improperly applied, may blur the lines in deadly force situations to the extent that officers will be placed in jeopardy in the interest of saving the perpetrator. A department's administration will certainly have to articulate clearly the rational, prudent, effective use of SIM before fielding any devices.

SIM necessitates the expectation that law enforcement officers will be specialist in the application of force. Given certain circumstances, deadly force may not justified, nor will it be safe for an officer to close on a perpetrator in an effort to control him or her with physical strength or close range impact weapons. Indeed, law enforcement professionals have come to realize that they do not have to take lethal action or initiate steps which may unnecessarily escalate the use of force when a subject is armed but non-confrontational. Thus, officers should be instructed to use less-lethal projectiles to deescalate potentially deadly situations, while reducing the likelihood of death or serious injury to all persons involved. Finally, officers must realize the value of a deescalation philosophy, to be used in all cases where confrontation does not further the mission objective.

Many police departments are already placing the use of SIM in the hands of SWAT units and training them to use SIM in these special circumstances. However, it must be remembered that many police agencies do not have SWAT teams; thus, all law enforcement officers should be trained in the use of SIM. The author already believes, at this point in time, that every police department, no matter the size, must start training SIM instructors, train officers to use SIM, purchase SIM systems for their inventories, field SIM systems for applicable use, and develop a clearly defined policy and procedure focusing on the use of SIM.

Finally, these munitions should be made available to security officers and/or school resource officers in order to fit legally and socially acceptable concepts of the appropriate use of force. When properly used, SIM reduce injuries to officers and subjects, reduce the cost of liability associated with the use of force, reduce personnel complaints and associated disability pension costs, and improves the public image of the concerned agency.

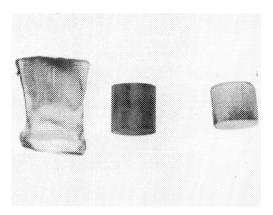

Figure 78. Specialty impact projectiles–37mm, beanbag, foam, and wood.

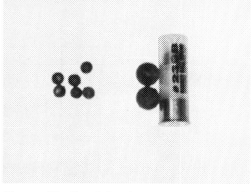

Figure 79. Specialty impact projectiles–12 gauge, multi-rubber and single rubber.

Chemical Agent Munitions

Chemical agents are available in a variety of chemical mixtures and devices for use in a variety of situations. These devices consist of area devices, chemical agent ammunition, hand-delivered devices, hand-launched devices, personal aerosol devices, tactical aerosol devices, and weapon-launched devices. Some devices are extremely specialized and may be dangerous to use in certain situations, while others are flexible and may be used in a variety of situations.

During school violence crisis operations, it may be conducive to employ chemical agents to the interior of the structure prior to breaching and entry. Hand-delivered devices may be thrown into the openings of rooms or through windows either singly or at coordinated multiple points in several different rooms. Another possibility is introducing the agent through an existing ventilation system (only OC should be used for this operation due to the persistent contamination qualities of CN and CS).

Chemical agents may also be used for spot control operations (after officers clear a room, they may deploy a chemical device into the room in order to discourage a

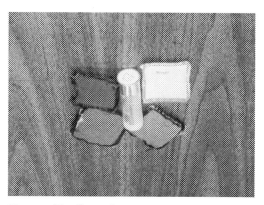

Figure 80. Specialty impact projectiles–12 gauge beanbags.

subject from room hopping). Of course, a room subjected to this treatment cannot be considered secure but merely neutralized to some extent. Frangible rounds may be fired in order to bore holes into the structure for the introduction of certain chemical agent device's spray nozzles. Entry personnel may use aerosol units in their weak hand to immobilize unarmed subjects or personnel who do not appear to pose an imminent or obvious deadly force threat (in a hostage rescue operation all personnel are considered suspects and must be restrained until positive identification is made).

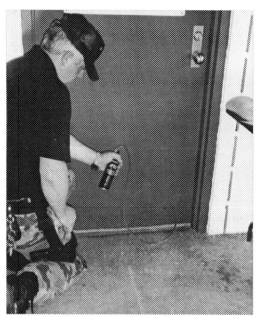

Figure 81. Chemical agent aerosol–tactical device.

Seeking School Violence Crisis Response Training

While many organizations would like to attend an off-site training facility, it is often beyond their logistical capabilities. Indeed, many organizations may have the funding available for off-site courses, but fall far short of other funding requirements which often prevent attendance. For example, other expenses include travel time, transportation expenses, per diem, billeting, and over-time requirements. Work loads may also be a problem, especially in organizations where employees are heavily involved in daily operations to the point where they may actually be over-worked. Work loads may be addressed by using flexible scheduling, substitute teachers, temporary employees, and/or special police officers/deputies to fill in for personnel earmarked to attend training.

Funding may be completely provided or partially provided by a number of grants set aside to be used for school violence training. The U.S. Department of Education is a good place to start searching for grant funding. Law enforcement entities will also find school violence grants through a number of criminal justice sources. Another good tactic is to contact state senators, representatives, and other politicians and request assistance in securing school violence grants. It does not look good on their record if politicians are reluctant to assist in either providing grant information or assisting in the grant process.

Probably the most difficult part of receiving grants is finding where the grants are parked. Indeed, it appears that some government representatives and organizations like to announce the fact that grant money is available for a specific program but are often reluctant to tell users where and how to apply for the funds. Of course, lengthy paper trails, assessment of grant requests by personnel unqualified to understand the scope of the grant, politics, and substantial amounts of "red tape" may be encountered. To counter these stumbling blocks, some organizations have personnel on staff who specialize in writing grants. Funding can also be effectively addressed, when both school administrations and law enforcement entities join forces and combine their grant funds on addressing school violence issues.

A final solution is to seek specialized training company that will conduct mobile training courses either at a requesting organization's facility or at a central location chosen by the customer to serve a variety of organizations. A quality training company will use specialists who are professionals in addressing certain topics; flex training hours and training schedules to meet logistical concerns (for example, training in the evening hours or on weekends); tailor training to meet the customers requirements (for example, provide a list of topics for a customer to choose from or offer different lengths of training to fit the needs of the customer such as 1-day, 2-day etc., or week-long time frames); and provide accompanying consulting services as required. Canned programs (strict regimented, non-flexible training subjects) are often undesirable especially when the customer has already developed and employed a number of school violence crisis response issues. Finally, some training companies will even assist the customer in finding and applying for school violence grants.

Figure 82. First responders training in a mock-up area.

Figure 83. First responders training in a mock-up area.

Figure 84. First responders training in a mock-up area.

Figure 85. First responders training.

Figure 86. First responders training.

Figure 87. First responders training–using a torch to breach a barricaded door.

CONCLUDING REMARKS

In conclusion, protecting those inside a school is a formidable task. Some experts label school security operations as "low probability high-consequence threats" due to the incalculable costs of death, facility destruction, disruption of classes, negative public perception, civil/criminal lawsuits, and the resulting embarrassment of these acts. Violence committed in schools is especially traumatic in nature because these acts are rare and unexpected. Nearly everyone in a community, if not the nation, is touched in some way. Indeed, the impact generated by a school violence crisis may be isolated or widespread, predictable or unpredictable, and result in damage ranging from minimal to major. Depending on the severity of the incident, the aftermath of school violence may generate a long-term impact on the schools and communities located in any given location. To date, there are no accurate predictions of exactly when an act of school violence will occur, precisely where they will take place, or the severity of the impact.

In the wake of such a crisis, members of the school community are asked, and may even ask themselves–what measures could have been taken to prevent the tragedy. There are no easy answers or solutions. Solutions run from ultra-conservative to extremely liberal. For example, some people condone arming teachers while others demand school administrators honor students' rights to the maximum degree negating all efforts toward implementing effective security/safety programs. Some people voice the opinion that school systems are too tough and lack common sense when administering security/safety programs, while others say educators are too liberal in their handling of high-risk students. One principle remains true and that is the willingness of many people to lodge lawsuits against schools no matter what the program and accompanying decisions may involve.

Solutions are hard to employ under these circumstances; however, effective programs may be realized by accepting the challenge of developing safe schools. Indeed the school community can be supported through school board policies that address both prevention and intervention for troubled students; school-wide violence prevention and response plans that include the entire school community in their development and implementation; training in recognizing the early warning signs of potential violent behavior; procedures that encourage staff, parents, and students to share their concerns about children who exhibit early warning signs; procedures for responding quickly to concerns about troubled children; and adequate support in getting help for troubled students.

The key to safe school environments places importance on the development of strong leadership, caring faculty members, parent and community involvement–including law enforcement officials–and student participation in the design of programs and policies. Research has shown that schools with strong principals; schools that are not too large; schools where discipline if fair, but firm; schools where teachers are imbued with high expectations for every child and schools where parents are drawn into the educational orbit are schools where learning takes place. For learning to take place, students, teachers, and administrators must feel safe. Indeed,

students have many things to contend with while in school and sitting in class worrying if someone might try to hurt or kill them or someone they know should not be on their list of worries or concerns.

Safe schools are also places where prevention and intervention programs are based on careful assessment of student problems. While school administrators and school resource officers cannot prevent all violence from occurring, these entities can do much to reduce the likelihood of its occupance. Through thoughtful planning and the establishment of a school violence prevention and response team, many crisis situations may be averted. Furthermore, when situations cannot be averted, planning will certainly prepare concerned parties for effective response measures.

Crisis response planning should be designed as a proactive tool intended to generate a detailed analysis of possible contingency plans available to response personnel. The plan should enable intervention during a crisis to ensure safety and also focus on responding in the aftermath of tragedy. This planning document should compile elements of essential information concerning a specific target and the surrounding tactical arena into a workable format. The planning document should be made available to respective SWAT teams, in order to streamline the planning effort for all SWAT entities; assist in developing the tactical operations center information display; enhance the formulation of the warning order and operations order; and assist with the development of tactical solutions.

Furthermore, a crisis response exercise should be held at least annually, in order for all operational entities to become familiar with their specific duties and to delineate the chain of command. A real-world crisis is not the time or place for operational entities to work out these issues. It is particularly important for a school's crisis response team to interface with police tactical response teams so that they can understand how important their contributions are to the law enforcement mission. All school violence incidents must be treated seriously and subsequent investigations must be given priority status.

Further, a crisis response planning document must be considered a living document and thus evaluated and periodically updated (at least annually). A properly designed, updated, practiced, and implemented planning document will ultimately increase a school community's success in (saving students' lives). A crisis response planning process will serve a proactive role in promoting peace and harmony within the community, and in ensuring the right of students and teachers to attend a safe school environment.

Additionally, teachers, SROs, school administrators, and parents should explain to students that there are situations where there are violent incidents, but that these situations are the exception and not the norm. When discussing these issues, one should explain to students the fact that the school has developed an emergency response plan designed to address emergency situations. It should also be stressed that precautions have been taken to prevent violence. While students should understand that there is no one way to prevent all occurances of violence, steps have been taken to provide as safe a learning environment as humanly possible.

Finally, school safety is everyone's job. One of the main priorities dealing with a possible school crisis is for the entire community to gain a better awareness and understanding of school violence. The benefits from this act are both long-term and short-term. Over the long term, community awareness and involvement will help reduce school violence. In the short term, it is vital that people realize that school violence can occur in their community. Only then can school violence be effectively addressed.

The relatively small number of school-site homicides is only a small part of what could cost children and the communities in which they live their civic health. Violence in schools—whether it involves threats, fist-fights, or weapons—is unwarranted and intolerable. Children deserve a safe learning environment and teachers and staff deserve a safe place to work. Communities deserve safe schools that educate students and help keep neighborhoods safer. Our society deserves and demands that our nation's most important asset—the next generation—is safe and secure. Thus, teachers, administrators, parents, community members, and students all have a stake in proactive measures focused on identifying troubled students, intervening when required, quickly and efficiently responding to school violence in progress, and addressing the tragic aftermath that is sure to follow.

APPENDIX

TECHNICAL INFORMATION SOURCES

Access Control & Security Systems Integration, Vol. 42, No. 14, Intertec Publishing Corporation, Atlanta, GA, December 31, 1999.

The Appropriate and Effective Use of Security Technologies in U.S. Schools, Research Report, National Institute of Justice, Washington, DC, 1999.

Basic Training Manual and Study Guide for Healthcare Security Officers, International Association for Healthcare Security and Safety, Lombard, IL, 1995.

Blumenkrantz, S., *Security Handbook*, Government Data Publications, Washington, DC, 1989.

Bullets, Bombs & Schools: A Response Seminar, Ohio University, Chillicothe, OH, 1999.

Early Warning Timely Response: A Guide to Safe Schools, U.S. Department of Education Special Education and Rehabilitative Services, Washington, DC, August 1998.

Emergency Preparedness U.S.A., Federal Emergency Management Agency, June, 1998.

The Emergency Program Manager, Federal Emergency Management Agency, June, 1998.

Exterior Intrusion Detection-101, Mcghee, Terry, Southwest Microwave, Inc., Security Systems Division, Location Unknown, 1998.

Gallati, R.R., *Introduction to Private Security*, Prentice-Hall Publishing, 1983.

Green, G., *Introduction to Security*, Butterworth Publishers, Location and Date Unknown.

Hand-Held Metal Detectors for use in Weapons Detection, Law Enforcement Standards Program, NILECJ-STD-0602.00, U.S. Department of Justice, Law Enforcement Assistance Administration, National Institute of Law Enforcement and Criminal Justice, Washington, DC, 1974.

Hazardous Materials: A Citizen's Orientation, Federal Emergency Management Agency, Emmitsburg, MD, 1993.

Hess, K.M., & Wrobeleski, *Introduction to Private Security*, West Publishing, 1983.

Hougland Steve, Conducting Searches on School Property, Police and Security News, Quakertown, PA, November/ December, 1999.

Indicators of School Crime and Safety, Bureau of Justice Statistics Clearinghouse, Annapolis Junction, MD, 1998.

Installation and Auditing of Security Technology, Session IV: Technical and Policy Focus Groups Group B, Cook, Peter, J., and Rodger, Robert, M., West Sussex, United Kingdom, 1996.

Jones, Tony L., *Booby-Trap Identification and Response Guide for Law Enforcement Personnel*, Paladin Press, Boulder, CO, 1998.

Jones, Tony L., *SWAT Leadership and Tactical Planning: The SWAT Operator's Guide to Combat Law Enforcement*, Paladin Press, Boulder, CO, 1996.

Justice Technology Monitor, Volume 2, No. 3, Capitol City Publishers, Arlington, VA., February 2000.

LEAA Police Equipment Survey of 1972,

Volume IV, Alarms, Security Equipment, Surveillance Equipment, NBS Special Publication 480-4, U.S. Department of Commerce, National Bureau of Standards, Washington, DC, 1972.

Magnetic Switches for Burglar Alarm Systems, Law Enforcement Standards Program, NILECJ-STD-0301.00, U.S. Department of Justice, Law Enforcement Assistance Administration, National Institute of Law Enforcement and Criminal Justice, Washington, DC, 1974.

Manual for the Responding, Investigation, and Prosecution of a Hate Crime, U.S. Attorney's Office, Cincinnati, OH, 1999.

Mercury Switches for Burglar Alarm Systems, Law Enforcement Standards Program, NILECJ-STD-0303.00, U.S. Department of Justice, Law Enforcement Assistance Administration, National Institute of Law Enforcement and Criminal Justice, Washington, DC, 1974.

Metallic Window Foil for Intrusion Alarm Systems, NIJ Standard-0319.00, Technology Assessment Program, National Institute of Justice, U.S. Department of Justice, Washington, DC, 1980.

NILECJ Standard for Mechanically Actuated Switches for Burglar Alarm Systems, Law Enforcement Standards Program, NILECJ-STD-0302.00, U.S. Department of Justice, Law Enforcement Assistance Administration, National Institute of Law Enforcement and Criminal Justice, Washington, DC, 1974.

(NOVA) National Organization For Victim Assistance, 1757 Park Road, N.W., Washington, DC 20010.

An Orientation to Community Disaster Exercises, IS SM 120, Federal Emergency Management Agency, Emmitsburg, MD, July 1995.

Penetrate Resistance of Concrete – A Review, NBS Special Publication 480-45, U.S. Department of Commerce, National Bureau of Standards, Washington, DC, 1982.

Perimeter Security Sensor Handbook, Space and Naval Warfare Systems Center Electronic Security Systems Engineering Division (Code 74), July, 1998.

Physical Security of Door Assemblies and Components, Law Enforcement Standards Program, NILECJ-STD-0306.00, U.S. Department of Justice, Law Enforcement Assistance Administration, National Institute of Law Enforcement and Criminal Justice, Washington, DC, 1976.

Physical Security of Sliding Glass Door Units, NIJ Standard-0318.00, Technology Assessment Program, National Institute of Justice, U.S. Department of Justice, Washington, DC, 1980.

Physical Security Systems, United States Department of Energy, Washington, DC, 1995.

Physical Security of Window Units, NIJ Standard-0316.00, Technology Assessment Program, National Institute of Justice, U.S. Department of Justice, Washington, DC, 1980.

Private Security, Report of the National Task Force on Private Security, National Advisory Committee on Criminal Justice Standards and Goals, Washington, DC, U.S. Government Printing Office, 1976.

Prothrow-Stith, Deborah, *Deadly Consequences: How Violence Is Destroying Our Teenage Population and a Plan to Begin Solving the Problem*, Harper Perennial, 1993.

Responding to School Violence: Legal Considerations in School Searches and Interviewing, ALERT and ABLE, St. Louis, MO, 1999.

The Role of Behavioral Science in Physical Security, Proceedings of the Second Annual Symposium, NBS Special

Publication 480-32, U.S. Department of Commerce, National Bureau of Standards, Washington, DC, 1977.

The Role of Behavioral Science in Physical Security, Proceedings of the Third Annual Symposium, NBS Special Publication 480-38, U.S. Department of Commerce, National Bureau of Standards, Washington, DC, 1978.

Rosenthal, Rick, Your Public Information S.O.P.: Where good media relations translate into good public relations, *Law and Order*, Wilmette, IL, May, 1996.

Security Lighting for Nuclear Weapons Storage Sites: A Literature Review and Bibliography, NBS Special Publication 480-27, U.S. Department of Commerce, National Bureau of Standards, Washington, DC, 1977.

Selection and Application Guide to Commercial Intrusion Alarm Systems, NBS Special Publication 480-14, U.S. Department of Commerce, National Bureau of Standards, Washington, DC, 1979.

Selection and Application Guide to Fixed Surveillance Cameras, NILECJ-GUIDE-0301.00, U.S. Department of Justice, Law Enforcement Assistance Administration, National Institute of Law Enforcement and Criminal Justice, Washington, DC, 1974.

Sound Sensing Units for Intrusion Alarm Systems, Law Enforcement Standards Program, NILECJ-STD-0308.00, U.S. Department of Justice, Law Enforcement Assistance Administration, National Institute of Law Enforcement and Criminal Justice, Washington, DC, 1977.

Stopping School Violence, ALLSTATE Foundation, www.allstate.com/founda-tion/1999.

Stopping School Violence, National Crime Prevention Council, http://www.ncpc.org/2schvio6.htm 1999.

Terms and Definitions for Intrusion Alarm Systems, Law Enforcement Standards Program, LESP-RPT-0305-00, U.S. Department of Justice, Law Enforcement Assistance Administration, National Institute of Law Enforcement and Criminal Justice, Washington, DC, 1974.

Test Methods for Detention and Correctional Facility Locks, NISTIR 4975, U.S. Department of Commerce, Technology Administration, Washington, DC, 1992.

Test Method for the Evaluation of Metallic Window Foil for Intrusion Alarm Systems, NBS Special Publication 480-34, U.S. Department of Commerce, National Bureau of Standards, Washington, DC, 1978.

Traits and Characteristics of Violent Offenders, FBI Critical Incident Response Group.

Violence and Discipline Problems in U.S. Public Schools: 1996-1997, U.S. Department of Education, Office of Educational Research and Improvement, Washington, DC, March, 1998.

Walk-Through Metal Detectors for use in Weapons Detection, Law Enforcement Standards Program, NILECJ-STD-0601.00, U.S. Department of Justice, Law Enforcement Assistance Administration, National Institute of Law Enforcement and Criminal Justice, Washington, DC, 1974.

Whitlatch, W.G., Toward an Understanding of the Juvenile Court Process, *Juvenile Justice*, Vol. 23, No. 3 (1972), 2.

ORGANIZATIONS INSTRUMENTAL IN COUNTERING SCHOOL VIOLENCE

American Association of School
  Administrators

American Counseling Association

American Federation of Teachers

American School Counselors Association

American Society for Industrial Security
  (ASIS)

Big Brothers/Big Sisters of America

Boys and Girls Clubs of America

Bureau of Justice Assistance Clearinghouse

Campus Safety Association

Center for the Prevention of School
  Violence

Center for the Study and Prevention of
  Violence

Council of Administrators of Special
  Education

Council of Exceptional Children

Eddie Eagle Program (NRA)

Education Resources Information Center
  (ERIC)

Federation of Families for Children's
  Mental Health

International Association of Campus Law
  Enforcement Administrators

International Association of Professional
  Security Consultants (IAPSC)

Justice Information Center (JIC)

Juvenile Justice Clearinghouse

Keep Schools Safe (Attorney General of
  each State)

National Alliance for Safe Schools (NASS)

National Association of Elementary School
  Principals

National Association of Police Athletic
  Leagues

National Association of School
  Psychologists

National Association of School Resource
  Officers (NASRO)

National Association of School Safety and
  Law Enforcement Officers

National Association of Secondary School
  Principals

National Association of State Boards of
  Education

National Center for Conflict Resolution
  Education

National Clearinghouse on Alcohol and
  Drug Information

National Clearinghouse for Educational
  Facilities (NCEF)

National Crime Prevention Council

National Criminal Justice Reference Service (NCJRS)

National Education Association

National Injury Control and Prevention Center

National Institute for Dispute Resolution

National Mental Health Association

National Middle Schools Association

National PTA

National School Boards Association

National School Public Relations Association

National School Safety Center (NSSC)

National School Safety and Security Services (NSSSS)

National Youth Gang Information Center

Police Executive Research Forum

Safe and Drug-Free Schools Program

Teacher's Workshop

Teens, Crime, and the Community

U.S. Department of Education, Special Education, and Rehabilitative Services

Youth Crime Watch of America

Youthinfo

INTEGRATED SECURITY SYSTEM TECHNOLOGY

MADAHCOM
50 West 23rd St.
New York, NY 10010
Telephone: 212-620-4413
Fax: 212-620-4439
Email: sales@madah.com
Website: www.madah.com

INTRUSION DETECTION SYSTEM SOURCES

Cortex Vision Systems, Inc.
P.O. Box 14282
Research Triangle Park, NC 27709
Phone: 919-361-9606
Fax: 919-572-2471

ECSI International, Inc.
790 Bloomfield Avenue, Bldg. C. Suite 1
Clifton, NJ 07012
Phone: 973-574-8555
Fax: 973-574-8562

FSI FLIR Systems, Inc.
9 Arrow Lane Amherst, NH 03031
Phone: 603-424-4752
Fax: 603-424-8941

Racon Security Solutions
12628 Interurban Avenue South
Seattle, WA 98168-3383
Phone: 206-241-1110
Fax: 206-246-9306

METAL DETECTION SOURCES

GARRETT
1881 W. State St.
Garland, TX 75042
Telephone (972) 494-6151
Fax (972) 494-1881

METAL-TEC
3500 Fairlane Farms Road, Suite #3
West Palm Beach, FL 33414
Phone: 561-790-0111
Fax: 561-790-0080

METOREX, Inc.
Princeton Crossroads Corporate Center
P.O. Box 3540
Princeton, NJ 08543-3540
Phone: 609-406-9000
Fax: 609-530-9055

EXPLOSIVE/NARCOTICS DETECTION TECHNOLOGY RESOURCES

IDS Intelligent Detection Systems Inc.
152 Cleopatra Drive
Nepean, Ontario, Canada K2G 5X2
Phone: 613-224-1061
Fax: 613-224-2603

ITI Ion Track Instruments
205 Lowell Street
Wilmington, MA 01887
Phone: 978-658-3767
Fax: 978-957-5954

ROBOTIC SECURITY RESOURCES

Cybermotion
719 Gainsboro Road, NW
Roanoke, VA 24016
Phone: 800-762-6848
www.cybermotion.com

INTERACTIVE VISUAL IMAGING

Interactive Tactical Group
Boston, MA
Telephone: 888-752-4205
Email: info@tacticalvr.com
Website: www.tacticalvr.com

X-RAY SCREENING RESOURCES

EG&G
4630 Montgomery Avenue, Suite 500
Bethesda, MD 20814
Phone: 301-951-0457
Fax: 301-951-0217

Heimann Systems GmbH
186 Wood Avenue South
Iselin, NJ 08830
Phone: 732-603-5914
Fax: 732-603-5995

Rapiscan Security Products
Washington National Airport
Hanger 3, Room 115
Washington, DC 20001
Telephone: 703-416-9571
Fax: 703-416-9573
Email: Bailey@rapiscan.com

SAIC Science Applications International
Corporation
16701 West Bernardo Drive
San Diego, CA 92127
Phone: 800-962-1632
Fax: 619-646-9718

VIVID Technologies, Inc.
10 E Commerce Way
Woburn, MA 01801
Phone: 781-939-7800
Fax: 781-939-3993

GRANT RESOURCES

Grants and Foundation Support (IP50G)

Catalog of Federal Domestic Assistance, Executive Office of the President, Office of Management and Budget, Washington, DC, 20503

Congressmen's Office, U.S. Congress, Washington, DC 20515, Phone: 202-224-3121

Foundation Center Cooperating Collections, http://www.foundationcenter.org/

United States Department of Education, 600 Independence Avenue, S.W., Washington, DC, 20202

Middle School Drug Prevention and School Safety Program Coordinators Grant CFDA 84.184K), United States Department of Education

FIRST RESPONDER TRAINING RESOURCES

North American SWAT Training Association
  (NASTA)
55 West Stafford Avenue
Worthington, OH 43085
Telephone: 614-848-8735
Web-site: www.nastal.com

INDEX

Note: Page numbers referencing photographs are in italics.